THE
SHORTEST
JOURNEY

Philippa Pullar

MANDALA
· BOOKS ·

UNWIN PAPERBACKS
London · Boston · Sydney

First published in Great Britain by Hamish Hamilton Ltd, 1981
First published by Unwin Paperbacks 1984

UNWIN®PAPERBACKS
40 Museum Street, London WC1A 1LU, UK

Unwin Paperbacks
Park Lane, Hemel Hempstead, Herts HP2 4TE, UK

George Allen & Unwin Australia Pty Ltd
8 Napier Street, North Sydney, NSW 2060, Australia

© Philippa Pullar, 1981

For Roy

British Library Cataloguing in Publication Data

Pullar, Philippa
  The shortest journey.
1. India—Religious life and customs
I. Title
291.4'4'0924   BL2001.2
ISBN 0-04-291018-8

Printed in Great Britain by Guernsey Press Co. Ltd, Guernsey, Channel Islands

Most of us live in a terrible muddle. Where are we going? What do we want? Apart from some vague theory of happiness, we have no idea. In terms of Western philosophy, Philippa Pullar seemed to be liberated. Her books were acknowledged. She lived a jet-set life.

The Shortest Journey is the story of her search for something more. In a quest for meaning she made three journeys to India, visiting the ashrams of several well-known gurus. Her introduction came at Allahabad at the Kumbh Mela, the oldest and largest religious fair in the world attracting hundreds of ascetics, some of them naked, who rarely descend from their retreats in the Himalayas.

This extraordinary book can be read on different levels – as an entertaining travel story or a serious study. Her encounters are often hilarious and sometimes horrifying. She draws such apparently unconnected subjects as Tantra, schizophrenia, vasectomy, sorcery, magnetism, healing, satanic possession, illusion and delusion into a fascinating synthesis. Some gurus are inspired teachers. What about the others? Are they simply businessmen making a profit out of their naive devotees or are they something more sinister?

Ultimately, Philippa Pullar sees that the way to freedom is within oneself – in effect the shortest journey of all.

·MANDALA·

·BOOKS·

By the same author

CONSUMING PASSIONS
FRANK HARRIS
GILDED BUTTERFLIES

Go to the pine if you want to learn about the pine,
or to the bamboo if you want to learn about the bamboo.
And in doing so, you must leave your subjective preoccupation
with yourself. Otherwise you impose yourself on the
object and do not learn.

Basho.

Acknowledgements

My thanks are due to the Society of Authors for awarding me a travelling scholarship.

I would like also to acknowledge the help of my editor Mr Christopher Sinclair-Stevenson, my agent Miss Tessa Sayle, Mr Michael Holroyd, Miss Jean Muir and Mr Stephen Pope.

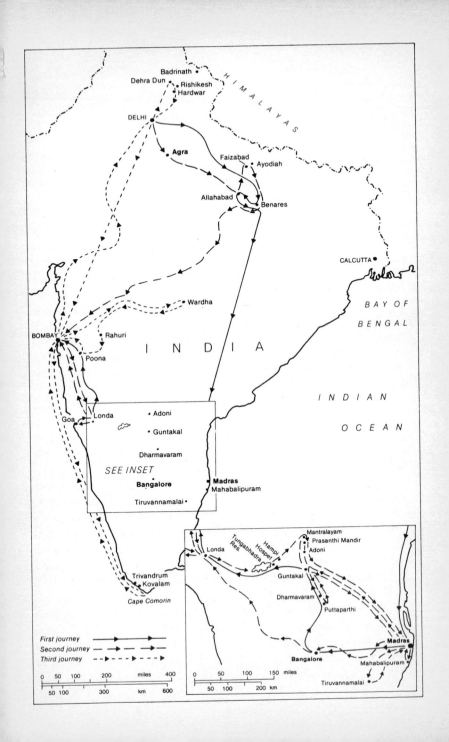

First journey
Second journey
Third journey

0 50 100   200   400
               miles
   50 100   300   600
                km

0   50   100   150
                miles
   50   100   200
                km

Introduction

As I was nearing the end of this book I came upon Peter Mattheissen's beautiful work *The Snow Leopard*, which describes a journey among the snow peaks of the Himalayas, charting at the same time his own spiritual wandering. Although I cannot claim to match this beauty, or the skill with which he has presented both his journeys, *The Snow Leopard* acted for me as a mirror. Until then I was not at all sure what my own book was saying. Now it is clear. Our lives are journeys and we are pilgrims who wander, most of us, not knowing where or why we are going; wandering, as Peter Mattheissen says, the future and the past, looking for meanings.

Most of us live mourning the past, which is magnificent in retrospect, and speculating on the future which fills us with a state of anxiety. Squeezed in between is the present. We live in a terrible muddle. Where are we going? What do we want? Apart from some vague theory of happiness, we have no idea. We spend our lives trying to piece together some order from the chaos. We pursue power, money, romance, religion, believing that one or all of these may provide the missing link. Mostly we turn outwards, as if we believe that by creating some sort of security from external matter inner harmony will follow automatically.

My kitchen floor is a microcosm of this. For years I have imposed upon my houses a most difficult floor. White and black tiles. And they must be of the purest black and white. No marbling effect here. The more disturbed my frame of mind the more I am obsessed with having an untrodden, or at least an unmarked, floor. Three cats and five or more people, to say nothing of chickens and rabbits in the past, tramp to and fro as I work to erase their stains. It is as though by wiping away these blemishes I will also wipe away the clutter that possesses my mind: my immaculate floor, glistening and still, will shine into my innermost recesses. But, as Jung has written, 'the externalization-culture of the West can truly clear away many evils, the destruction of which seems to be very desirable and advantageous. . . . It is undoubtedly more comfortable to dwell in a well-ordered and hygienically furnished house, but that does not answer the question as to *who* is the dweller in this house, and whether his soul enjoys a similar state of order and purity. . . .'*

Although as a child I was remarkably unaware of anything, there was one fact of which I was conscious. I was two people: an inner and an outer person. The inner person was always being trapped by the outer. There were times when it seemed the very sky closed down like a blue bowl to suffocate both of us. My poor parents had, with the best possible intentions, fabricated a prison. I spent much of my life a victim of claustrophobia, rebelling against authority and obsessed with liberation, trying to escape from physical and emotional traps. How could I get out? How could I be free?

Always I looked outside and my efforts to break free simply reinforced my prison. It was only when I had made three physical journeys out to India that I began to realise the way to freedom lay not through getting *out* but getting *in*. I had to turn within and dive deep into my source – in effect the shortest journey of all.

When it comes to writing about religious matters it is certainly easier to hold the attention of your readers by reacting against your subject thereby creating a nice tension and injecting energy into the prose. Agreement is far more difficult and needs an exact tone. In writing about esoteric things, there is a danger of cliché. To turn your attention from the material world is not easy; to find a vocabulary with which to describe the unearthly is more difficult still. The English language for exploring these realms is limited. We would be better off

* Dr C. G. Jung's introduction to Dr Zimmer's *Der Weg zum Selbst, The Way to the Self* – the Life and Teachings of Sri Ramana Maharishi.

working in Chinese or Sanskrit which are far more comprehensive. English forces us back on words which to some people seem suspect. 'Negativity' and 'negative', for example, smack of an American earnestness (although I find the halitosis of cigarette-smokers disgusting, to hear smoking described as a 'negative oral situation' as I did recently makes me long to smoke a whole packet). Finally I will mention 'ego', which makes certain hackles rise. 'Have you nothing in English?' queried one reader of my typescript. 'It strikes me as a ludicrous word, reminding me of the things that hens lay'. I can find nothing better. In Sanskrit the meaning is 'chit-jada-granthi' indicating the knot between the Self which is pure Consciousness and the physical body which is inert and insentient. Thus 'ego' must stand as a technical term signifying part of the human mechanism, just as 'sump' is a technical name for part of an engine, and which may for all I know fall as a disappointment on some ears.

The rich and reverential note that is adopted by many, especially in India, is quite disagreeable to most Western ears. I have tried to find a style which will be acceptable to everyone, but I am aware that tone is as subjective as humour and music. Likewise I am aware that my selection and shaping of facts may strike interested parties as being unfair. I have not consciously set out to fashion my view of any person or event and have done my best to present a true picture as it appeared to me. But the mind acts as a tailor cutting the material so that the final creation may fit some better than others. If anyone is offended then I hope to mollify him or her with this apology.

One matter strikes me as being of exceptional importance. To have a sense of humour does not imply a lack of seriousness, nor a want of compassion. Humour is a gift as subtle as music and as various in tone. To be able to laugh – above all at oneself – is in essence a spiritual quality: it is a witnessing and detaching agent which stops one becoming involved, immersed either in oneself or one's subject. One is enabled to stand back and observe the situation for what it is – often ridiculous.

Everything in one's life and in the world about us can be reduced in essence to energy – or the lack of it. All tension, unease, unhappiness, whether in one's own self or in the world, amounts to an imbalance of energy of one sort or another. Art, weather, economics, war, music, the oil crisis, sex, personal illness, all are expressions of energy. To manage energy is the enigma of life. All neuroses are rooted in worry over dissipation of energy – money, security, vitality, sexual powers and so on. The dwindling of the world's resouces is well-advertised but nowhere is the crisis more real than within ourselves.

I would like to suggest that this book is a modest exploration of human energy. Anthony Burgess has told us that he presents his books in the hope that the reader, who is immersed in life, making history, may be able to see through the light of the novel that life more clearly. In the same way I would like to think that I am presenting my life. It would be encouraging if it enabled some readers to see their own lives more clearly – at least it may provide some laughs.

PROLOGUE

I was four when war was declared. The next five years were spent scuttling from one rented house to another round counties which my mother hoped would be safe from the bombs: five years of living among other people's ugly belongings. My father had already served in one war and, being too old for active service, was in the west country carrying out duties suitable to his rank of major. My mother, who was of a nervous disposition, had been told she could never have children, and then when she was on the wrong side of forty I had been conceived. I was a delicate child and a constant worry to my mother. She had transported her staff from London and now here she was conducting three elderly servants and a sickly child through the perils of war somewhere in the depths of the home counties; somewhere as safe as possible, but not too isolated, the place must be on a bus route for the servants. My mother tried to do her best for everyone.

There was my nanny, Agnes Hodder: 'I've got a bone in my leg,' she would say when she did not want to do anything, and 'I'm as old as my tongue and a little older than my teeth,' if you were bold enough to ask her age. There was James the butler, past his prime now, huge, red-faced, malodorous and lame and his wife Mrs Grant, the cook, soft and sweet and cosy. As for myself I lived in a complete daze. I had no idea what I was meant to be doing, least of all at school, where I would sit in front of my books with no notion of what should be happening. I lived in constant dread of being ill, while my mother lived in constant dread of my going out without changing my shoes,

1

thereby getting my feet wet. Life was a rhythm of meals, lessons, walks and bicycle rides, which was interrupted by my illnesses, holidays in Cornwall and the air raids. We would crouch under the stairs and the flimsy houses would rattle and shake about our ears. Later on there were doodle-bugs, more frightening than air raids; one moment they would be flying overhead and the next the engine would be cutting out and they would be plunging down out of the sky.

In those doodle-bug-days we were living in a nasty little house somewhere in Surrey (with the bus route passing the door). Away at the back stretched flat fields where in my memory it is always winter: stark brown plough. But there was another place nearby: Penny Pot Lane. Here I remember summer. Penny Pot Lane was redolent of hot tar and cow-parsley, further along there was a cool brown stream whose banks were covered with wild garlic. Here stood a cottage belonging to an old lady called Miss Curtain. She made jam, bread and – a rare treat in wartime – home-made butter, all laid out in little curls glistening with tiny bubbles of water. No, I would have no butter. Why? they asked afterwards. I had thought the water was Miss Curtain's spit. I was a fastidious child and horrified by anything to do with spit. I was particularly horrified by babies, which seemed synonymous with spit. I was told that when I myself had been one if I even so much as spotted another I would scream and scream. One of my first memories is sitting in my pram in Regent's Park, one in a circle of babies and grown-ups having tea. One of the babies removed its sandwich from its mouth and then, to my disgust, its mother, or whoever she was, put it in her own. I could not believe it: that anyone could do such a sickening thing – eat a sandwich that had been in a *baby*'s mouth!

What I really longed for was a friend. My mother did her best. She played a lot with me, imaginary games involving an exotic lady called Zenobia, and our holidays in Cornwall were spent with a cousin of my own age. Sometimes my half-brother's nanny's son would be brought over for the day to play. But they were not friends with whom one could share one's life. I kept a small diary at this time, covered in soft red leather, to whose pages I confided my longing. I wanted to meet this friend, this boy, with whom I would share my life,

2

we would be together always.

When I was nine we moved once again, this time to an old farm house. Its rooms were furnished with large open fire-places and low beamed ceilings – indeed the entrance to my bedroom was so low that some people had to bend double to get in at all. Outside there was a cowshed, stacked up as usual with other people's stuff, but the original stalls were still there. This place seemed marvellous. There were vegetable gardens, orchards, fields, a pond and, best of all, an old caravan in which to play; not even the bus route was wanting. Now there was Children's Hour on the wireless. I ate baked beans and poached eggs and listened to 'Dick Barton' and 'Toytown'. Then came the famous cold winter of 1945. The country was transformed into landscape of unbelievable beauty, or so it seemed to me, trees blazed dazzling pink against that brilliant blue sky. Everything sparkled. This was the first time I was aware of light. At last I was beginning consciously to enjoy myself, rather than being in a state of inertia. With the best intentions in the world my poor parents had created bound-aries that were so limiting I had stagnated. Very little from outside had penetrated through to me.

Actually I cannot remember much of those years: from an early age I possessed the capacity to erase what I did not like and substitute a fantasy world instead, but the contents of that fantasy world are as much a blank as the other, apart that is from one extraordinary experience. In the doodle-bug-days I had a private place, a small fragrant nest inside a clump of macrocarpa. Once when I was there the air raid sirens howled. Then I performed a magic spell. I whirled a special twig and recited an incantation consisting of abracadabra a number of times. There was inside me a funny sort of click, as though some connection had been made, a stream of confidence flowed through me. I absolutely *knew* that the all clear would ring out when I gave the signal. I cannot explain that absolute knowing, but I had no doubt at all, just as I would have no doubt at all of my ability to raise my hand and scratch my head. I waited for five minutes before giving the appropriate sign and sure enough the all clear sounded immediately. The power I felt from that experience was quite stunning. And when I ran to the house it seemed that I was flying. But there was no one with whom I could share that experience: no one at all.

At last the war was over. Victory bonfires blazed out and my father returned from the outposts of Somerset. Now I went daily to a convent. My father however did not believe in God. 'Do you drum religion into these children's heads?' he asked the Mother Superior crossly. The Mother Superior was very shocked. My mother believed in God, just as she believed in the importance of one's daily bowel movements. Every morning one should 'try', every night one should say one's prayers: 'God bless Daddy, God bless Mummy, God bless Wu' (my half-brother who was certainly in need of blessings since he was held a prisoner of the Japanese), 'God bless Nanny. Help me to be a good little girl. Amen.' I believed in God all right, and now because of the convent I believed in the Virgin Mary. I treated them rather like the air one breathes. I took them for granted. They were there, but you could not really say that you loved them. Besides, at the convent their celebration involved such long arduous services, kneeling in clouds of incense, propped for hours on hard little chairs.

What I really did love was my pony. He was by no means my first animal. There had been Bobtail, a rabbit I won in a raffle, which gave birth to large litters that she and sometimes we ate, much to the distress of my mother. And there were two cats: Moppet, which my father insisted should not be castrated and then spent the rest of its life persecuting on the grounds that it smelt (which indeed it did), and Bimbo, a sweet timid stray, soon to develop suppurating feet. None of these did I love so much as my pony. He was dun-coloured, called Chocolate – none of my animals had original names – and my first real teacher. He was young, fast and wild from the Highlands of Scotland, quite unsuitable for one whose experience had been gleaned on tame ponies with names like Beauty. I can only suppose that he had been drugged the day that I tried him. For there was nothing quiet about Chocolate – even his field manners were appalling. He chased my mother, who very understandably was terrified of him, he bit me and stamped on my foot. It was not that he was vicious, he was a tease; someone as nervous as my mother was irresistible and someone as inexperienced as myself needed to be taught a lesson. As we

4

hurtled grimly through the country he would rear, swerve, bolt and buck – his bucks were rendered more terrible by the loud farts which accompanied each eruption. I fell off him so many times it would be impossible to count. But that pony opened up a new horizon. It was as though a door had opened. Now there were smells: the crushed turf of the downs redolent with wild thyme; damp earth mixed with bluebells; gorse; hay; the tarred string of hay nets; saddle soap and the warm sweaty breath of Chocolate himself. Celandines shone in the spring, the ground drummed in winter with hard white frost.

There was furthermore a whole new social spectrum open before me. Now I had countless horsey friends (girls, though, not the longed-for boy). We shared together a world where a new nose-band was one of the finest things you could imagine, smelling so marvellously of fresh leather; where a new bit glittered as precious as a jewel. And there were gymkhanas! You would wait in the collecting ring with excitement knotting up inside the chest. Jumping was the worst. Chocolate was a good jumper and the first round would usually go well – more often than not it would be clear. But one round was enough for him, after that he played up. He would refuse to enter the ring for the jump off. Eventually after much arm waving from the stewards he would career in – backwards. For a time he would whirl about like a circus horse, ears laid flat on his head, eyes rolling; at last he would consent to jump, but between the jumps he bucked, those frightful bucks accompanied by the terrible farts. Round the ring we would go, bucking and farting. The audience loved it. They roared and clapped at the comic turn we provided.

My father viewed my new companions with the gravest suspicion and scowled ferociously at them. He was a creature of convention, my father, a victim of respectability, or so it seemed to me. He lived in horror of what he called the hoi polloi, together with hooligans, Jews and socialists. My new companions fell into the category of hoi polloi. He disapproved of them and particularly of my closest friend, Rita Rock, the baker's daughter, who rode an elegant Arab pony called Shakespeare. Nevertheless we were inseparable. We rode together, jumped together and ate tomato and bovril sandwiches together on every possible occasion, and when we were not

5

together we maintained our communication with long telephone conversations. Rita Rock was a reservoir of dirty stories, most of which I could not understand. There was one I remember about someone being exceedingly weak on account of his having been strained through a sheet. I repeated this to my mother. 'You must never say rude things like that again,' she said. 'Never.'

Perhaps it was to get me away from Rita Rock that I was sent, aged eleven, to Bartrum Gables, a boarding school in Broadstairs (it was thought that the sea would be salutary for my health) run by two fat old ladies called Olive and Winifred Crittall. I missed Chocolate, but quite contrary to all the other pupils I felt as though I had been *released* from prison. The moment I entered that building I turned from a timid child into a bumptious tomboy. Such behaviour was unheard of in a new girl, who was expected to mope around, tear-stained and homesick. But I became wilder and wilder, engaging in pillow- and water-fights and midnight feasts. I felt quite liberated, or rather I felt liberated by breaking the rules.

Broadstairs, however, I hated. For a start I found the place and the school building horrible (eventually the premises were bought for a lunatic asylum, a function for which they were eminently suitable). Twice every morning we had to trail out on a constitutional run round the dog-stained pavements, whose sourness mingled with the stench of rotting cabbages emanating from the surrounding fields. Every Sunday we trotted along in a crocodile to a long boring church service. Any rapport with God seemed to have stopped behind at the convent, now I felt nothing but ennui. After some terms I was confirmed. Not only was everyone confirmed but it seemed to me that the ritual carried with it a certain cachet: on Sundays the communicants trooped in late for breakfast after early church, so that food and a table had to be kept especially. Perhaps it was not surprising that during the celebration I was visited by nothing more than a virulent attack of hay fever.

Every so often there were school dances: embarrassing occasions attended by my parents mainly so that my father could quiz the other parents to see what they were like – Jews, socialists, hooligans, hoi polloi...? My career at Bartrum Gables came to an abrupt end when I was thirteen. During certain periods of prep. I had been engaged in a work of fiction: a correspondence between myself in the role of a dashing young lover and my best Bartrum Gables' friend as my beloved. The epistle began innocently enough, yet grew more lurid with the blossoming and consummation of our imagined affair. Apart from Rita Rock's stories I was ignorant of the facts of life, but my friend was more precocious and could furnish me with some details. 'It was so lovely,' I wrote at one stage, 'to feel a bit of me inside you.' I forget the rest of the composition, no doubt my friend was equally abandoned with the script. Certainly we were both careless because somehow our papers fell into the crabbed fingers of the Misses Crittall. They were appalled. We were expelled, but not before a terrifying interrogation. Where had we come across such filth? the Misses Crittall wanted to know. It did not enter my head to confess that I had imagined it. In the school library, I said. I had come across filth like that in the school library. The Misses Crittall were appalled again. *The school library*! And which books, pray? Mercifully the rest of the interview is blotted out. I was collected and driven home in embarrassed disgrace by my parents who as far as I can remember never referred to the incident again.

I was escorted to my next establishment, Brondesbury-at-Stocks, by Chocolate. But he unfortunately was even more subversive than I and only lasted one term. No one apart from myself and the head girl, herself from the Highlands, was allowed to ride him. He chased the riding mistress up a tree and swerved, bucked and bolted his way across that ravishing country. I loved that school, mainly perhaps because of its situation: the marvellous hills and woodlands of the Chilterns near Tring. In January the beechwoods surrounding the school were famous for their snowdrops – one year, the photograph which, in those days, appeared on the back page of *The Times* featured three or four of us in our gym slips evocatively seated among the white drifts. In June the fields were fragrant with hay. Less wonderful was the stench emanating from the rookery bordering the road.

Once, the place had belonged to that famous hostess Mrs Humphry Ward; somehow it still retained the soothing atmosphere which belongs to an ordered country house, incorporating security and continuity, pot pourri and log fires. Our education also lingered on from the nineteenth century. We danced and curtsied with Madame Vacani, we hunted, we acted in pageants; on Sundays we enjoyed 'drawing room'; we sat in Mrs Humphry Ward's salon and worked at our embroidery while Miss Forbes Dunlop, the headmistress, read from Elizabeth Goudge. Her assistant Miss Rose supervised the sixth form, conducting it round the Tate Gallery and initiating it into the mysteries of soufflés.

Here in this peaceful setting I waxed wilder than ever. Liberation still came (just as it came for Chocolate) by defying all rules and regulations. Off I went again: midnight feasts in cellars and heaven knows what else. It was heady stuff and I was filled with euphoria except for one thing. Everyone at Brondesbury seemed to have boyfriends. And their holidays were so glamorous. They went to dances. They kissed their partners in the bushes. Their lives seemed an endless round of gaieties. My best friend was always descending from her bedroom window and going off to rendezvous in haystacks with her father's stable lads. Everyone eagerly awaited the post. Some girls had as many as three boys writing to them, passionate letters, postmarked Eton, Harrow, Radley, Winchester. Everyone, that is, apart from myself. I even started writing to my half-brother's nanny's son so that at least I would receive a letter from a boy, but it was not satisfactory. You could tell from the writing that he was not in the same class as Eton and Harrow. So I started making up compensatory stories about my holidays, my 'experiences' becoming so daring that they quite matched those of my best friend. It was rather confusing. Soon I could not remember whether the events I was describing, or anyway the more commonplace ones, had happened or not. In my mind they were indistinguishable from fact. For some years I had difficulty in seeing what had actually happened and what I had imagined had happened.

Meanwhile, my behaviour grew steadily sillier. So did that of my friends. Somehow we made it to the top of the school and became prefects. Now we were sitting for our school certificate examination – school cert., as it was called. But instead of devoting our time to studies we spent most of it descending from the window and stealing over the cow-patty fields, either to meet American boys or to attend dances at Pendley Manor – an establishment for further education, mostly equestrian, under the direction of the famous Dorian Williams, who happened to be an uncle of a girl in our form. In those days the Hokey Cokey was popular. One evening we joined the end of the line as it hopped and jumped its merry way through the kitchen regions of the manor. So tortuous was the route and so long was the line of dancers that at one stage the leaders doubled back through the bootrooms encountering those of us at the rear. There leading the revelries was Miss Rose.

Thus began a run of bad luck which concluded eventually in our being expelled – or rather we would have been expelled had we not been leaving. I was sent off to a finishing school in Switzerland and then to a domestic science college at Lyme Regis where I gave much time to hitch-hiking along the fox-glove lanes to Weymouth to pick up sailors at the Navy Days. Once two of us went as far as London where we had a rendez-vous at Battersea Fun Fair with two American ratings. In those days the white slave trade was at its height. Old ladies, it was said, would approach you in the lavatory and before you knew it you were waking up in some foreign port, a concubine. In the circumstances it was surprising that nothing like that happened either to me or to anyone I knew. Instead we lived to grow wilder and sillier than ever, much to the horror of my parents, who had hoped by now to find all of us transformed into manicured and sleek adults.

My poor parents, how little I resembled their ideal daughter and how little did they approach my expectations! There is a marvellous passage in Maurice Sachs' autobiography. He closes his eyes: there is the drawing room of a large country house whose fireplace holds three logs. His father enters muddy from hunting, his mother rises from the piano where she has been singing a simple ballad and his (virgin) sister leaves her embroidery. How little did these fetching people resemble his own family. Like Maurice Sachs, I lived with my mother and father in a perpetual state of friction caused by each wanting the other to be different. My father was a serious, taciturn man; sometimes when he drove me to the country the hour-long journey passed in total silence without our exchanging a word. Clearly I was to him the most frivolous thing he had ever clapped eyes on: no vocabulary to speak of and interested only in having a good time. My mother loved to be fine, or rather what she called attractive. Dress was her passion. Good appearance was the complexion by which she judged people. If they looked attractive, were prettily dressed, *soignée*, with well-set hair, then they would be nice to know: *comme il faut*. She would have liked a daughter with equal interests, who cared for the cut of her hair. My hair was one of my mother's neuroses. She would have wished for her daughter natural curls rather than straight wisps. 'Your trouble is that you've got very bad hair,' she would say. I on the other hand would have liked my parents to be relaxed and to live in a large country house surrounded by charming neighbours with *sons*. At least we were united in desiring for me suitable male companions; both my parents believed that the only resort for such a tiresome girl was marriage, and eventually, in Coronation Year, with my full agreement I was launched into the London Season.

While I had been in Switzerland my parents had removed to London, a ground-floor flat in Ashley Gardens, Victoria, convenient for every possible bus route to carry my mother off to Harrods, Woollands, Harvey Nichols and Fortnum's, while the Army and Navy was just round the corner. I found the cement of Victoria as confining as a strait-jacket. And after the heady mountain air of Switzerland, to say nothing of the sea breezes of Weymouth, the atmosphere in the flat was stifling. Life was lived against the ticking of several clocks; strictly ordered like those wartime years. Part of the day was allotted to the *Times* crossword puzzle and several parts to meals. Mrs Grant and James were no longer with us, neither was Nanny; now we had Winnie, who was prone to deep fits of depression although she had a great sense of humour. 'Where's my hair brush, Winnie?' might be countered with: 'Hanging up on the wall with the bike, dear;' or it might be met with no reply at all, just gloomy silence. Another favourite came to 'What's for dinner, Winnie?' 'Bread and pull it, dear.' The food was good if a little repetitive. You could tell the day of the week by what there was for lunch. Mondays, cold meat, Tuesdays, shepherd's pie, Wednesdays, rissoles, or, if the joint had been small, haddock, Thursdays, liver and bacon, Fridays, stew, Saturday, chops, and Sundays, joint, so that it could happen all over again. I began to experience claustrophobia. I felt the whole weight of the building was crushing me, that my body was a cage in which I was trapped. I would lie in bed writhing, feeling as though I were bound up like a cocoon.

But as soon as the season started I was in very rarely. Every night as the light thickened I would zip myself into those awful foundation garments we called stays and whirl out to my dinner party and then on to the dance. This is not the place to describe the London Season, but the result of it was that like all good debutantes I soon became engaged, at least unofficially. My husband-to-be was called Robin and lived in Carmarthenshire: a marvellous green rolling country with huge skies filled with purple billowing clouds. The house was beautiful, designed by Nash and illuminated by old-fashioned gaslights. The view fell away over fields and hills to the blue distance. There were acres of daffodils, forests of rhododendrons, and at dusk hundreds of rabbits grazed.

I was as much in love with the place as with the man himself. In my mind I was already playing the role of hostess and country landowner's wife. I thought only about Robin and our life in Carmarthenshire. I cared for the trees, the gardens, the tenants' wives. I was excellent at it. Everybody said so. I played that role for a summer. That year the rabbits died, swollen and festering from myxomatosis, and in October Robin was admitted to hospital. After a week he was transferred to London. I had had no knowledge that he was ill; he had never said anything – although afterwards I remembered how he would sometimes cough and look down at what must have been blood. Never before had I seen a serious illness: the fear, the blood transfusion tubes, the struggling for breath, the vomiting. Three days later he died: Bright's Disease, T.B. and leukaemia. It was unbelievable. Outside the hospital, people were talking, living as though nothing had happened. It seemed extraordinary that they could continue like that. My world had shattered; it seemed impossible that theirs had not also – that my shock was not universal. For death is a subjective affair. One mourns one's own pain, one's own loss. I was distraught. Now there was no future. I would dedicate my life

11

to others. I would become a nurse. Certainly I would never marry. That is what I said and what I believed, but what I did was a different matter.

Somehow I never got round to being a nurse and I passed the next three years more foolishly than ever. I had departed from my parents' flat and moved with two girls (one of them my friend who had descended each night to meet her father's stable lads in the haystack), two cats and a dog to a studio in Chelsea for £5 a week. I worked in King's Road coffee bars and in the first bistro to open in London. The food was a revelation after the war (to say nothing of the camp waiters): succulent fillet steaks served with garlic for 7s. 6d. It was in fact horse-meat. I knew this because it came from the shop where I bought the cat's liver: the men were friends of mine.

Every so often I would pause to reiterate that I could, would, never marry. Then on I would dash. I did the season all over again, gate-crashing the parties this time with an equally silly friend. Sometimes we would dance at a club called the Condor. Georgie Brown would sing 'Sweet sweet the memories you gave to me', everyone would get up to shuffle round the floor and we would go round swigging their drinks. By now I was drinking too much. The bottles of wine and whisky would sink as my friends and I sat into the night discussing and wondering. Now my interest in God was intellectual. I read books by Christmas Humphreys, Ron Hubbard and Rudolph Steiner. We would sit in our basement sitting room with its striped wallpaper discussing reincarnation and regressive hyp-notism while Bing Crosby and Frank Sinatra sang: 'You make me feel so young.' We had mended the flower bowl, I remem-ber, with fish glue and its reek mingled with the sweetness of white hyacinths and the acridity of tarred road blocks we were burning in the grate. Once a month we would give a party and invite all the men who were likely to ask us out to dinner for the next month. This was how we existed: working in coffee bars and restaurants by day, dinner parties by night.

All this time I had a constant admirer whom I had known since that summer in Wales. He had been a good friend and, enticed no doubt by the unobtainable, by my reiterating that I would never marry, he had fallen in love with me. He too had felt stifled at home. His father had died (from drink) and his mother idolised him. Cambridge had been his passport to freedom – and liquor. Certainly we were well matched in our silliness. We stuck pots of jam on chairs in tea rooms so that people would sit on them, we poured water everywhere and we consumed countless bottles of alcohol. To impress me he read the books I recommended – which had mostly been suggested to me by friends. Through the same process he listened to music reflecting my ideas – or my friends' ideas – back to me. Life continued in this aimless drifting way for three years and the notion of becoming a nurse finally perished. By now all my friends were getting married, the flat was being given up and my job as an air hostess had fallen through. What was I to do? I decided to accept the long-standing proposal of my admirer. After all, what could possibly go wrong? But alas! What could go right was more like it: how little that marriage was to resemble the ideal union I had envisaged in that little red diary!

No sooner had I committed myself than I knew the alliance was not right. I would wake up in the night screaming from nightmares of being trapped. My parents did not like it either. A nice enough fellow, they thought, but weak, with no sound prospects. But just then we were getting on worse than ever, they despaired of my frivolous and alcoholic ways which seemed neither *soigné* nor *comme il faut*, and there appeared to be no point of contact. Besides I was obstinate. I had made up my mind to marry and that was that. The arrangements went ahead and I never had the courage to stop them.

The marriage was not a success from the start. Soon we moved to Devon. Just as Mrs Humphry Ward's place had had a blessed atmosphere, this one was disastrous. That it was cursed I am now convinced: this house was, and presumably still is, haunted by some evil that penetrates all those who live there. Superficially, though, there was nothing wrong and at first I was not conscious of anything. Indeed visually the house was attractive with a long thatched roof and sunny rooms; wistaria and honeysuckle filled the air with fragrance, there were groves of magnolia and rhododendron and a stream ran through the garden. Yet from the moment that we put our feet across that threshold things went from bad to worse.

To begin with we had not been practical. The house, as my parents had pointed out, was too large for our income. My

13

husband had a job with an agricultural company. He invested a thousand pounds and was supposed to receive shares and instruction into the skills of farming. The company eventually turned out to be totally incompetent and after a few years he lost his thousand pounds, receiving little more than several harsh lessons in what not to do. Meanwhile, however, he was forced to work long and hard hours. He drank more and more and arrived back in the evenings later and later. We lived through a perpetual cycle: rows over finance followed by restorative drinks. The refrain 'can't afford it' would ring out over and over again. My husband was weak and I was impossible – heading for a nervous breakdown. My philosophical ideas belonged to the past. As for my husband, he no longer could bear my reading and wondering. Now I was a pseudo-intellectual, so were my friends. What we all needed was an honest day's work, that would stop all our rubbish! Even for my friends, of whom I saw less and less, the only reality seemed to be money. Mostly they had stayed in London, living the gregarious, ambitious lives of the young married. They needed money to buy drinks, furniture, clothes and food, to impress people in order that they might in turn receive invitations and meet more people to invite and impress. Energy now meant money. Behind each mouthful, each drink, lay a great deal of energy expended: the tiresome hours at the office, the struggle to get back home again. Under the circumstances it was very reasonable that people wanted a return on their money. We did not live my friends' lives, we were not going to give the sort of parties where they could meet interesting or useful people. We were good for a free weekend, it was true, but as they pointed out they could go to Paris for the same money.

Matters were not helped by my being pregnant. Some mornings the sense of isolation and irritation was such that there was a strange knocking in my ears. The only way to stop this was to drink, sometimes as early as eleven o'clock. I felt incarcerated, always exhausted, shut into myself with this strange sensation as though the blood had curdled in my veins. It seemed that nothing worked harmoniously within myself, that there was a series of blockages as though my system was knotted up. In the house the roof hung over me threatening to fall and crush me. In the garden the weeds and the willows advanced, the sky seemed to lower, reaching down and fitting against the land so tightly that it made a blue bowl over my head. There was no release anywhere – or at least only in drink, then for a while it seemed that my mind, my consciousness, could slip out through the two round holes in the bone and away. I would wonder how it was possible to be so miserable, every part of me ached and felt clogged. Everything felt absolutely wrong. This was hell, that at least I knew. Even at night I dreamed that a great heavy weight was crushing me, smothering me, pushing me down and down.* As for the expected child: that I believed was a devil. It was all part of the conspiracy: Satan was planning to take over the world. One of his techniques was to flood women with chemicals so that they became cows. I absolutely *knew* this. I could feel those poisons flooding through me, separating my blood, causing that strange curdling sensation. I knew that I had been especially selected for this purpose, that I was steadily being taken over. I wrote pages on this in my diary:

'With his hands spread out like talons he [Satan] presses his buttons so that hormones can flood through me. He swirls up the drive and straddles over me. He arches his back and lowers himself, supported on bent hands, he breathes in through my mouth, through my nostrils. Misery tingles through me. There is only great pressure forcing me down, I have sailed so deep into a depression it is too dark to know anything. I only know that the baby looms like some huge rock blocking the way. No sun shines under its shadow. I am without energy. Already the devil's spawn inside me is sucking my strength, savaging the sense of humour. This is the centre of Satan's attack. He knows very well that once the sense of humour sinks it is shipwreck: time to jump overboard, leaving the body empty, arms and legs spread-eagled, hair streaming out like strings, a floating puppet ready for him to operate. The dark waters of melancholy close over me, swirling and eddying like a whirlpool. One moment I am plunging down to the green depths, then up rising to the light, crystal, translucent on the

* See pages 251–3 for psychic attack. What is not stated here is that one of the symptoms of a noticeable attack is a sense of weight, another is nervous exhaustion.

surface.'

The case was not improved by my doctor who had never in his life had to deal with such a thing. Cows and devils indeed! I was to pull myself together, snap out of it! And when I failed to do so he resorted to purple hearts and every other kind of pill – only stopping by some miracle at thalidomide which was then newly on the market. The tablets heightened my illusions. I knew that I was mad. Doomed. I felt that I had been completely taken over by the devil who was sweeping me away in a swirling black river, banging me en route against rocks and cliffs. I must escape. But how on earth could I?

Summer had turned the Devon lanes into tunnels, cutting deep into the country. Dog-roses, foxgloves, honeysuckle and cow-parsley made sweet-smelling walls out of which cats, dogs, children and old men would suddenly jump. The grove of purple rhododendrons hummed with thousands of bees. Sometimes I vibrated with excitement; my nerves tuned to an absolute pitch, I was brilliant. I soared above my body and watched it unreal and swollen, lumbering below. Strange incantations ran through my head. Once it was 'sun is light'. The esses floated like gold snakes. I became conscious of different dimensions in sensations. When I gazed into my cats' eyes I could feel the texture of glazed butterfly wings that I saw therein. They were completely tactile: luminous aquamarine wings fading to the most delicate yellow. Once on a brief trip to London I went into St Paul's cathedral. I saw the shaped sound of the music pouring up and curving against the painted domes and crescents, overflowing from the aisles through the arches until it reached the altar. A note swept through on the current, it turned, others joined it and fell thundering on the stones by my feet, spraying up into my ears, echoing inside me. Now it was all quite clear why people sanctify parenthood. It is then that they can play at being God. Looking down from their great height into their child's face they can thunder or shine. For the child they are the whole world. But what if they are not the material of gods?

As summer progressed I saw few people other than the devil. I loved my cats, dogs and parrot. I enjoyed the vegetable garden with its young green lines of succulent vegetables

which I stewed up on a large erratic Aga, but most of the time I
was locked up in a private world. My real communication was
with the devil and the diary:

'It is nine o'clock. I am drinking. During the day I am dead. I
live only at night. Then the body is forgotten, there is no smelling, seeing, touching. The senses sleep. There under the
blankets the mind can work to expel emotions. Fear, sadness,
sex and even sometimes happiness all emerge with astonishing
force. On waking the mind holds them and they dominate the
morning until familiar articles, sensations and the light make
them fade. Now wistaria drapes on either side of the window.
In front of the willows there is a solitary Christmas tree. It
stands black against the ink blue sky. I have in front of me the
gin bottle and I am going to tip it down my throat until I am
drunk. I hate myself. I hate this prison which is the body. I can
feel myself pressing inside my cheekbones, inside my chest,
trying to get out and away. I am alone and now I have drunk
neat from the bottle. The gin is thick and pungent. It attacks
my tongue, burns down my throat. As I look at the spike it is
no longer one, another has joined it, erect beside it. I shall
examine myself.
Examiner: Why do you wish to leave your body?
Me: Because I am alone with myself, because I hate myself,
because I am afraid.
Examiner: Afraid of what?
Me: Myself.
Examiner: Why?
Me: Because I am evil, meaning that part of me which is
usually safely hidden away – the self – the true self. . .
Examiner: Ah ha!
Me: . . . only in extremes does this force make itself known.
Examiner: What do you mean by extremes?
At this point I looked away from the examiner to the spike. It
still has a second beside it. Most tiresome. I must remember to
look in the morning.'

The situation did not change when the baby was born. I
remained in a state of extraordinary sensitivity. All my
chilhood horrors of babies and saliva were still with me and so

17

was the devil. Matters got even worse when my husband left the agricultural company and set up batteries of chickens at the bottom of the garden. For a start he failed to make any provision for the manure – and manure from five thousand hens is quite something. This was simply shovelled, or rather mechanically propelled, out of the sheds and dumped. The summers were no longer fragrant with honeysuckle and hay, but stank of ordure; so did my husband.

Then, the suffering inflicted on those birds was excruciating. Even before they were crammed into their cages, their beaks must be electrically amputated so that they should not attack their neighbours. It was a most harrowing process: ghastly with gasps, sizzling and blood. Soon those pullets turned red and raw from the constant friction against the iron bars. From morning to night it seemed to me screams of distress rose up the garden from those awful prisons. Hundreds went blind; hundreds more suffered some respiratory disease and the kitchen was filled with hunched up birds, moping and malodorous, in boxes. 'It's horrible,' I said and refused to have anything to do with the chickens at all. 'It's money,' retorted my husband, reiterating that I should do an honest day's work and stop 'all that rubbish'. An epidemic of fleas added to the torture, infesting everyone and everything. The last straw came when I had to drive a load of poultry to their slaughter. Hundreds of fowls were squashed squawking into crates. At their destination they were hauled out and hooked upside down on a conveyor belt and, flapping what was left of their poor wings, they rotated to their death. On the other side of the building the belt re-emerged, still with the chickens suspended, but now they were quite naked, limp and dangling, their eyes white, their throats cut, only their hooked feet were as before. Now to a certain extent they and other food animals replaced the devil as the focus of my hallucinations. As I ate I could hear the knife ripping into their flesh. I would flinch, feeling the pain. The gravy turned to blood in the dish and I watched fascinated as the meat grew whiskers and ears. Sometimes the steam seemed to turn to breath, and there, reflected in the shining sauce, calves sucked the men's hands as they shot them, larger cattle kicked and jerked as they died.

In due course the chickens lost so much money that we could

18

not afford anything at all. It was the final irony: those poor birds living those awful lives to lose money! Eventually the house had to be sold to cut the losses. That was it. The end of the marriage. And I bought a house in Deal and moved there with the children (by now there was another baby) and the animals. There was hardly any money to live, let alone to buy a house, which I had to paint myself from top to bottom. For two ghastly years my husband lived there as well. At last he moved to London.

Now, marriage was a most ugly word. I felt that under no circumstances could I ever consider it again. For me it was associated with worry, rows, debts; in a word, hell. As for jealousy I could not believe that it existed. The last thing I wanted was to belong to anyone, or vice versa. And in this frame of mind I fell in love. Horace (I shall call him Horace after Horace Walpole) was the perfect antidote to my husband: gentle, sensitive and intelligent; an author working on a long biography of an eminent man of letters. He educated me, introduced me again to music, books and ideas. Sometimes during the past years I had struggled through *Encounter*, I had even subscribed to an anarchist magazine, but most of the words had remained on the page. I had been unable to absorb them. Now, gradually and creakingly, my brain began to function, but not by any means clearly. I was perceiving the world through a thick veil, thick being the precise word for what I felt: there was a barrier between myself and what I was trying to understand. When Horace and I were together it was as though an electrical spark flew between us, igniting some force that was both invigorating and clearing. We were both of us stimulated, full of verve, and we *laughed*. I calmed down considerably and, although I lived in the grips of financial anxiety, my contact with the devil, my hallucinations at the dinner table and the curdling feeling in my blood were all things of the past.

Horace was my second teacher. The pony Chocolate had opened up a whole world so that I could feel and see and smell. Horace altered my way of thinking. Horace altered my attitude of mind. Certainly I did not want to marry, but I did want to be with Horace.

In London we lived in a rather seedy maisonette in West Kensington, which was infested with mice – encouraged no doubt by our guinea pigs (someone had given us a pair which multiplied at an alarming rate and lay expensively in hay purchased from Harrods). It seemed that scaffolding was forever being erected or dismantled in that street; clatters and clangs reverberated day after day. The lower floors of the house were occupied by two old ladies, one of whom at least was at war with herself and everyone else in the world. Mrs Harvey wrote poetry and, it was said, had once been imprisoned in China. She wore a strange brown habit, bubbled evil-smelling concoctions in her kitchen and piped abuse to all and sundry in a terrible quavering wail. She planted wooden cats' heads in her window-boxes and watered them, their drips combining with those from the lavatory brush suspended from the window-sill on the other side of the house to enrage Mrs del Rio in the flat below. Mrs del Rio was rather a dear old lady who wandered each day very slowly round her tiny garden followed by her elderly cat.

No one was unaffected by Mrs Harvey's delusions, which were quickened alarmingly by the full moon – it was rather like living in a sea resort and being governed by the tides. Next door there lived some hippies. Mrs Harvey certainly could not bear them: lowering the tone of the neighbourhood, she screeched, and what a noise they made in their fireplace all day long, bang, bang, bang, with their poker. Once towards the end of the moon's last quarter we invited a venerable man of letters to lunch. He arrived complete with spats and cravat. The collation was a success, lasting long into the afternoon. As the winter dusk drew in and the cries could be heard of children returning home from school, we said our goodbyes in the street below, nodding together over the delightfulness of the occasion. Mrs Harvey loomed above us on the balcony.' Vile woman,' she bellowed. 'Your morals match your vermin, madam!' Again it was nearing full moon when Horace's father came to dinner. She shot out of her front door as he was climbing the stairs and arrested him. 'Come to place *another* bet,' she roared. She fancied then that we were running a betting shop. Next she supposed we were spies and locked up her letter box. 'PRIVAT LETTER CAGE,' she wrote, and posted all our letters back to the Post Office marked 'not known here'. That almost made Horace as mad as she was: he had just had his book published and by every post was receiving congratulations, commissions and requests to appear on this and that.

Deal was, by comparison, peaceful. The house was eighteenth-century, facing east and west. On the west side you looked out through the scented conservatory to a garden which was surrounded by mellow tiled roofs. In summer the vine was heavy with muscat grapes; jasmine, tobacco and datura, whose white bells hung over the pond, filled the air with heady fragrance. But it was a house that changed with the seasons and from the middle of November to the middle of February no sun made its way in, being too low to shine above the roofs on the south side. This had a most depressing effect: it was a real descent into the underworld and for four months you felt incarcerated in darkness. On the east side you commanded a view of the car park and then the sea; at low tide you could distinguish the masts of ships that had been wrecked on the Goodwin sands – space was one of the reasons I had elected to live here. But in winter iced gales howled through every crack of the house and transformed the narrow streets into wind tunnels which shut one in more than ever.

Yet there were times of unbelievable beauty. Autumn was particularly good, sometimes a mist would lie over the sea, glowing pink in the evening. The fragrance of buddleia would fill the garden, the starlings whistled, pigeons chanted in rhythmic waves. It was nostalgically, yearningly, beautiful. People would park their cars outside the kitchen window, lay their picnics out on the bonnets of their cars and eat, gazing out at the seabirds bobbing on the calm waters. Sometimes there would be foggy mysterious days when the fog horns would blare out; sometimes again long lines of ships would shelter in the lee of the land between the Goodwins and the town and it would seem that the slanting rays of the sun set them ablaze. Those early years were the stuff of romantic dreams: walking together along the cliffs in August, floating, it seemed, in the dusk above the sea, seeing the ships sailing below. One hot still evening a cricket sang in the garden, bringing with it the essence of the Mediterranean, olives, thyme and rosemary. And again there was a month when the garden moved with butterflies, tortoiseshells, cabbage whites, chalk blues and purple emperors, hovering above the lavender, cornflowers, fennel and savory. As we ate dinner one night we watched the harvest moon rise up out of the sea, a yellow ball with a red band, turning from gold into a huge corn-coloured orb which seemed joined to us by a white triangular path of light shining in the sea.

Horace understood my fears of being trapped. He believed that by living in two places this would to a certain extent be alleviated. No sooner would you begin to feel enclosed than you could get into the car and move to the other place. In theory this should have been ideal. In practice, like so many things, it did not work out. Much of the time was spent stuck in a traffic jam on the M.2 which was just being constructed, with the car overflowing with bowls of soup I had not wanted to waste, children, guinea pigs, flowers, cats, dogs, endless papers and typewriters. Torn as I was between longing to be free and wanting to be secure the latter had prevailed and I had assembled around me plants and animals, which in their turn ensnared me – as of course did the children. Quite often I had to stay at Deal to be with the children, during their school holidays for example. Then the house on which I had worked so hard would seem like a prison and my plants and animals jailors – especially during those sunless winter months. As for those children they constituted the nub of my neuroses, requiring endless resources of finance and energy, above all pinning me down so that claustrophobia overwhelmed me.

I had neither the stability nor the finances to sustain this double life. I became frantic, swinging wildly from one place to the other, growing unconfident, uneasy, incompetent, continually running out of things, petrol, salt, lavatory paper, time, energy. I was always exhausted, always irritable. As Horace grew increasingly articulate, I grew correspondingly less so. I was in a constant whirl of anxiety, always late and losing things. On top of it all I was writing a deeply depressing book based on those diaries written during my marriage which infected me all over again. I began to relive the horrors. Very often when I was alone in Deal with the children I felt completely isolated. I did not see people out in the streets, but so many islands with orifices out of which to push words and communications: ropes of fragile communications; little strings of words, little strings of emotion. I became depressed,

22

rattling with sleeping pills, sedatives, anti-depressants and heaven knows what else, all mixed up with alcohol. Everything seemed grey. Nothing seemed funny any more. When I looked at my roses I saw only greenfly; when I peered through the window my gaze was stopped by smears on the glass; when I cooked I tasted only grease. All the feelings of doom returned. I resented my children. I resented Horace's success and I resented my failure – my depressing book had made the rounds of the publishers and had been rejected. Above all I resented my resentment. I was shocked at my unfairness and my uncivilised behaviour. I knew how unfair I was being. It was precisely of what I most disapproved. Once again I experienced the sensation of my blood curdling in the veins.

I was crippled by nervous exhaustion and particularly exhausted by intellectuals. All those ideas batted round the room like tennis balls, the mind thundering like a heart after a fast run, thoughts whirling, racing up and down the nervous system so that I could hardly sleep, waking up exhausted. I reverted to the other extreme, wallowing in nature and animals. I began to be more and more affected by the ugliness and horror that was being created in the name of profit. 'Progress' made me feel impotent and angry. Factory farming was my first horror but next to it property speculation was running a close second: all those awful tower blocks, those acres of concrete, stifling the land, perching people up in the sky, making them dependent on every whim of the establishment. I hated scientists and economists and men of progress. I hated them. They seemed to me to endorse so much suffering in the name of profit. They reduced animals to machines and reality to paper. I hated the education system which seemed to produce unbalanced freaks, lacking any sort of common sense, their limbs of specialisation sticking out like goitres. I felt isolated and crushed by an uncompassionate system, trapped by an infernal circle, confined to a paper world which squeezed out individuality and was geared to the making of money and the spending of it. Always the economists, or the industry, had some argument ready to justify their horrible schemes.

And how altruistic they sounded! Factory farming for example: 'the world was full of starving people and by the year 2000 .... People are more important than animals,' they said, 'there is no room for sentimentality, one must live with realities.' Anyone who rebelled against 'reality', in other words the commercial interest of some company or other, was called a crank. Factory farming, tower blocks, aircraft noise, anyone who disliked them was a crank. One evening a man lectured me on how nature was obsolete: we must abandon all romantic notions of the countryside; we could not escape from the realities of life (factory farming and property speculation). It was absolutely contrary to what I felt. It seemed to me that reality was nature. Continuity and security came with the seasons, with the lilacs and the roses returning each year. The values of the economic society seemed to me not only false but excessively evil. Exploitation was being sanctioned in the name of money. Furthermore I felt the system was not even practical. Not only was society invaded by industry, which poisoned, created shoddiness, ugliness and excruciating noise in the name of profit, but people were being turned into robots to manufacture machines which would make them redundant. It was an Alice in Wonderland situation.

I hated the economists and their materialistic values yet I was too caught up in the cycle to drop out to an alternative world as the hippies were doing. Nor would I have dreamt of doing so, all that was quite foreign to me. I was part of the machinery, part of a society in which it was virtually impossible to live without a substantial income. As usual the idea of escape obsessed me but my agents for liberation were standard – sex, holidays, food and drink – and in turn these became obsessions, traps, requiring financial resources to pay for them. I felt more than ever that my inner self was a caged lion, rampaging round inside my body, up and down the bars of my mind, using the orifices through which briefly to escape before being hauled back and trapped as before.

I do not give space to these afflictions for motives of self-pity but to underline the malevolence of my nervous system. That there was something very wrong with this I have no doubt. The symptoms that began in that cursed house in Devon were now recurring ten years later. The delicate mechanism had tipped over and my life was out of control: the source of bad luck and unhappiness. That chemical imbalance was so strong that I experienced the strange sensation of inner curdling as acutely as any external pain. At the same time it was accompanied by delusions. I knew, for instance, that when Horace said he had taken the car to collect some books from the library he was really having a drink with a girl. I believed this implicitly, quite regardless of Horace's assurances that he had not been having a drink with a girl at all, but had been collecting books from the library.

Meanwhile I was writing a second book: about food; about why the Victorians ate so much. But I could not begin until I had understood against which pressures the Victorians were reacting. Because of my motley education I was unequipped to use standard analytical processes. The scientific practice of extracting a part and examining it seemed to me not only unsatisfactory but impossible. I went deeper and further back into British history until at last I arrived at the Roman Empire and could grasp a picture of the whole. I had to make a study of England through the ages incorporating agriculture, social history, superstition, attitudes towards sex and pleasure: all these seemed to me an integral part of why the Victorians ate so much. Thus the book had several aspects. One was an attack on the Church: I saw the Ministry, with its crusades, its doctrines of hell-fire and sin, its burning at the stake and torture of heretics, as the source of bigotry, guilt and fear, all in the name of God. Another was a study of British cooking and its development, starting with Romans and ending up in the present day with a harangue against factory farming. It seemed to me that the Roman and Victorian style of entertaining (the *nouveau riche* one, that is) had much in common with modern dinner parties. There was little here of the aristocratic notion of hospitality, where entertaining was a duty of the rich man who provided food, shelter and entertainment with no view to self-interest. Romans, Victorians and modern hosts had, it seemed to me, several motives other than altruism. Money = success = energy = virility: this equation was interchangeable and equally applicable to all three groups.

Consuming Passions, as the book was called, was my education. Every day I researched at the British Museum and during those hours established some sort of grounding in British and European history. I combined paper with practical research, rummaging through the hedgerows, wallowing in

25

spices, pot herbs, puptons, pickles, jellies, fritters, ragouts and custards, bubbling mediaeval potions, tasting such rareties as messes of pottage, frumenty, civet, charlotte, wild carrot, glasswort and skirret. Writing the book was however something else. There is a marvellous image of Carlyle's: the machinery of the mind like some giant rusted crane lumbering, grating into operation. My mind must be one of the most cumbersome and corroded that has ever tried to make a book. It was nerve-racking. Building it up piece by piece; like a jigsaw puzzle, fitting in the parts, unable to see the whole. It seemed that all round me in thin air ideas whirled. I would clutch at a thought which, like straw, blew off in the wind, often never to be recovered. All those blank pieces of paper on which I scribbled the ideas, all those stacks of exercise books filled with illegible notes waiting in chaos to be set in logical order and narrative! 'What is your book about?' people would ask. I dreaded this. Actually I did not know what the book was about. Like any jigsaw puzzle I had to wait until each piece was in place before I could see the picture.

In 1968, in this state of intellectual and physical exhaustion, I went along to Caxton Hall to a lecture on Transcendental Meditation. By now Maharishi Mahesh Yogi had appeared a few times on television, bursting often into convulsive cackles of laughter. Horace had thought him ridiculous. I however found him marvellous. He and his T.M., as it was called, carried an appeal for many people. You were not required to give up anything. You were not even required to believe in God. It was simply a technique that anyone could learn which would lead automatically to inner peace. Caxton Hall was packed that night and wreathed in a cloud of tobacco smoke. The large audience was mixed. A woman in front of me seemed to be unravelling a red bath mat. There were ladies in fur coats, gentlemen with pipes, girls with flowers in their hair and boys with long curls. Meditation, the lecturer told us, would bring us energy, intelligence, happiness and perception. Perhaps, one member of the audience suggested, it would prove so delightful that people might want to meditate all day long, not wanting to go to work and live normal lives? And could the lecturer reassure the audience on the ethics of the thing? If people were getting in touch with so much energy the swindlers would be able to swindle more people, twelve, say, instead of eight, and so on.

Unlike so many of my contemporaries I was insensible to the promises of T.M. About two months later I swallowed a cocktail of tablets and, to the accompaniment of Mrs Harvey's roars was rushed in a coma to hospital where my stomach was pumped out. After this I plunged into despair and nostalgia. I made the mistake of centring myself on Horace since I had lost my own equanimity. He obsessed and possessed me. I saw him when I looked at the sky, the sea, the garden and the roofs. Our beautiful love affair once so liberating had turned into another trap, an emotional one, polluted mainly by me, riddled now with jealousy and neurosis. All the joy and delight was gone and the friction created between what he wanted and what I wanted dissipated our last dregs of energy. I still believed that a change of circumstances would clear away the poison, and eventually we struggled into a large Victorian house on the borders of Putney and Barnes. It was not ideal. Aeroplanes roared by at what seemed to be eye level, a train hurtled past at the bottom of the garden, and a vast hideous block of 'luxury' flats blocked out the sun in winter. But there was a huge mulberry tree, there was space, and now I could have all the animals in one place.

I began to pull together. It was discovered that the cause of my depression was a particular brand of contraceptive pill which I had been swallowing along with all the other tablets. Furthermore *Consuming Passions* was published and surprisingly well received. Horace, rather with his tongue in his cheek, had added to the jacket of the book the information that, besides being enthusiastic about guinea pigs and Greek dancing, I had received a Cordon Bleu Diploma in Cookery and that I was a Fellow of the Royal Horticultural Society. Upon these two 'qualifications' the reviewers pounced, citing them as the necessary certificates authorising me to write such a book. I do not wish to carp at the reviewers to whom I am extremely grateful for their enthusiasm, but must point out the fallacy of paper 'authority'. A Fellow of the Royal Horticultural Society meant simply that I had paid an annual subscription to that body, in return for which I received the Society's magazine and two tickets for the Chelsea Flower Show. As for the Cordon Bleu Cooking course, I had indeed received a certificate but for the bride's course, lasting only three months. I did have knowledge but it had nothing to do with these paper sources. It was empirical, gleaned from the homosexual cauldrons of the bistro, the vegetable garden of Devon and from putting theoretical material in the British museum to practical experience.

In any case the net result was that we were received as a sort of literary couple. I appeared in newspaper features written about Horace. I even appeared in newspaper features written about myself. But neither of us had the sustenance to hold on much longer, our affair had been too polluted. Two years later we parted. For a month I could not leave the house. Then my reaction was to become wildly, crazily, promiscuous. About six months later I was visited with a mysterious illness. My temperature rose and stayed at about 103 degrees for about three weeks. T.B. perhaps? V.D. even? Who knew? Certainly not the doctor who was never inspired at the best of times. Pints of sour yellow sweat poured out of me, day and night. The sheets were so wet they could literally be wrung out. When I recovered, my depression had more or less left me for ever. It seemed that something had streamed out in that yellow liquid and I felt light and euphoric.

For the next few years I lived between spates of intensely hard work interspersed with wildly irresponsible holidays. I was now reviewing books for the *Sunday Times* and researching for a biography of Frank Harris. For my subject I felt great compassion. There were, it seemed, two essential points of interest arising from his whole enigma: one was energy; the other was reality. As to the latter Harris was a marvellous raconteur, with his voice like the rasping of iron leaves he could hold his audiences spell-bound. His stories, especially his accounts of the Wild West, were one of the reasons for his being accepted into the salons of society hostesses, who were always on the look out for anything new. Yet even at the height of his success he never quite made it. The criterion of social success was to be received by Mrs Humphry Ward, but Harris was too unreliable even to be introduced to her, he was likely to blurt out anything. For the pioneering hostess, however, his stories were brilliant. He would recount his adventures and those of other people and in their telling he would embellish them; he would hear some story told by someone, it would lie dormant for years and then suddenly it would come back again and Harris would tell the story as though he had been present, inserting himself in the role of hero. And, as he told the stories again and again, they became real to him. Like myself with my own compensatory stories he could not tell the difference between what had actually happened and what he said had happened. He himself admitted that his mind would colour incidents dramatically.

As for energy he was born with exceptional resources. When well into his seventies, an admirer recalled, he was like a stallion, so dark, so charged. He had a magnetic presence which could mesmerise his beholders. In his early years he struck people as a remarkable and original young man. Certainly he struck himself as such. His creative energy he saw working like some fermenting brew, throwing off too many bubbles, it was true, and in a state of too much commotion: would it ever settle down to produce a strong and generous wine? he wondered. Alas, it never did. It bubbled away and finally subsided, leaving inside him an emptiness. He tried to fill the vacuum with reverence for great men. In this he adhered faithfully to the text of Carlyle's *Heroes and Hero worship*. His heroes in turn were men of letters, men of action, poets and deities: Carlyle himself, Shakespeare, Christ. It was logical to suppose that having moulded himself on such company he would himself become a hero, a deity. He identified with each of his teachers and, as much as his personality would allow him, modelled himself in their shape, becoming outraged when others failed to spot his metamorphosis. Society was in the grips of hypocrisy and inhibition and Harris spent much of his energy in trying to liberate himself from these. One of the agents for liberation, he believed, was sex, which he saw as an ennobling experience, especially when enjoyed with himself. He saw himself as the teacher, the liberator, of women. Take me, teach me, one of his heroines sighs. Sex was a sacred ritual into whose mysteries he would be the initiator; from his ladies he required devotion and surrender. He was inordinately proud of his virility according to Bernard Shaw and believed that it could be maintained by lunching on at least two entrecôte steaks and a mix of highly-flavoured cheeses, washed down with plenty of burgundy and several liqueurs. But, like his creative energy, his potency too bubbled away and subsided. He longed for love, power and money and he spent his life dissipating his resources in their pursuit. In his quest he burnt himself out. He ended with nothing: no money, no power, no grace, no success. And he was impotent, too, with a disgruntled and frightened wife, martyrs both of them to his cause: liberation from sexual inhibitions in life and literature.

The biography was received with lead reviews. On the whole the reviewers were most kind to me but Harris himself came in for a beating. And I learnt something. You can spend four years on a book, elaborately proving how someone was such and such, yet people will continue to see the character from the point of view of their previous conditioning. Most of the reviewers presented in their columns their own idea of Harris which had already been formed and which had become part of their intellectual furniture – as Harris himself would have called it. Their concepts had become to them truth, they believed them, just as Harris believed his own stories. It seemed to me that even though one might sincerely believe that something is true, it is not necessarily so. The mind is no criterion of truth, it can play too many tricks.

With the publication of *Harris* I achieved a certain literary success and a certain measure of financial security. The aeroplanes and trains still hurtled excruciatingly through the garden but I was secure in the house, I could centre myself, and I could rest. The garden grew lush, roses poured through the trees, honeysuckle and clematis rushed up the walls and over the windows obscuring the 'luxury' flats. I dug a pond in the conservatory and kept chickens, cats, a rabbit which attacked the cats and a fierce black cockerel which attacked everything. The children were far less dependent, they were at school and away for much of the time and I felt less trapped. I went off to Ireland, Greece and Italy for holidays, I had a large circle of friends and an assortment of lovers – some of them attractive. In one aspect my behaviour was not unlike that of my subject, Frank Harris. It seemed that I was making up for the parties I never had in the school holidays. Night after night

30

there were dinner parties. Bottle after bottle of drink would be consumed while we behaved idiotically into the night. And just as I had done at school I enjoyed this silly behaviour very much indeed: the sillier we were, the more liberating I found it. One would wake in the morning with a hangover, stagger through the day, struggling with one's work, begin to feel better by the afternoon, clear, if a bit muzzy, by six when one would have a drink to gear oneself up for the evening ahead . . . and it would happen all over again. Sometimes I would hardly remember what had passed the evening before. We would spend much time on the telephone marvelling at our drink consumption, trying to retrieve the events of the night. We even had competitions at parties to see who could behave in the silliest way.

Drugs were commonplace, not however taken for any transcendental purposes, just for further sensation and foolishness. Cannabis was the most usual, but cocaine was sometimes available, so was Thai stick. There was one particularly dreadful episode just before Christmas spent with a neurotic Moroccan friend who was always announcing that people were the bane of his life and it was impossible for him to see them unless he were drunk. We had made a good job of it that day: champagne for breakfast, heaven knew what at a Christmas rag-trade party in an East End warehouse, cherry vodka on the bus home and quantities of wine and Thai stick at dinner. At one o'clock in the morning one of the guests was pleased to present a capsule of L.S.D. to my neurotic Moroccan who insisted on sharing it with me there and then. Green horns shot out of his head, the chairs got up and danced and the cobwebs swung round the room; then everything dissolved in a swirling mass of energy; the furniture, the pictures, the cobwebs and my neurotic friend melted into vortices of whirling matter. And there was such a noise, a booming resounded in the air – to say nothing of the great roaring emanating from my friend who had thrown all his clothes into the fire. He was having a major hallucination, he shouted, and all I was having was a middle-class trip. Indeed I was. I was struggling round sweeping down those swirling cobwebs with a broom that kept dissolving in my hands. The only thing that got me through was my companion shouting out every hour like a night watchman: we've only got eighteen hours left of this trip; seventeen; sixteen, and so on

31

until at last the nightmare was over and everything was still.

What with one thing and another I was, I suppose, in the idiom of Women's Lib liberated. I was more or less free of my children and reasonably successful both in my career and my sexual life. I had regular 'relationships'. I had one-night stands. I had orgasms. I write this not to boast, but to show that at a certain level of society I was free, in that I was free from any inhibitions. Indeed so 'free' was I that my spontaneous sexual adventures were the source of some amusement to my friends. Once in the course of some researches into Russia and Russian wines I ended up swallowing an extremely liquid dinner with two Russians, after which I found myself on the last number 14 bus home and in bed with the bus conductor. Certainly I never felt guilty about my promiscuity. Sometimes the encounters were lovely, sometimes funny, sometimes just boring. Sometimes I was so drunk when I went to bed that on waking I could not remember who was in bed beside me – although I never hit the limits of one poor friend. Are you a man or a woman? he asked. Besides, there could be a marvellous cosiness about sex; there in the room with the fire blazing you could make someone secure, if only for a brief moment, for it seemed to me that many men were haunted by sadness: they yearned for contact, communication – some even longed for love. And for a brief interlude sex gave them release from their isolation.

To some people then it might have appeared that I was free, successful. I had plenty of friends, plenty of invitations, plenty of sex. I travelled. I earned an adequate income. I liked my house and my garden, and my books were well received. Yet something was lacking. I was beginning to feel how pointless was my life. All this rushing about, all this energy spent in order to make money to spend on more rushing about, to pay for energy consumed in the form of petrol, oil, electricity or on quantities of drink. For like my neurotic Moroccan friend I needed drink: without alcohol, or some sort of anaesthetic, I would not be able to face most of the people with whom I spent my evenings. The truth was I had to anaesthetise myself before meeting people in order to establish any form of communication. I began to want to see people less and less. We were all of us just passing the time by wasting it. Even while I was working on *Harris* I had recognised that I needed some sort of direct experience. Cooking? Gardening? In a sense they were on the right track. Smells? Scents? I experimented with medi-aeval unguents. I made an Elizabethan pomander out of gum benzoin, mixed up with musk, civet, rose oil and ambergris. It was a dark, ominous-looking thing, but it did smell wonderful and it was soothing, malleable, something to play with rather like tactile chewing gum.

But the only way I felt I was going to find this new dimension was through my work. It was not, however, going to come through the mind. I had had quite enough of received information, digested and regurgitated. Again I knew that I needed some sort of direct experience. I felt that it would have something to do with nature. Travel. A journey in some remote country? That was it. I needed to travel. There is an irony here. I knew that I required knowledge that could come from no mind, yet I felt unable to embark upon a journey without the justification (and financial backing) of 'work'. I was too much of a coward to set forth without a sponsor. I knew that I needed experience that would come from no paper-research yet ultimately I would have to put down my findings in a book.

Three countries attracted me: Arabia, India, and Georgia in Russia. I had no particular idea or views on any of these countries, just some strange attraction towards them. My publisher and agent were patient. India? No. Not commercially attractive. Arabia? Yes, now that was a possibility. I saw it in the ancient sense: myself travelling along the incense trail on a camel in the steps of the Queen of Sheba, passing through ravishing untouched ruins, redolent still with exotic unguents and spices. My agent saw a more modern journey: from the interior of an air-conditioned Cadillac I would interview various oil sheiks on how they were adapting to their new power. A preliminary contract was arranged. I began some primary research, purchasing a cassette course in Arabic. Besides the alphabet it taught you (in the wrong dialect for the incense trail) to pronounce such phrases as 'the oil tanker is in the sea'. The idea died.

Now Georgia? What about the wine trade? a dissenter suggested. Georgia was one of the oldest wine-producing countries in the world. I should become an authority on wine.

33

I could then apply to the trade delegation. I would be escorted to all the most remote corners of that country – and *en route* the smart thing to do would be to take a large suitcase of jeans to Moscow and sell them, everyone did this. So *this* was the reason I was considering a career in wine and researching so wildly into Russian affairs.

I had meanwhile decided on a year's freelance journalism. At least, I reasoned, research for this would not come from libraries. My first assignment was a piece on the dustbins of England. Rummaging through rubbish in snow-swept Glasgow was a far cry from the exotic places I had in mind, but at least garbage made a change from verbiage.

The majority of my articles however were taken up with attacking commercial greed – to say nothing of factory farmers and property speculators. The reason I mention this here is on account of the response. People wrote on the state of society, the Church, morality, and our spiritual and social leaders. 'We are so grateful to read your article,' wrote one, 'there are so many thousands who are revolted by what is going on but we seem totally unable to do anything about it.' 'Do not fear!' wrote another. 'There are many who sympathise with you, who want to build a new world and not prop up the ruins of the old. How long will we have to endure the folly of the present illusion that now dominates reality? Do you think the truth will ever emerge?'

But what on earth *was* the truth? What was reality? What for that matter was normality? Perhaps the most touching letters came from those who in their isolation were trying for some sort of contact by 'writing to the papers'. Some of these could only be described as mad. What vast numbers must there be, disappointed, hurt, persecuted, like these my correspondents, swept by pressures into subterranean worlds of fantasy, paranoia and delusion?

Another outcome of my year's journalism was that I received a small commission from a well-known newspaper to travel to India and write a piece on the Kumbh Mela at Allahabad, the largest and oldest religious fair in the world; and thence to travel to the ashram of a particular guru, Saitha Sai Baba, who had been attracting a certain amount of attention in the West. No one could have called this proposal economic: my expenses were not paid and the fee hardly covered the outlay. However the commission was the goad I required and in the middle of January 1977 I embarked for Delhi. Ironically, I could only spare three weeks in all, since I was due back in the second week of February to begin my wine course.

PART I

The Kumbh Mela dates back to the seventh century and is probably the most notorious fair in the world. According to astrological conjunctions it is held every three years, rotating between four holy places: Ujain; Nasik; Hardwar and Allahabad.* Hindus believe that to make a pilgrimage on these astrologically auspicious occasions, to bathe in these holy places, will purify their bodies from sin. Furthermore the occasion offers an opportunity to meet hundreds of holy men, many of them ascetics, who rarely descend from their retreats in the Himalayas. For hundreds of years pilgrims have made their way across India, braving dangers that have included cholera and plague epidemics, elephant stampedes and murder (certain sects, it is believed, for whom murder is a religious duty may perform their sacrament without fear, finding their victims easily on the ghats and banks). This particular year, 1977, the conjunction of stars was said to be the most auspicious for a hundred and forty-four years. Record crowds, the largest gathering of people ever assembled together, were expected to bathe at the Sangam – the confluence of the Yamuna, the Ganges and a third invisible river, the Saraswati. 'There will be nowhere to sleep,' an expert told me gloomily, 'nothing to eat; hygiene is non-existent and elephants stampede all over

* According to Hindu mythology the gods and demons, once upon a time, churned the ocean, and a pot containing amrit, the nectar of immortality, emerged from the deep. The demons ran off with the pot, resting in the course of their flight in four places – Ujain, Nasik, Hardwar and Allahabad; according to another version these are the four places where the nectar spilt.

the place' (Kumbh mêlée sounded more like it). Equipped therefore with a cooking stove which fitted into a match box, a sleeping bag purchased from a shop specialising in mountaineering gear, some garlic, a tea egg, a bag of bran and an expensive mohair rug from Harrods which would, I planned, double up as a travelling cloak and blanket, I was ready for anything. I had this idyllic vision of sleeping under a leafy tree on the banks of the moonlit and gently-flowing Ganges. The only person to be alarmed was my mother who was convinced that my feet would get, if not wet, something in them.

Before my departure I had made some researches. I needed, I knew, some kind of direct experience, yet, ironically, the first thing I did was to turn to books. *The Autobiography of a Yogi* by Paramhansa Yogananda was quite unlike any work I had ever encountered. It engendered an atmosphere of marvellous calm. From an early age this boy, Mukunda, had a deep trust in God. He was, it seemed, guided by some mysterious presence. Everywhere he went he was protected and his material needs provided for. Saints would recognise him and reveal that they were intimate with every detail of his life. Fragrances would spring from handkerchiefs and fingers; Sanskrit verses would materialise at auspicious moments enabling him to pass exams. But what he longed to do was to meet his guru. At last he did. 'Ah! you have come,' this beautiful man in his orange robe said to Mukunda. 'How many years have I waited for you?' And from that moment it seemed like a love affair. The guru assumed all responsibility, cured the boy's illnesses, protected him, guided and guarded him, was always there when required: a soothing, strong father figure.

This book created for me the frame of mind in which I approached India; invading, pervading, the pages was the feeling that nothing ever happened by mistake, everything was some sort of sign. It seemed to me that I had been called (saints and gurus were always appearing in the pages of *Autobiography of a Yogi* and telling people they had been called). There was one particular guru – the guru of Mukunda's guru's guru named Babaji. He sounded quite extraordinary. He worked in the Himalayas with a secret band which included two advanced American disciples. This Babaji was apparently deathless. He would remain in his present body during the

37

present world cycle, but he was elusive, appearing only to select people who were in a sufficiently evolved state – and often these revelaions occurred at the Kumbh Mela. His message was that between the East and the West there must be a bridge established. I saw myself travelling to India to be that bridge. First however I would meet my guru – whom I would instantly recognise. The rapport would of course be mutual: 'So you have come,' he would say. I should also add that shortly before I set forth for India I had smoked some Thai stick; just as the effects were beginning to wear off and I was going to sleep I heard a strange music – music I had never heard before in my life: melodious, undulating notes that carried with them a central vibrating tonic.

The moment the plane landed I was aware of a strange undercurrent of soothing harmony. I felt absolutely at home. I was aware of the confusion, babble and bustle, the crowds rushing here and there, transporting, it seemed, whole households piled up on their heads, yet underneath was this peace. Here we were, with a great distance to cover and very little time in which to do it, and it did not seem to matter how or what happened.

I was travelling with a friend whom I had known for many years. Ian was a researcher into such esoteric matters as levitation and kundalini, or, as he put it, mumbo jumbo. He was a marvellous escort for this, my début, into the world of Asia. He made most of the arrangements and I could enjoy myself. I was absolutely delighted by India. The train steamed across the Ganges plain towards Benares and never, it seemed, had I seen such beauty. I had not imagined that India could be a green land, yet the brilliance of young wheat, mustard and sugar-cane was overwhelming; and everywhere were women swathed in saris of scarlet, blue, gold and emerald, scattering seed, carrying curved water jars on their heads and tending herds of goat and buffalo. Small winding paths and dusty tracks led invitingly over the land. Sometimes the fields were cut by canals, there were glimpses of peacocks, long-legged white birds, monkeys, pigs, parrots and elephants. 'Never,' I said, 'have I seen such peace, never have I seen such light, such brilliant beautiful light.' 'Your window is coloured,' Ian said drily. 'You are observing India through coloured glass.'

Indeed we were travelling in luxury by air-conditioned carriages whose windows held tinted glass. Meals were delivered to us and when we stopped at stations we enjoyed tea and toast and watched monkeys run up and down the pylons. Long lines of crows flew into the sunset, light thickened, then suddenly the illusion was shattered, a gust of vomit spattered the glass, followed shortly by a stone.

At six in the morning we arrived at Benares station. The morning was cold and a white mist covered the town; the sun was just rising, infusing the cloud with a red glow. I had never in my life seen anything like that platform: so many people in one place. Some were apparently cooking their breakfast in the middle of the station, some were drinking tea, most had not yet got up. They were lying in bundles everywhere, with just a thin cloth under them to protect them from the ground and another wrapping their bodies completely from head to foot like a shroud. There they were, these bundles, lying side by side, like mummies in a museum. Outside the station, the crush was astonishing and all the people so gracefully draped, the material marvellously swathed not only round the women but the men as well, and everyone balancing their luggage on their heads – one man had four yellow plastic chairs and an orange table all piled up there. Our own luggage as well as ourselves perched precariously on a cycle rickshaw. As we passed through the streets, smoke mingled with mist as breakfast began to cook. Here, the doorstep was the kitchen. Families squatted round their brick ovens eating chapatis and vegetables, surrounded by pigs, cows and dogs. It was the most harmonious atmosphere all in that dusty rosy morning light. The rickshaw man turned round to make some remark and suddenly his mouth filled with blood, it flowed over his teeth and lips. It seemed we had been too heavy for him and that he was struck down by a haemorrhage. But it turned out that he was only chewing betel; what we saw was quite commonplace, one minute a fellow is quite normal and the next he appears to be dripping blood like a werewolf.

From the map, Benares had seemed the most suitable place whence to approach Allahabad. We enjoyed grand accommodation complete with bathroom at Clark's Hotel. When you turned on the tap only cold water gushed forth. 'Yes, yes, yes,' said the housekeeper, who had been summoned and who was rolling his head in the strange way with which Indians indicate the affirmative. 'It is coming, isn't it?' It was not. Several people congregated, shaking their heads now. Allahabad? More head-shaking. The catalogue of difficulties seemed copious. The day after tomorrow is the most lucky day, you see. On 19 January everyone is wanting to take his bath at that time. Trains? Most probably they are stopping because of the crush. Buses? Please no. You cannot imagine the squash. Taxis? Now they are very scarce. We sat waiting, discussing over glasses of whisky the price of maintaining elephants. No one can afford them these days, they are more expensive than Cadillacs: all that hay and banana plant – not just plant, whole trees, isn't it? Then, miraculously, the press officer appeared to adopt our cause. It was his problem, his duty, to find us a car. Everyone rolled their heads happily over more glasses of whisky.

'This is something every Hindu is doing, rich or poor,' said the press officer; 'taking his bath in the Ganges when his mother is asking him.'

'Excuse me, please,' the hotel P.R. man had joined us. 'You are having trouble with your water, isn't it?'

'I am asking you what will you see?' the officer ignored him. 'Beautiful brothers washing their sins together? Or dirt? Dirty people?'

'Please, you must turn on the taps also,' said the P.R. man anxiously. 'It is very cold outside. Everyone is wanting his bath at this time. It is taking a long time to come down, I am telling you.'

'All the cars are stopping far from Allahabad,' the press officer said next morning. 'You must walk seven kilometres with the pilgrims. You cannot possibly imagine the crowds. It's extraordinary the faith of the people. Ten million people can't be wrong. Ten million people can't be mad. Goodbye, goodbye.' He pressed an envelope into my hand marked 'ON INDIA GOVERNMENT SERVICE: Take B.C.G. vaccination'.

That journey to Allahabad was extraordinary. Again I was amazed by the country's lushness, we passed through villages with huge heaps of shining vegetables laid out for sale. The tree-lined road was crowded with pilgrims, travelling by horse and bullock cart, foot, rickshaw, camel, elephant and bus – which drove in their hundreds along the middle of the road, horns blaring. One man, holy apparently, was walking along with his arms attached permanently to a crossbar, so for anything he required to eat or drink, or any function he needed to perform, he must rely on the passers-by. By mortifying himself, putting himself to such inconvenience, he hoped to receive illumination, according to our drivers who, being the owners of some shop, 'Curio Cottage', in Benares, were extremely anxious that we return and purchase their curios.

We approached the Mela from what seemed to be an escarpment and looked down over a great sandy plain which, with its patterned tents and coloured flags, spiked by watch towers manned by soldiers, resembled a giant war camp. Organisation of this Mela had started months before and now a canvas town covering three thousand acres had been erected, complete with flood-lighting, hospitals, piped water, chlorinating plants, latrines, loud-speakers and disinfectant. Posters offered one thousand rupees for each identified rash of smallpox, and all beggars and lepers had been bustled off to special colonies – very nice homes, as one lady described them – where they make baskets. Away in the distance across a sparkling river packed with boats the bank teamed black with people. The sound was extraordinary: whistles, car horns, loudspeakers, mounting in crescendoes of hysteria, shouting out names of lost people; and then the voice of that crowd rolling in, great waves over the white sand, like roars of an ocean. It was only after some time that we discovered that we had arrived at the wrong place on the wrong side of the wrong river and that we should be five miles away somewhere in the interior of that human forest. It took us all day to get there, encouraged by a band of volunteers with red caps and whistles whose duty it apparently was to provide us with a personal escort service, row us across rivers and hack our way through the human undergrowth. At last the crowd became less dense, people had space to hold out their saris, like sails to dry in the sun, and we were on tarmac joining a flow of traffic – pony carts overflowing with sometimes as many as twenty people, army jeeps and pedestrians kicking up dust and disinfectant – passing shops

41

and side-shows which included a laughing booth emitting howls of laughter. 'What happens if it rains?' Ian asked our guide. 'No. No rain,' he replied.

At last we came to our camp which, sighted at sunset, was the scene of some confusion. In the left-hand corner of a tent a man wearing beads and a white dress was trying to use the telephone to arrange a talk on kundalini. In the centre was an official endeavouring to use the same telephone to reach a certain extension 117. In the right-hand corner a second official was dealing with an Australian television crew who were hoping to climb something called the Nose Tower. 'No. No. It is forbidden. Absolutely forbidden,' this official was shouting. The Australian film crew were here to shoot scenes of the holy bathing and naked sadhus, only to find that it was forbidden to photograph either the holy bathing or the naked sadhus; recently a photographer had tried to photograph a naked sadhu and the naked sadhu had bashed him over the head with his trident, and the photographer was still in hospital. At this point I delivered my letter to the central official who crumpled it into a ball and banged it down in front of the second official. 'Hopeless,' he bellowed. 'No hope for you here. It will be definitely impossible for you to find accommodation. No, there is no accommodation whatsoever.' Unfortunately the press officer at Benares had applied his dispatch to the right-hand official, who turned out to be called Mr Singh, rather than this central figure, whose sense of protocol was deeply offended. This was my first taste of Indian bureaucracy. Some time passed.

Meanwhile Yogi Shantisgaroop, he in the white dress, introduced himself. He knew all the saints. There was one over two hundred years old who lived naked on a platform and who had manifested an orange for Mr Singh. The latter in spite of all his difficulties with the television crew and his colleague, now revealed that he was not at all tired because he had this special advanced meditation – he could go for seventy-four hours without food, sleep or water. India had been inverted, he explained, forever asking: What am I? Who am I? Why am I? Here he broke off to deal with an American, a scholar from Harvard, who was writing a thesis and having difficulty with his pass. Just then the bureaucrat rose to his feet. Our acccommodation was now ready, he said, and we were shown to a fine patterned tent complete with carpet, camp-beds and a bathroom. All night the chanting, the loud-speakers, the police whistles, the car hooting, the excitement and the roars of laughter from the laughing booth continued.

Nothing is considered more auspicious for the holy dip than a light drizzle. At midnight the rain started. As the lucky day dawned the mercury fell to four degrees centigrade and water flooded the floor of the guest accommodation and dripped steadily through the sagging roof of the press tent. One of the highlights of the festival was the spectacular for which the press had come: the procession, which started at dawn. Sadhus made their way down to the ritual bathing accompanied by carved wood chariots, elephants, bagpipes, conches and drums. Members of the press were to be escorted through the crowds to special towers from which to watch the pageant (the mere sight of the sadhus in cavalcade is believed to cleanse one instantly from sin). But the rain was so heavy that it had thrown the programme out of gear. No one appeared to escort us and a few members of the international press hung around soggily, making plans for their immediate return to Zürich, Paris and so forth. 'Soft morning,' said one reporter wittily. 'More like the bloody monsoon,' said another who came from Delhi. And like the monsoon it continued all day.

A steward hurried up beaming through the drips. 'Six thousand people are arriving per minute. Thirteen million are in this area, already one million have taken their bath this morning.' It was like a racing commentary, and the more the merrier. Every few hours the press authorities released statistics revealing how many trains, buses and pilgrims had arrived, how many had bathed, how many had been treated for cold. In the gathering light most seemed already to have been immersed, drenched to the skin they flowed down towards the Sangam, silent for the most part, their feet churning the dust and disinfectant into chilled mud.

Ian, Shantisgaroop and the hotel P.R. man, who had mysteriously appeared, were enjoying meanwhile a cloud of incense in a neighbouring tent – which belonged to a lady from Kuala Lumpur, and which was dryer than ours – while awaiting a police escort to drive them to the Ganges. The lady from

Kuala Lumpur and Ian had stayed up talking late into the night, during the course of which she had revealed that she had met the ageless Babaji on three separate occasions. But I had no chance to talk to her. Yogi Shantisgaroop commanded my attention: 'I am getting very beautiful vibrations from you. You are being an artist, isn't it? Recently you have had an occult experience?' He would, he said, take me for his sister. and his guru, who was three hundred years old, would teach me to feel happier, to work for peace in the world. . . . Here the lady from Kuala Lumpur suddenly flew at Shantisgaroop. 'Why do you call yourself a yogi?' she demanded in really quite violent tones. 'You've got a long way to go yet. You dress yourself up like that, you are nothing but a phoney.' Shantisgaroop took no notice at all, just addressed her with what I suppose was meant to be a loving gaze. At this point the police escort appeared.

What a crew we were, setting out in the pouring rain! Shantisgaroop in his white, Ian phlegmatic, the P.R. man, joined now by his colleague the housekeeper from Benares, myself in a bedcover, and the lady from Kuala Lumpur who was trying to remove her pink petticoat so that I might wear it for bathing. 'Now all India will be very nice,' said Shantisgaroop happily, eyeing the saturated crowds. 'All purified.' We alighted from our escort's car at a fortress and encountered a grand vehicle flying an ensign; inside, his forehead lined with white sandalwood paste, was Jagadguru Shankaracharya, one of the most illustrious holy men of all – the Hindu equivalent to an Archbishop. Shantisgaroop presented his dripping group through the window – the lady from Kuala Lumpur still struggling with her petticoat. 'Now we will be very lucky,' he said. An even grander car appeared, containing a gorgeous figure in red: the governor of Uttar Pradesh. 'Very, very good omens,' carolled Shantisgaroop. 'Two very lucky meetings.'

Our boat was less buoyant. Shantisgaroop lusted after one with a blue awning. We were propelled however towards two decrepit shells awash with bilge. 'No problems,' cried the housekeeper gaily. 'I am your housekeeper in life also, not only in the hotel. No problem with the bath.' 'Which bath is that?' Ian asked gloomily, peering into the swirling waters. 'Goodbye, goodbye,' the lady from Kuala Lumpur, still wrestling, was vanishing in one of the covered boats.

All round us boats were moving towards the Sangam. People were chanting, singing, beating drums. There was the fragrance of incense, the rattle from a thousand oars. We floated low on the water, moving down on the grey Yamuna, enveloped in a haze of rain. Soon Shantisgaroop and the house-keeper were left far behind. Every so often we passed small sta-tionary craft on which lone men crouched over flickering fires. What a sound there was! The chant of bhajans,* echoing, reverberating into the distance, the soft hum of millions of people, the hiss of millions of feet through mud; mile upon mile of people moving gently, softly, all with one goal in mind.

At the Sangam the crowd was so dense that, apart from the jungle of masts, you could not tell where the water began and the boats finished. Eighteen million people, we were told after-wards, had come to bathe that day. Eighteen million people! Jammed between shivering people struggling to change their clothes I perched on a heaving deck and, feeling a bit like Nanny at Frinton on bank holiday, held Ian's things while he bathed. I am sorry to say that I did not immerse myself, but to reach land we had to wade through water which was waist-deep. You could hardly squeeze through, it was so packed with people. Some were so old they were bent double, some were babies, some looked absolutely dazed: all were shivering with cold. As each of us climbed up on to the land, steam rose off our millions of bodies to blend with the mist and the rain. 'From where are you coming?' people called, again and again. 'Where are you coming from?' In the middle of it all, waist-deep in the Ganges, there was a bazaar going on: men with buckets of milk were selling cups for one rupee, not for pur-poses of refreshment but for dropping into the holy river; others sold coconuts, red powder for putting on the hair and garlands of marigolds. All along the edge of the water little piles of incense smoked and the bank was covered, as far as one could see through feet, with garlands of flowers and tufts of hair – many shave their heads before the holy dip and drop their hair in the Sangam.

On land we planned a visit to the camp of Ananda Mai Ma, one of India's most famous saints. Unfortunately when we

* Devotional songs.

45

tried to ask directions we omitted the 'Ma' (mother). 'Ananda?' We struggled through the wall of people. 'Ananda?' Puzzled faces agreed politely. Decorated entrances would be indicated or the smoking banks of the Ganges. It was only later that we realised we had been mouthing the Hindi word for bliss to people who must have imagined that we were making some sort of salute. 'Ananda? Ananda?' Through the wind and rain, we paddled, through the mud, past lines of beggars, escaped apparently from their homes and baskets, past a man who pursued us, pointing an erected cobra into our faces, past dripping straw temples. 'Ananda?' Up came a boy dressed in white who escorted us into a tent. 'Brahmacharya, brahmacharya,'* he kept on saying. What a muddle there was in there! A row of men taking money, while a sage in a saffron robe with lustrous eyes received a line of women. 'Come out, come out,' ordered the boy in white. 'He will be very angry with me.' What seemed to be a religious play with painted actors, in crowns and jewels, jumping up and down, gongs, cymbals, drums and conches afforded brief shelter. Nearby was a sort of temple with logs of wood burning, into which only special initiates could enter. Over a pontoon bridge, soldiers beating people off the sides, swept into a steaming mass, forced like cream through a funnel, rotated, warm mud oozing under foot, breath crushed from lungs, people falling, gasping, eyes staring, mouths gaping. Expelled into the cold once more. 'I don't know what Nanny would say about all these wet feet,' Ian said.

Now we had arrived in the sadhu's area. Here were the nagas, naked but for a covering of ashes and the occasional bit of sackcloth, squatting in front of the fires, blessing pilgrims who came to touch their feet. A man indicated that we should follow him. He led us to his tent, inhabited by his mother, daughters, sons, brothers, sisters and grandchildren who were all here for some weeks making their pilgrimage. They served us with delicious food: sweet stuff like fudge, crisp spiced lentils, puris, peas, fried chapatis; all of which we ate with our fingers from leaves. We had little language in common, but their gentle eyes, their kindness in offering two bedraggled strangers food and shelter did not need words. Here was our food being provided spontaneously, straight from the pages of

* Celibate religious student

46

Autobiography of a Yogi. Shortly after this something else happened which seemed too to be sent by providence.

I had abandoned the search for Ananda Mai Ma and, leaving Ian, I slipped and slithered, drenched to the skin, back to the camp which was about four miles away – or rather this is what I tried to do, but it was not easy to find anyone who knew where they were, let alone who spoke English. Soon I was lost and in quite the wrong direction before a stone temple. Here the crowd was not so dense and a man was tying a rope to a jeep, in order to extract a car stuck in the mud. Not only did this man speak English but he knew the area intimately since he was some part of the organisation. Furthermore he even drove me back in his jeep to the camp.

Vijay was certainly a gift from the gods. Not only was he a source of information but his language was a joy, comprising a sort of 1930s vernacular, which belonged in the world of P. G. Wodehouse. People did not make mistakes, they made howlers. The government had only today made a howler. Vijay had been allotted the government quota of a scooter for the quarter July to September 1976, but the letter telling him this had only arrived that very morning, six months late – indeed the Indian post sounded no better than its British counterpart, one letter had taken eight years to arrive. There was nothing, it seemed, that Vijay wanted more than to place his government jeep, together with himself as driver, at our disposal. He left us with firm plans for the morow to escort Ian and myself on a tour of the saints.

Meanwhile we spent the rest of the evening with a journalist who now lived in America, but who had returned to gather material and to escort his mother on this pilgrimage. He had spent the day talking to people. Did they have any complaints? (He, himself, had plenty, he thought it was quite irresponsible the way the government had advertised the Mela, drawing by every possible means people, scores of whom had fractured their limbs and been trampled in the mud.) He had interviewed some groups who had stopped by the side of the road and made a fire. Like thousands of others they had come for miles (many pilgrims were away from their villages for as long as a month), they had been walking for days and were exhausted, drenched to the skin, with nowhere to go as they lay on the Allahabad pavements with only a wet blanket to cover them. Did these people have any complaints? No. no complaints.

This was the story wherever he went. Nowhere was there the least sign of crossness or irritation. The journalist had interviewed a barber. For the latter the Kumbh Mela is the highlight of his career. He could, on a major bathing day, expect to shave as many as one hundred and fifty people. That day he had shaved fifteen. The journalist had sympathized: very bad. *Bad*? The barber had been astounded. If God had ordained it, how could it be bad? Another had lectured the journalist: 'You travel everywhere by air; you dash about all over the world; you see nothing but concrete; everywhere is the same. I have travelled along the road from my village. I have seen every grain of sand, every blade of grass, every person on the way.'

There was much to be learned from this Mela and one thing at least did not require translation: here, one was led to believe, were eighteen million people gathered together, most of them poor villagers. Here were eighteen of the starving millions we were always hearing about. But how tough these people were! Whole villages, old people some of them, who must have been well over ninety, enduring rain and discomfort that few Western people, let alone geriatrics of ninety, would face. Malnutrition and debility were not conditions that were evident, it seemed to me: fortitude and strength, however, were.

Next day dawned cold but dry. Shantisgaroop in a most beautiful ochre robe, hurried in: God had wished that we should not bath together, but today we would make a tour of the saints, isn't it? His entourage consisted now of two photographers, the journalist and the journalist's mother. Vijay arrived. Who were all these jokers? he wanted to know. They seemed a boring lot to him. Nevertheless, jokers and all, we piled into the government jeep and set off on our conducted tour. Apart from the special area that was allocated to nagas there did not seem to be a special locality for saints. Those on our list were to be found in different corners of the three thousand acre area. It is doubtful we would have found them without Vijay. You needed someone with a clear picture of the

48

layout in order to navigate the crowds which had the same effect on visibility as dense fog.

Veena Baba, a scholar of music, was first on this whistle-stop tour. The moment we entered that tent a feeling of peace stole over me. It was extraordinary in there. The floor was lined with straw and the fragrance of incense mixed with the all-pervading disinfectant. The man himself was seated cross-legged in front of an altar playing the veena. His expression and his eyes were gentle, his head was bound in a red turban, his chin was covered with a luxurious beard, and his music was ravishing – a marvellous plucked rhythm accompanied by the vibrating hum of a harmonium coming in great waves of melody. This was the sound I had heard that night of the Thai stick. There was nothing I wanted more than to sit there quietly, listen to that wonderful music and establish some sort of contact with this man. Here indeed were shades of *Autobiography of a Yogi*, but that is where the resemblance stopped. The two photographers jumped about rustling the straw with their flashlights. Could we sit here? Could we sit there? The journalist tried to interview Veena Baba in the middle of his raga. Vijay dispensed cough lozenges and Shantisgaroop autographed and distributed compositions which actually belonged to Veena Baba, who after a while, showing visible signs of relief that we seemed to be departing, handed round some sugared seeds. 'Let's beat it,' said Vijay, confiscating the seeds. 'No please, they may come from a dirty place.'

Our second objective was Aghori Baba, a sage who has lived wrapped in blankets up a tree for twelve years and is a member of a sect which, to conquer worldly feelings, once every twenty-four hours must eat some noxious morsel, excreta perhaps, carrion, a sliver from a corpse. We all paused under his tree, while he peered at us through red-rimmed eyes. Was there anything he required today? Vijay inquired – it seems that he often runs small errands for him. Aghori Baba wondered if he could have an umbrella.

We moved on to Vishwa Guru Pandal who sat sniffing loudly in a beautiful dry tent. We arranged ourselves in front of him. 'What medicines have you brought?' Vijay asked me. 'I will give you a list of all the medicines you should buy in India.' A line of people came up to touch Vishwa Guru

Pandal's feet which were tucked away warmly under him. He gave a grunt, exposed his sandaled extremities, then addressed a few grave words to the line of devotees. 'He is now discussing what sugar to buy,' Vijay explained. 'How they should get some for all the people who have arrived: now it is bedding, he will give these people bedding to sleep on.'

From here we proceded to the camp of the famous Ananda Mai Ma, who was nowhere to be seen. The tent was crowded with detectives preparing against the arrival of Mrs Gandhi who was lunching with the saint. We waited a little. Vijay produced his certificate of vasectomy. This, it seemed, was a document of some importance, carrying advantages beyond the obvious. If you required a commodity which was in short supply, a motor car for example, your chances were considerably improved if you produced this magic docket; and though obtaining merchandise had not been Vijay's motive for agreeing to the operation in the first place it made a nice bonus. On this note we left Shantisgaroop and his entourage waiting for a sight of Ananda Mai Ma and moved far away to the other side of the river where the crowds were thinner. Two camels lay resting, loaded still with huge piles of wood. We crossed the Ganges where it flowed down towards the Sangam. 'Many pilgrims are drowned,' said Vijay in a voice of doom – he was always coming up with intelligences like this. You never could tell how many had been drowned, policemen were pushed in, voluntary helpers, Vijay had seen their red hats floating on the waters.

Now we had arrived back at the nagas' area. Vijay thought very little of the nagas. A dirty lot, he called them. Fools. The lowest. They just sat about wearing nothing, having a good time in front of their fires. Soon we arrived at the platform of Deoraha Baba, who is said to be over two hundred years old (some say three hundred), and who lives naked, with long flowing hair, so bent with some affliction that he is unable to stand upright, in this strange little hut on stilts. Deoraha Baba has a large following among government officials – different gurus, it seems, attract different types, different groups of society. Today there was no telling what group of society was here. Hundreds of people were round the platform. They stretched up their arms, their fingers dark against the sky, to receive bananas, mangoes and oranges which had been blessed by his touch and came showering down upon them. Then the crowd in turn peppered the balcony with money and more fruit, the latter returning to them again, a storm of sanctified comestibles. Bent double, the saint retreated into his hut, and liquid of an unknown quality trickled down through the floor boards. The crowd rushed beneath, stretched up their hands to receive the drops, in their eyes, their hair, their open mouths.

Our lunch was for the second time provided free, this time by the Marwaris, the Jews of India, who provide many services for the poor. Long lines of people seated cross-legged were served with chapatis, rice, vegetables and chillis which they ate with their fingers from leaves sewn beautifully together; when they had finished, second helpings came round. We were placed a little separately, we all ate with our fingers while Vijay lectured us on corruption. People spend ages apparently fiddling their electricity meters, changing over all the wires, many of them so incompetently that at the end of the quarter they end with a credit and Vijay has to go round and disconnect them. When we had finished eating, the Marwaris gathered round thanking us for eating their food; their ultimate hospitality being to introduce us to their guru Dharam Dassji. We sat before him, drinking tea, and there is no doubt that from his presence there did emanate a delicious calmness. But suddenly this was disturbed, a stir ran through the tent and a man dressed all in black dashed in. This was Kali Kamli Wale Baba – The Black Blanketed Fellow – who was asking for Dharam Dassji's guidance with his Character Building Foundation, whose main aim is – appropriately enough – to halt corruption. 'This is a very famous saint,' cried Vijay excitedly. 'People have been waiting for years to see him. It is very surprising that we were just sitting here and he came to us like that.' The Black Blanketed Fellow however was clearly not interested in us, he proceeded to shuffle through his papers; and shortly we left – not only the Marwaris' encampment but the Mela itself.

Ian was anxious to return to Benares and did so during the afternoon by train. Vijay volunteered to drive me in the government jeep back along the tree-lined road to Benares later that evening. As we drove away from that huge area, the

51

Ganges was pink in the sunset and all the sand very black. It was like a spectacular shot from a film. Indeed the whole night was like a film.

For a start the attitude that Vijay adopted towards me was far more familiar on the screen than in real life, quite unlike that of most Englishmen I knew: he was so protective. We ate dinner in the little back room of a restaurant, dahl in a delicious tomato and garlic sauce, seated on benches on which you were supposed to sit cross-legged. We drove on, the trees dark now against the sky. Here and there the road was full of holes – some jokers had taken the stones to build their ovens in the villages. We never reached Benares that night, we spent it instead in an official inspection bungalow somewhere along the way – Indian nights, it seems, are very like Arabian ones.

After the Mela the inspection bungalow seemed the epitome of luxury, the staff rushing about: yes, sahib, no, sahib, three buckets full, sahib. They kept on bringing in beautiful hot buckets of hot water and next morning delicious hot samosas were carried from the village nearby, vegetables and jalebis, which are a kind of syrup fritter, a breakfast speciality in the villages. Then all the staff brought me roses to wear in my hair.

The day was bright with sunlight, the sort of morning that comes in England at midsummer when the grass is drenched with dew and there is an early morning mist; everything expands, one's spirit lifts and the trap loosens. So there it was, this optimistic morning after such a night. To add to the oriental flavour Vijay claimed that we had already been married in our past lives. And now God had arranged that we should meet again at the temple. This was why I had been drawn to India, to Allahabad, to the Kumbh Mela. It had been ordained that we should meet again. This, according to him, happened sometimes. Souls met up with their true partners and were united again. And indeed when we parted I did feel as though something had been torn away.

There was however no time for languishing. Next day we rose at dawn so that we could watch the famous Benares sunrise in the company of a holy man Ian knew, who was experimenting with levitation. Muni Baba lived up a labyrinth of small winding streets lined with tiny shops selling scented oils, spices, kohl and coloured powders. He had not spoken now for several years and communicated with the aid of a very grand pen. 'Are you well?' Ian asked him. 'No,' wrote Muni Baba. He had a soft pain where his third eye was and could not eat or drink, furthermore he had nothing to tell Ian on the subject of levitation. He slept on a carpet under the roof of what smelt like the public latrine. Sai Baba? We were going there? Sai Baba's favourite devotees were extremely rich, he penned. 'Sai Baba appreciated only for capitalists.' 'Competition' Ian remarked afterwards. Marvellously spiced tea was served and then we squeezed our way through the narrow passages that intersect the old town of Benares, packed that day with pilgrims who, having visited Allahabad, were now taking in Benares. We came to the banks of the Ganges and from a wooden pier jutting out into the water watched the sun rise, a great red balloon climbing slowly out of the water, while down below on the bathing ghats ladies wrapped themselves in their saris and washed their clothes. A boat carrying an enormous load of hay was rowed slowly past.

From here we proceeded to the burning ghats. Benares is the Mecca for Hindu death, everyone who can afford to comes here to be burnt: it costs fifty rupees. It seemed to me that the attitude towards dying is more healthy than in the West, were death lurks, the unmentionable monster of the twentieth century, filling us with fear. Yet it is the one thing of which we can be absolutely certain: we all have to die. Here in the East it seems to be treated in a more intimate way: it was a bit like going home, one Indian told me. Little children played round the burning funeral pyres, a few hens scratched and plenty of cows wandered about – those cows are more like goats than cows, they eat anything, one was busy swallowing a long red sari. The bodies are wrapped in material and carried on stretchers of green bamboo poles. In the adjacent street there was quite a queue of corpses lined up waiting till there was pyre-space available. The mourners wait too, squatting patiently in small groups. First the bodies are dipped in the Ganges and then they are ignited. The pyres flare up sizzling, there are pops and explosions as skulls burst and gases escape. Yet I found the scene less macabre than the performance at modern crematoria when the coffin slips away, a curtain is drawn over and unseen the body is precipitated into subterranean furnaces (the coffin, it is whispered, having been appropriated before-hand).

From Benares we went south by Indian Airways to Banga-lore, where we were to visit the ashrams of two holy men: Tiruchi Swami, the guru of the lady from Kuala Lumpur, and the renowned Saitha Sai Baba. Bangalore seemed sweltering after the winter of the north, and after Benares rather like America. There were plenty of modern buildings, fewer cows, no cycle rickshaws but hundreds of noisy scooter ones with puritanical slogans inscribed on their backs: 'Work more', 'talk less', 'the need of the hour is discipline', and so on. To get to Tiruchi Swami's ashram you go through country which is rather like suburbia, with large housing developments. There were some monkeys, but very few cows, just oxen with painted horns, for the people here in the south decorate their bullocks; with their doe-like eyes and their huge pointed horns, all brightly painted and topped with tinsel baubles, they were more like reindeer ready for Christmas than beasts of burden. A pair was being shod in the leafy clearing on the side of the road as we passed, one man made the small oval shoes, while another knocked over the animals, tied them with a rope and sat on them.

We arrived at the ashram just as the most colossal din was starting up. The noisiest discotheque imaginable had nothing on this blast. We were shown into the temple where bells and gongs were crashing, reverberating in the ear-drums. Men kept on approaching with items with which I had absolutely no idea what to do. When in doubt, I thought, eat it, accordingly I did so: white powder, red powder and bananas, only stopping short at some flowers and a flame on a plate which was being circulated in the air – we had had the good fortune, I learnt afterwards, to attend a Hindu service of worship, a pooja, and the powders were supposed to be applied to the forehead.

The ashram was beautiful, with tall fruit-bearing trees and pigeon-lofts and a charming dog which was particularly fond of one rather fat devotee, who drove up in a car just after the pooja, the dog looking sheepish sidling away after him. Outside the walls, stone-chippers were at work, banging away at huge rocks. A regular line of ladies came to draw water from the well; their activity contrasted with the still air in the ashram garden, peaceful now that the din had died away.

Soon we were ushered into the presence of the guru, who was sitting on a Western chair in a quiet room. He was a sweet man, but I was not aware of any rapport between us. It did not seem that it was he drawing me to India. He spoke a few words. Everyone was united, he said, to find God and the Self. As soon as money was involved peace of mind evaporated. Ambition was particularly bad. We must go round experiencing, meeting people until we found the right one to guide us to God. We must not meanwhile fill ourselves to the brim with food. We must eat the right things: avoiding meat – because animals had the right to live for themselves – and alcohol. Soon after this Ian and I were given lunch in a clean shining hall: a huge meal dished by servers from buckets on to banana leaves while we and the ashram inhabitants all sat cross-legged on long mats stretching down the hall and ate with our fingers. After lunch we talked to a devotee. Everyone should have a guru, he said. Previously his uncle had been his, then one day he had come to this pooja, had met this swami and had had the feeling that he should return. He was remarkable, this swami, a great soul. Years ago he had performed miracles. Now he performed none. Don't worry, he tells his followers, I am with you always, everything will be all right. This devotee's sister had had a dreadful accident, she lay in hospital with her skull fractured, quite unconscious. The doctors said they didn't know how she would be. Our friend had thought of Swamiji. Soon, after three hours, his sister had recovered consciousness and she had been quite all right. For three years he had been coming. All the time he has had extraordinary experiences. Sometimes he sees his guru's face wreathed in a divine white light. He has completely changed. He used to get angry. Now he is quite calm – certainly his expression was delightful: clear and serene. Here again straight from the pages of *Autobiography of a Yogi* was the idea of this parent figure, guarding one, protecting one, radiating love, teaching one, above all caring for one's well-being. It was a seductive prospect. I longed for the experience myself.

Disciples refer to their gurus by special names. Tiruchi Swami is known to his devotees as Swamiji. Saitha Sai Baba is named variously Baba, Swami and Bhagavan. He has millions of followers from all over the world. On one occasion when he was in Delhi crowds surrounding the place where he was staying were said to have stretched for one mile in all directions. He claims (along with at least two other gentlemen) to be the reincarnation of a famous Indian saint – Shirdi Sai Baba. He claims also to be an avatar, God, reincarnated in human form to save the world from the moral and spiritual crisis into which it has fallen; come down to distribute liberation and bliss and to establish a life of morality and virtue. He has been the subject of several books, a few of which I had read before my departure. I had been very impressed. I felt this extraordinary link, this bond. Saitha Sai Baba was exactly in keeping with *Autobiography of a Yogi*. I had felt that it might be he who was going to say: 'So you've come.' And as the train had steamed across the Ganges plain to Benares I had tuned in to him, or imagined that I had done so, and a stream of energy had shot through me swelling my head so that it was like a huge balloon. It was not altogether a nice sensation. According to these books Saitha Sai Baba had performed an enormous variety of miracles and manifested a huge assortment of physical objects. Indeed these books were catalogues of marvels, their authors testifying to the manifestation of carved glass bowls, sweets, photographs, emeralds, rubies, crucifixes, statues, fruits, necklaces, rainbows, rings, pendants, books, and, of course, his speciality: ash – vibhutti. These authors had seen him cure cancer, paralysis and stomach ulcers; they had seen cripples throwing down their sticks and walking. Saitha Sai Baba had rescued disciples from wells full of water, flaming railway carriages and frying-pans. He had raised them from the dead and materialised surgical instruments with which he performed miraculous operations – once a mislaid cheque-book had saved a couple by mysteriously turning up in a suitcase.

He was stopping just then at Whitefields, his establishment just outside Bangalore. It was not possible to stay here and his numerous Western worshippers – many of them middle-aged American ladies from the mid-West – were putting up in various luxury hotels and travelling comfortably to darshan* each day by taxi. (Ian's theory was that they were all divorcees

* Seeing a holy person or image.

56

spending their alimony – this was how they could afford to come for two months and keep a room in expensive hotels.) They seemed to spend their day in Edwardian style, constantly changing their clothes: special silk saris for darshan (Baba insists that his ladies wear saris), special loose clothes for shopping, special casual robes for listening to Indian music in the evenings and so on.

Before morning and evening darshans the route to Whitefields was a bit like the Kumbh Mela on the most auspicious bathing day – crammed with people. Darshan was held in a large open space before a building which was like an enormous iced cake, all blue and pink and white plaster elephants, tigers, gods and lotuses; everywhere there were lotuses and everywhere strange hieroglyphics sketched in the sand and decorated with coloured powders.

It was evening when we eventually arrived at Whitefields. By then I had worked myself into a state of suspense. This was going to be the great moment of my life. I was going to meet my guru. The scene was stunning. The energy of that crowd was rather like that engendered by a football match, a great flow of electricity, yet one that did not erupt into violence, it ran through in a highly, charged, controlled tension. There was very sweet singing going on, accompanied by drums, bells and harmonium, nothing at all like the din from the other ashram. The shadows were growing long, dogs were lying in the dust and we all sat on the ground waiting, women segregated from men. We must have been there for about an hour. The tension mounted. Smoke spiralled upwards from the incense and then a hiss ran through the crowd: Baba was coming. He stepped through the long lines of people, wearing an orange robe and a frizzy Afro haircut just at the moment that the sun was setting. He stood under the banyan tree on a dais rather like a bandstand and the sun set behind him so that it gleamed through his lips. Then from the air he produced a flow of fluffy silver stuff – vibhutti – which flowed out of his hand into the open palms of a man. And then he turned towards me. Now, I thought, would come the great moment of recognition! His face was rubbery, his expression the most gentle and compassionate I had ever seen. It was as though he glowed with love. For a brief moment his eyes rested on mine and I experienced something like an electric shock running through me. That was all. He stopped and spoke to very few people. It was something of an anti-climax. Yet there was no doubt that Saitha Sai Baba did have a remarkable magnetic presence – even Ian was impressed. Just as he was disappearing from view an orange, exactly matching the orange of his robe, appeared in his hand and he threw it to the driver of a car parked in the compound. Gradually the crowd dispersed. 'Heavenly!' breathed the ladies from the mid-West. 'He was heavenly!'

The highlight of the ladies' trip was to be Shivaratri.* This was to be celebrated at Puttaparthi, Sai Baba's birthplace in the hills, where every year he performs two of his public miracles: ash flows unceasingly from an upturned urn and a lingam,† sometimes of crystal, sometimes of other materials, shoots out from his mouth. The proposed journey had all the Western disciples in a fit of jitters. 'That avatar sure makes me nervous,' exclaimed one, speaking for them all. Words flew about: he is leaving for Puttaparthi tonight ... tomorrow ... in a few days' time ... Monday ... Tuesday ... Wednesday. The days passed. The disciples were as blown and confused as leaves in a gale. Was he going? Wasn't he? Could they not go to Puttaparthi and wait peacefully until he arrived? No, certainly not. No one must leave before him. Rumours grew more fantastic. He is going to inaugurate a state bank; the trees are

* The festival of Shivaratri celebrates the night that Shiva saved the world by swallowing the poison which threatened to envelop it. The story is that Indra, king of the gods, had been cursed by a great rishi and had lost his powers. Vishnu promised to return them provided he could produce the liquid of immortality by churning the sea, using Mound Mandara as a stick and the serpent Vasuki as a rope. So he began, but the gods pulled the snake by the tail and all the devils pulled it by the head and a torrent of venom escaped from its jaws which poured down in a vast river threatening to destroy everything. In their distress, everyone called upon Shiva who heard them and swallowed the poison, thus averting a world disaster.

† A lingam, according to Howard Murphet, one of Sai Baba's disciples, is a Hindu symbol, mathematical in form: an ellipsoid, symbolising Siva-Sakti which is the primary polarity principle of positive and negative forces. The lingam therefore is the basic form lying at the root of all creation, just as 'Aum' is the basic sound. It lies at the base of all matter within the atom where the electrons apparently move in elliptical course round the central neucleus.

being cut down; there will be no more darshan as we know it; he will walk along a high wall; he will appear as a red ball in the sky.

At last the day dawned. Definitely he would be leaving today, although the hour was not yet known. The American ladies spent all morning packing, unpacking again and balancing articles on top of taxis. At half-past one news came: he had left in his white Mercedes.

We all set off in pursuit – apart that is from Ian who was returning to England in some pain having dislocated his knee while availing himself of the Indian lavatories. The American ladies were equipped as if to penetrate a jungle: cooking stoves, mosquito nets, beds and heaven knows what besides were all wobbling about on top of the taxis. The journey, though ravishing, was anything but peaceful on account of the tenseness of the passengers. The country was rather as I imagine Mexico to be, red rocks, red tree trunks, palm trees and strange shaped hills all bathed at sunset in a soft warm light. Oxen with their painted horns worked water-wheels in leafy groves as we drove along the narrow ribbon of road leading on and on into the interior.

At Puttapatthi the narrow street was lined with shops that seemed to comprise a Saitha Sai Baba industrial centre, selling photographs, medallas, vibhutti, cool drinks, saris and so on. And there in that remote hill village was Prasanti Nilayam (The Abode of Great Peace), a huge plaster palace, all domes, pavilions, temples and halls, decorated like Whitefields with gods, elephants, tigers and countless lotuses.

There were a thousand guest cells alone into which we were duly shown. And they were literally cells, small bare cement rooms, approximately eight foot square with adjoining lavatories and taps. Now one could see the reason for all the equipment. My cell mate was from Los Angeles, called Denise. She had ridden horses bareback at the circus and performed some strange trick with a rope in Las Vegas. Now she runs a Saitha Sai Baba centre in L.A. Sai Baba sets great store on bhajans: when she started she had never sung a bhajan in her life, yet the rhythm and the intonation came to her automatically. In her metamorphosis she looked more Indian than the Indians, adorned with nose-, toe- and ankle-rings. She maintained a high standard of material comforts, however, travelling with a store of protein pills, vitamins, sugar and coffee to which I added my match-box stove, bran, tea egg and garlic. Soon she had converted our cell into a mixture between a laundry and a temple. String lines carried our saris hung out like coloured scarves while the alcove was transformed by candles and incense into an altar, underneath which lay all Denise's pills and make-up, my cooking pot and travelling stove. It was a strange sight. The fragrance of rose oil mingled with that of incense and flowers. Soon two cockroaches emerged and made themselves at home.

One thing was certain: there was a great deal of red tape in this particular kingdom of heaven. Rules abounded. One must cover oneself at all times and, in that sweltering heat, wrap one's sari round one like a blanket so that one's shoulders were not visible; one must never approach the men's quarters; one must walk in line; one must have permission to do anything and everything; above all one must lead a very pure life – no pop music, no television, no films, no meat, no alcohol, certainly no drugs, smoking or promiscuity. Sing bhajans, be good, see good, do good, notices exhorted from the walls. It was like being back at school again, yet a school that was charged with this strange energy. It was curious to see these middle-aged ladies from the mid-West, submitting to this discipline: one aged about sixty tried to get permission to go to Bangalore and buy some deodorant, a commodity which exercised them all a great deal. 'You stay,' Baba had said. She stayed.

Apparently one had to have a lot of merits* from past lives to get to Puttaparthi at all. Denise has had many lives before, she says; some unhappy ones in France and England, many in India, some in Egypt (she looks rather Egyptian), some were in Atlantis and some on the Steppes of Russia. Sai Baba, she explained, can be anything you like: mother, father, child, master, lover – you decide the relationship you want and he'll go along with it. Denise had selected lover. And it was by no means an unconsummated affair. He visited her by night in the

* Karma, the law of cause and effect, decrees that one carries from one's past lives all one's merits and demerits, for which one is rewarded or punished accordingly.

wildest, most passionate dreams. Clearly she was in love with him. 'He was so beautiful tonight,' she would sigh. One evening she saw a white aura round his head: 'Oh! you're cute, you dear little lotus face.' When she was not eating cookies (she was, she explained, a cookie monster) or meditating, she was concocting long letters to 'little lotus face', and then the ensuing days would be spent wondering whether he would or would not take them. 'I thought he wanted it and then the little stinker never took it,' she grumbled irreverently. It appeared she had done something with which he was displeased.

It seemed that we were all obsessed with Baba. He had bewitched the lot of us. I was occupied with my own fantasy. As each day dawned, I felt that this would be the one in which he would show some recognition. He would come up: 'So you've come,' he would say. I was still sure he would say that. 'I've kept you waiting, a little test, but now we can talk, come along with me' – or something of that nature. Yet he never did. There was however this strange force circulating through the place, this highly-charged, electric atmosphere. We glowed. I felt the sort of well-being that comes from being in love; this even with a particularly disagreeable cold, caught in the rain at the Kumbh Mela. Yellow fluid was pouring from my sinuses. 'Baba is clearing you out,' explained Denise. 'People get awfully ill here, it's all the impurities draining away.'

Every morning at first light devotees would be up brushing and combing the sand, sketching those strange hieroglyphics, decorating them with coloured powders and watering the trees and jasmine bushes which were planted in special beds protected by packed mud walls. Outside the walls of the ashram, shopkeepers and flower-sellers were also up at dawn selling freshly-gathered garlands and vegetables. Our day began at four o'clock with meditation in the temple (not that I had any idea how to meditate), then as dawn broke the sky turned pink and birds began to fly out of the trees and everyone was supposed to process round the ashram chanting bhajans. Breakfast was at seven, darshan at nine, bhajans at eleven, then lunch, one slept through the heat of the afternoon till five when it was again darshan, bhajans again at six; bed and lights out at 9.15. Silence was supposed to be maintained, but what a racket there was! People chattered incessantly and one person sounded as though he were clipping a hedge all night long. 'It is always like this before festivals,' said Denise, with the air of a veteran.

The day was geared to darshan – the focus of all our fantasies. Some people arrived as much as two and a half hours early to secure a 'good' position, and they would sit on the ground waiting, under scrutiny of the Sai Baba police who patrolled continuously to see that no one was doing anything without proper permission. It was never certain what a 'good' position was, since as always Sai Baba set out to confuse. No one ever knew what he was going to do next; no one knew where he would go or whom he would select for interview. Sometimes he would go only to the men's lines, sometimes to the women's. Sometimes he would smile at a few people, sometimes he would address them with a few words, or take their letters; sometimes he would select a few lucky ones for interview: 'You go,' he would say, and they would get up from the ground and go to a side-room. There was no question of applying for an interview. Either he selected you, or he did not.

Every day more people arrived, bringing the halt, the lame and the sick: frail sticks of bodies lying out on stretchers. You did not often talk to people but I did meet two Malaysian ladies who were displaying all the symptoms of paranoia. One, called Malu, was very annoyed indeed. Have you had your interview yet? she asked me. No? Well, neither had they. They'd arrived on Monday night and still no interview. 'I'm not like you people,' said Malu. 'I'm not a believer. I sit here and I say, what the hell do you think you're doing?'

'Are you enjoying yourself?' I asked, foolishly, under the circumstances.

'No, certainly not,' said Malu. 'If I get my interview I shall go home immediately. My friend here held out this handful of letters we've brought from our friends: *he* just touched them.'

'Yes.' The friend was indignant. 'I said: "Bhagavan, these are for you." Nothing. There I am having to carry all these heavy letters round and he never took them.'

'He comes up and looks at me with hate,' Malu said. 'They all told me: the first time you see him it'll be the most marvellous sensation. I saw him. Nothing. I say to him: what the hell have you brought me all this way for, Baba, if you're not going to call me for an interview? You'd better give me a jolly good reason.'

Several of the Americans did not seem too comfortable either. One called Marybeth set up a great yelling one night about the cockroaches; she and her daughter were moved to another cell and the next night they yelled about mice instead. One lady, who was inclined to be bossy, was growing increasingly agitated at the shortage of deodorant. 'You'll smell like an Indian,' she told a colleague who had completely run out. 'Do you *want* to smell like an Indian?'

The country round Puttaparthi is beautiful with its mauve mountains and brown and orange landscape. Every so often I would play truant from the bhajans – together, I noticed, with several others who could be seen slinking away *smoking cigarettes*. Nearby was a curious hill on which there was a holy tree. The story is that when Sai Baba was fourteen, or so, he used to take his friends to the tree and ask them which fruit they would like to pick; no matter what they selected, apples, pears, mangoes, oranges, figs or any other variety which might not necessarily grow in the area, there it would be ready for plucking. Obsessed by my lack of contact with Sai Baba, I climbed the hill and sat on the top watching the sunset. A boy was bringing in a herd of goats, girls carrying water pots on their heads were returning to the village for the night and huge dark birds were wheeling against the glowing sky. Away in the distance lay the dried-up river bed with a few remaining pools where the villagers washed their clothes, the coloured saris laid out on the sand to dry. Up there in that highly-charged atmosphere I prayed for a sign. I prayed that I might know what on earth I was doing. And I was filled with elation, again the sort of joy that comes with a love affair; not quite secure, rather tense, but that sort of feeling. From below the sound of bhajans floated up to my hill. It was a moment of stillness. I climbed down to the tree and there I found a holy man, a sadhu, who gave me a packet of ash. I should always say 'Sai Ram', he said – the greeting, the salute of all Sai Baba devotees – because this would remind me that Sai Baba was always with me to take care of me. I walked back in the night, the crows wheeling, the sky very pink. And in my state of mind this seemed to be the sign I had asked for. In that atmosphere even the most trivial encounters seemed infused with some deep meaning, incidents appeared ordained: omens, signs, portents.

Not far from the village, down the road near a small cluster of thatched huts in a leafy grove where peacocks called, is Sai Baba's dairy farm. It is the most singular dairy farm I have ever visited. I went one day at dawn. Hibiscus, oleander, jasmine and marigolds bordered the drive, which like that of the ashram was beautifully swept with circular brush strokes and hieroglyphics sketched in the sand. The cows were very docile, sleek and shiny, and there was a large brahmin bull with a hump, more like a camel than a bull, very beautiful, his horns all painted red, and beside him, grunting, his friend which was like a Friesian. At the end of one of the sheds was Sai Baba's menagerie, consisting of a strange bird with feathers sticking out of his head like a mop, a young camel and an elephant. The elephant seemed out of sorts and fretful. She waved her trunk backwards and forwards weaving like a frustrated horse. Once there had been a nightly ceremony at which she garlanded Sai Baba; now she had been dismissed to the cowshed where she seemed bored and lonely; this in spite of her keeper who lived with her. His washing was hanging out to dry before an altar made of camel and elephant fodder, decorated with photographs of Sai Baba. Even the fields seemed immaculate; all the cows were lying down, some with crows balancing on their backs, some attended by long-legged white birds. Even outside there was an altar with a white brahmin plaster cow suckled by her calf and the god Krishna playing his flute. Suddenly from out of a small hill opposite the sun rose exactly in line with the altar and the whole scene was flooded with light. The morning and all the hills glowed.

The ashram became fuller. A German lady arrived in our cell. Like everyone else she was under Sai Baba's spell. 'I have wanted to go back to the Aurobindo ashram at Pondicherry,' she told us, 'but Baba won't allow it. "You stay," he says.' Her health was not too good, plainly she found these spartan living conditions difficult, nevertheless she endured them with determination. Her daughter apparently was horrified. What? You live in a room with no chairs, no table, no *bed*? I'm certainly not going there. As for the Malaysian ladies, they continued in gloom.

'If you're hoping to have something nice for tea,' Malu said, meeting me on the way to the dining-room one afternoon, 'there's nothing left to eat. We just had a drink.' She seemed very chatty that day. 'What do you think of India? What? You love it? That's unusual, if I may say so, for a white person. You're very race-conscious in your country.' Her friend was still weighted down with the bundles of letters. 'We are saying things about Baba over there.' I met them again next morning. 'Did you sleep well?'

No, Malu had not slept at all. Her friend had snored and when she had stopped, the person three doors along the landing was snoring even louder. They were still obsessed with the delivery of their letters. Always they went to darshan early and always something happened; either *he* went to the men's lines or *he* ignored them. But on my last morning Malu herself was called for an interview. 'You go,' he said. Malu was very frightened, her friend said. She would not look at him at all. She just sat gazing at her feet. I never did know what happened. I had to catch the bus before the interview was over.

My own night in the Abode of Great Peace had been anything but peaceful. The mangy dogs – of which there was an abundance – set up a frightful howling. 'They drag them away with wire loops and strangle them,' said Marybeth. 'They hit them with sticks stuck with nails. It's very distressing to us Westerners who are used to dogs being so pampered. I woke up the other night and cried.' There had furthermore been a mysterious rustling all night long in our cell. A cockroach was eating Denise's cookies. 'I never knew a bug could chew like that,' Denise remarked.

Although it did not seem that I had made contact with Sai Baba, the sense of his presence on my journey to Bombay was overwhelming. This was the first time I had travelled alone in India. In the ordinary way this would have been nothing, after all I knew very well how to shift for myself. However, when proceeding into the unknown, it is all too common to be met with a catalogue of dangers. Vijay, for example, had been full of stories. Only recently, he said, six buses and two coaches had been ransacked near Barelli and two passengers killed: to travel alone was to lay yourself open to rape and pillage. The amount of difficulties promised for my journey seemed insurmountable. It was apparently impossible to buy a first-class ticket to travel by night without a reservation. You had to wait until the train arrived and since this happened at midnight there was every likelihood that it would be full. But in fact the journey went like clockwork. I safely negotiated the stages by bus and pony cart and reached the station whence the single guage track would carry me to Guntakal, the main line junction. The platform was crowded with devotees, all come that day from Puttaparthi, all filled with optimism. Tales of miracles and healings were fresh upon their lips. This one had a son who had been cured of a skin disease; that one had himself been healed. We were all united in this flow of energy. Baba will take care of you, they said. Baba will see that you get safely to Bombay.

And he did: or so it seemed at the time. At the first stop three men entered my railway carriage. Officials no less, they turned out to be, of Indian Railways. At every stop cups of tea, coffee and delicious snacks appeared – by courtesy of Indian Railways, all hospitality extending to myself. They would, they said, arrange everything for me. And so they did. When at midnight the Madras-Bombay express thundered in to Guntakal everything was settled. The din and confusion as those huge trains steam in has to be seen to be believed: everyone rushing with their baggage on their heads; up and down the train go the coffee- and tea-sellers, the vendors of pens, books, fruit and nail-cutters; everyone shouting and yelling. And there I was being escorted through it all into a first-class sleeper where two Indian ladies like angels looked after me, tying my sari, ordering me food and drink and helping me in every possible way. Far from being in danger I had never felt so protected. One of the ladies was herself returning from an ashram, a remote place right down in the south called Tiruvannamalai. The guru was dead, but his spirit lived on, and the ashram was very beautiful, at the foot of a holy hill round which disciples were recommended to walk every day. You could see that she was not impressed by Sai Baba. She didn't like to say anything, she said, but ... She gave me two books to read: *The Path of Shri Ramana*, Volumes I and II. When we arrived in Bombay she took me to her flat and gave me a delicious lunch, followed by a siesta on her bed. I coveted one of her pieces of furniture, a marvellous swinging seat suspended from the ceiling by ropes, you could sit there, gazing out to sea, swaying backwards and forwards, the warm air fanning your face and body.

I was sorry to leave that generous and gentle woman. This sort of welcome I felt would hardly ever happen in England. Here again was the question of hospitality. At home there was rarely either the time or the inclination to offer shelter to strangers. People lived to tight schedules – to say nothing of a calculating rota of cutlet for cutlet. But for this lady nothing was too much trouble. She even drove me to the flat of some people with whom I was to have drinks before my departure. These were Parsees. The man was a typical product of Harrow and Oxford: sophisticated, cosmopolitan and sceptical. It was a ridiculous situation: there I was in a crumpled sari and sandals, shining with credulity, and there were these Indians, more international than many Europeans, cold with rationality. The ladies were trendily dressed – or they would have been trendily dressed about ten years ago – in high platform shoes and trouser suits. My experiences were all coincidences, said my host. Nothing to do with Sai Baba at all – indeed my host had himself had similar experiences in Germany one Christmas when some people had taken complete charge of him, driven him hither and thither and finally paid for his railway ticket. It had nothing at all to do with God – in whom he did not believe. What good were these miracles anyway? What do you do in that ashram all day long? What does he do, this Sai Baba, if he's so remarkable? He produces ash? You *eat* it? ugh! ugh! ugh! and they all made exclamations of disgust, turning with relief to discuss the niceties of Eaton as opposed to Grosvenor Square.

PART II

I had set out for India in much the same frame of mind as for any previous work of research. I had returned bewitched. I was the archetype of a person who is swept off his feet by the place. I had been delighted by Vijay, dazzled by Sai Baba and astonished by the Kumbh Mela. Never had I seen anything so exotic; the crowds, the feeling of awe and reverence were stunning. Nothing would ever be the same again. I think the reason for my being so affected was that this strange new world had absolutely nothing to do with anything I had ever known. The experience was similar to that sense of adventure you feel on moving to a new house. An air of freshness hangs over rooms uncontaminated by memories. All too briefly you enjoy a certain space until the clutter comes crowding in.

Before going to India I had been consciously active in all that I had done. I had exerted myself strenuously, with the result that I was usually exhausted and often ill. India changed my attitude to life. It made me change gear. Now it was as though I had entered a theatre. I sat back in my seat and watched the play of life passing before me. I moved from being active to passive. Of course I did often get up from my seat and join the actors on the stage. But for the most part this passive mood stayed with me.

India made me realise that the dimension I lacked was a spiritual one; that I had been operating (and indeed still was) on a restricted basis. Spirituality however was something decidedly foreign, something that happened abroad. It had to do with sackcloth and ashes; with sadhus up trees; holy men dressed in orange. It was extremely exotic and it had nothing to do with England, where it seemed to me that faith in God was non-existent, having been replaced by trust in the human mind.

Just then I was reading an anthology of love letters which contained some written by men about to be executed. You could see that it was their confidence in God that had given such men as Chidiock Tichborne, Thomas More and Walter Raleigh the strength to face their deaths – and in the case of Chidiock Tichborne a dreadful death it was too, by hanging, drawing and quartering. God was to them a certainty, whom they would meet in heaven. He granted repose, comfort and lasting riches. He would be a husband to their widows, a father to their children. Indeed the attitude towards death had been, it seemed to me, far healthier in those days. One accepted that it was God's will that one must die. Nowadays, each man was his own god, creating his own world and terrified of the death that would end it. And the culprit seemed to me to be science. It was Darwin (who himself once aspired to take Holy Orders) and the evolutionists who caused the fissure between religion and science. At the first glimpse of evolutionary theory God was hustled out of the back door and numerous scientists were shown in through the front. Now, on the one hand, science was was standing for free thought, free speech, liberation; and, on other, the Church was the symbol of bigotry. But science, though devoting its energies to making human beings comfortable, subduing matter, fighting diseases and taming nature, cannot after all overcome nature's final solution: death. Furthermore, by splitting the atom, it has dealt the final blow, it has devised a means of totally destroying us all in the twinkling of an eye.

In this vein I went off to my wine course. I sampled the finest vintages, but not somehow with the same zest. The wine seemed to curdle my new energy: I did not feel so well after a few glasses as I had done before them. On the last day there was a grand passing-out lunch – which in my case was quite literal. We started at ten in the morning tasting the rarest madeiras, ports and sherries; with lunch came superb vintage clarets, burgundies and brandies. We adjourned to the Ritz for champagne cocktails; by eight o'clock I was slumped over the wall outside my house – crying drunk, as my father would have said. A wine career was not for me. I had neither the constitution nor the control. Georgia faded from my mind.

I knew I must return to India. By now I had read the two volumes of *The Path of Shri Ramana*, of which it must be admitted I had not made much sense. But then I had read Paul Brunton's *Search in Secret India*, which had much the same effect on me as had *Autobiography of a Yogi*. Paul Brunton was a sceptical journalist who had travelled across India. He was always having chance encounters which were to change the direction of his life for ever. All along his route people came to him declaring that a higher power had stirred him to travel to India; that he was on the brink of illumination. Those who search sincerely, they would say, will most assuredly be led towards God/the guru at the appointed hour; whatever destiny had been allotted must be fulfilled. Like the *Autobiography of a Yogi*, it was a marvellously soothing book and very exotic. Fakirs pierced their cheeks with nails, extracted their eyeballs so that they dangled bleeding from their sockets, trapped scorpions within magic circles. Yogis wound themselves into strange contortions; revived dead sparrows so that they rose up and fluttered round the room, and projected strange streams of energy into Paul Brunton himself – forces which poured through his body, stiffened his neck, drew up his head. Others told him how they had met their masters; there would be this venerable man with lustrous eyes, anything from four hundred to one thousand years old. 'So you've come,' he'd say (naturally). 'Six months ago I was directed to take you as a pupil. . . .' This higher power had drawn Paul Brunton eventually to Tiruvannamalai, to Ramana Maharishi and the ashram at the foot of the holy hill whence the hospitable and gentle lady on the train had been returning. Fifty years ago tigers had lived in the jungle, there had been huge snakes, cheetahs and scorpions, and Ramana Maharishi had been alive. There Paul Brunton had found his guru and had been precipitated into a spiritual trance lasting two hours; in the midst of an ocean of blazing light he experienced a delicious sense of absolute freedom.

I saw myself as a sort of 1970s Paul Brunton. I would be doing the same thing fifty years later, wandering through wonderful green valleys and over mountains, very peaceful, very soothing. My agent and publisher were loyal, if luke-warm. No one, they reiterated gloomily, wanted to read about India. Nevertheless they came up with a commission, but also put forward another idea altogether. Why didn't I write an illustrated book about debutantes? This was exactly the sort of book I did not want to write. Nevertheless I agreed and then regretted it. It involved long hours of research: hours of digesting and regurgitating other people's books. And to make it worse it had to be done quickly, rushed out in time for the Christmas season. I started in April and by November the book had struggled to a conclusion, leaving me wrung out like a dish-cloth. I was growing increasingly tired of words, whether uttered or written.

Two other incidents added considerably to the year's difficulties. One was Roy. Roy is not his real name: he said he wanted to be called Roy because he had once known a Roy at school who was madder than he. I had first met him just before I departed for the Kumbh Mela. He had himself just returned from India and been recommended to me as a source of information. It was with him that I had smoked the Thai stick. It was not a conventional liaison. For a start he was twenty-six when I was forty-two. I am prepared to admit that the bond that I felt between us may have had something to do with the Thai stick, nevertheless I did feel this curious and intangible connection. Sometimes, power appeared to surge out of him. At others, strange forces seemed to emanate from his presence. Sex was important – it had been the cause of much trouble in his earlier years. He had this concentration of energy which, it seemed, had nowhere to go, no direction; it needed to explode in the cleansing force of orgasm.

He had been travelling in India for three years and was quite disorientated. He could settle at nothing. My heart is dead, he kept on saying. Yet he had a rare sense of intuition and when we were together, or sometimes at least, peace would envelop us. His skin seemed that spring to grow darker and as the year progressed he became wilder and would jump into the air uttering Indian ejaculations. He went off to Wales on an archeological dig and somewhere in Newport was beaten up by a gang of hooligans – as my father would have called them.

Next he departed to Dorset to some establishment where he believed he would be healed by the discipline of manual work.

Meanwhile my youngest son's speech day approached. Speech days were anathema to me, indeed anything to do with those schools was anathema (and it was I who had to deal with them and my poor mother who had to pay for them). Once I had gone to discuss my eldest son's academic progress and the master had tried to remove my dress. This particular occasion proved to be no less awful. Since Roy's establishment was near my youngest son's school, it had been arranged that he should escort me. We were to meet in Salisbury. It was wonderful weather. Heat shimmered over the lush June downs. The cathedral close was fragrant with roses. My escort however was less engaging. As he came into view it was clear that there was something very wrong. He was unshaven, wild-eyed and almost speechless. He waved his arms about: 'Shakti!' he kept ejaculating. We went then into the country to picnic on that balmy midsummer's night. We ate a little, drank a little and then suddenly something triggered off an explosion inside Roy. His heart thundered and some strange force shot through him, rather like water boiling up in a kettle. He grabbed me and bit my arm so hard that his teeth nearly went through to the bone. After a little he became calmer and we could return to the hotel, which was an old coaching inn converted in the worst possible way, all plastic fittings, hideous annexes and the inevitable fire-doors. Here Roy removing all his clothes, wandered off through the corridors.

So there we were! And as if that were not bad enough speech day loomed ahead on the following day. I had to get to that speech day and I had to get back to London after it: the car was borrowed and I had to return it. The only hope, I felt, was to continue as though nothing odd were occurring. So next day we set forth again. There it all was: cricket and strawberries and chablis; England at its most romantic; the stuff of tradition and nostalgia. The speeches were held in the Greek theatre. The headmaster of Westminster, I remember, was the speaker. I was very impressed by his powers of oration, although his message escaped me since my attention was wholly taken up imagining Roy careering naked over the cricket pitch. All was well, however, or anyway until he reached the train (for he insisted he must return to his manual work), then somewhere along the route his suit vanished. Next day he was back in London – having walked all night – ranting about great princes and adventure playgrounds and how he loved everyone and it was his job to help them. He accompanied his recitation by a tuneless composition thundered out on the guitar which he called 'The March of Angels'. He was taken off to hospital and treated with electric shocks. When after some months he was released he was totally obsessed with his body: with sex and eating. Like most of us he did not get on with his parents who were the unwitting source of much guilt and tension. Quite unaccountably it seemed the most natural thing in the world that he should come to my house in Putney. Apart from the fact that he had been diagnosed as schizophrenic I had absolutely no idea what was wrong, no clue as to whether he should or should not be given any special treatment, no clue, for example, whether he should drink alcohol. As a matter of fact I had no clue what schizophrenia was: nor it seemed had anyone else. His doctors refused to discuss the case at all. The psychiatrist's unhelpfulness seemed quite as bewildering as Roy's fits.

One thing was very clear, however. No sooner do you have anything to do with one who is mentally ill than everyone turns up with stories of their own lunatics. One had a cousin who thought he was God, always rushing into Brompton Oratory and taking off his clothes behind the altar. Another, a curate whom we all called 'the vicar', had known a lady who, whenever she passed All Soul's College, Oxford, would observe: 'You may think that's All Soul's College, Oxford, but it's not, it's my husband's palace and he's the king.' Another thought she was the Princess of Uganda and if 'the vicar' would ring the Ugandan Embassy and tell them that she was being held prisoner in the mental hospital she would give him an elephant. All of them were visited by delusions of grandeur: either they were gods and kings or their relations were.

The other tribulation that year was Vijay. Our separation had done nothing to lessen his certainty that I had been his bride in a previous life. He communicated on writing paper that was illustrated by misty figures romancing in leafy glades. Each drawing was embellished by a verse, if it could be called a verse.

> I can live each day
> hoping and believing
> and reaching out
> for new tomorrows
> all because you're the
> keeper of my dreams.

and another:

> I can't remember
> how or when it started –
> but somehow you and I
> came together –
> and suddenly love's dream
> came true.

In the cold light of England his written word did not seem to carry the charm his oral tones had held. I cared neither for his style nor for the situation which was clearly getting out of control. As I saw it our romance belonged in the exotic world of the Kumbh Mela. It had nothing to do with home whither it appeared to be approaching. In his first missive, dispatched soon after our parting, he reiterated long-windedly that it was God's will that 'your body and soul had to meet me as we have definitely been associated in our previous life and such souls must meet their loved ones again if there is true love and affection'. If I had the chance to live with him, he said, I would know and appreciate how much he would love and care for me. He was sure I was a sincere and true person and would not like to forget him, or to let him down. Then after a lapse of three months he wrote again. He was a Hindu, he wrote, plus a Rajput, who once a thing was decided never turned back. He would forever remain mine and I must be his as well. He was writing to tell me that he had applied for a passport so that he, his wife, his son and his daughter could come to England and we could all live together. Now we were all one family. His wife was very co-operative, he added. 'My wife and I' would be writing to me again very soon. Meanwhile would I write an affectionate loving letter to his wife also. At this point the thing became too much for me. I did not answer that letter and I did not hear from Vijay again until about three weeks before I was due to set out again for India, when he sent a Christmas card on which he proposed that he and I should enter into some 'business work' together: importing and exporting carpets. I had replied that I would be coming to Allahabad very soon, within about three weeks.

When finally I embarked for India I was not alone. I was escorted by Roy. It was rather ironical. I was being accompanied by someone who had recently collapsed, largely, it was thought, due to his own travels in India. Nevertheless it had been felt that the journey would be as good a convalescence as any. Besides, it would be interesting: if there was any truth in these gurus being healers they might restore Roy's equilibrium. So there we were: Roy in search of food, while heaven only knew what I was after. You could say I was in search of spiritual material. I was a spiritual materialist. By now my link with Saitha Sai Baba had more or less evaporated, although it was on my list to return to Puttaparthi and witness the manifestation of the lingam. I hoped I would feast my eyes on countless marvels; that my head would be filled with a wealth of visions, my nostrils with fragrances emitting from no known source. I hoped to witness a sort of spiritual peep-show, a cosmorama, while at the same time undergoing an astonishing metamorphosis. In short I was travelling to India with spiritual expectations and I was impatient of anything or anyone not of a spiritual disposition.

Even before we set foot in India, the diversions, the voices, started. Roy was wandering about on the aeroplane eating bread rolls, one after the other with great concentration, and a Sikh came and sat down in his seat. 'It's nice to find somewhere to sit,' he said. That seemed droll since presumably he had travelled all the way from Kennedy Airport, New York, sitting in a seat. Why was I going to India? Here I made the mistake of telling him I was writing a book. *Writing!* What about? Poverty? Art? *Religion!* Now if I really wanted to find out about religion I should go to the Punjab, or to Delhi, behind the Golly Market (they always give you directions like that,

Roy said afterwards). Yes, I should go to the Gurdwara behind the Golly Market and to the Golden Temple in Amritsar. In all these places one could live free. 'Left you live FREE,' he scrawled in large letters in my notebook: 'TAKE THE BUS.' That done, he got down to business. Now I could tell him: how do the English kiss? I could tell him that. 'Yes, I can tell you everything about India, you give me a kiss and I tell you about the woman goddess Kali – everything.'

'I'm not coming to India to kiss people,' I said primly.

'Don't talk,' said the Sikh, 'all the people will hear. Do.'

Goodness knows what he thought we were going to do, kiss all the way to Delhi and vanish into the sunrise on the bus to the Golly Market. Luckily, Roy turned up just then with his mouth full and put an end to it.

In Delhi we attended mostly to non-spiritual matters. A tailor was making us shirts. His cupboards were full of clothes for shops in the King's Road. He knew them all. 'Forbidden Fruit'. 'Mr Rock'. He made many things for 'Mr Rock'. Did I know 'Mr Rock'? Unless this was Mr Rock the baker, father of my friend Rita Rock, trying his hand at clothes in his old age, I could not say I did. Junkies, the tailor said, those Western people, they were all junkies – which seemed to cut out Mr Rock the baker. They owed the tailor thirty thousand rupees. For myself I was not au courant either with Indian money or the art of bargaining. An Irish girl who bought old clothes told me later that everyone started off with prices far too high; when someone asked her for one hundred and fifty rupees she would offer three, eventually she would get the thing for ten. She would not, I suppose, have paid twenty-five rupees for a shirt, neither no doubt would 'Mr Rock'. But at least that was an advance on the thirty rupees that Roy had paid that morning to have his shoes cleaned against a visit to one of his gurus.

For one to qualify for the position of guru in Roy's eyes, I discovered that one must look completely outlandish, as far from being middle-class as possible – much of Roy's energy went in to escaping from the middle class. One must have a great deal of hair, the more matted the better, and ideally be veiled in clouds of cannabis smoke. Yogiraj Siyaram Sharan, with whom he returned to polish off the duty-free whisky brought from Heathrow, qualified on the grounds of physique. He looked splendid: huge clear eyes, long shining hair and lean tall body. In the evening we were conducted to his ashram, which consisted of three rooms in as many buildings situated in a suburb of Delhi. We should stay here five days practising yoga, he told us, and then we could all proceed to Allahabad, where the Maga Mela, a small annual version of the Kumbh Mela was taking place. 'You come and live here,' he urged. 'Here you can have this room.' He threw open a door and we trooped in. There was a bundle of dirty washing in one corner, which on closer inspection turned out to be a man sleeping. We climbed over him to examine the pictures on the wall. Here was the master in every possible contortion, together with his wife, less contorted. He has experimented with everything, he told us, breathing, mantra, bakti, every sort of discipline, every sort of diet, now he does everything, drinks whisky – everything. It was rather hard to make head or tail of what was going on. Two little girls called Baby ran in and out bringing cups of tea, roasted vermicelli and smartly headed writing paper, accompanied by a noisy little puppy which bit their dresses. After a while we left in some confusion. 'My guru,' Roy said afterwards, 'is not very remarkable.' What was remarkable, however, was his special correspondence course which he had pressed into our hands: a masterpiece of misprints.

Here, for the benefit of the general public, Yogi Raj Ji had presented an extract of his forty years' experience. Yoga was the secret key to Beauty, Health, Success and Prosperity, it said, and for the 'last many years' H. H. Yogiraj Siyaram Sharan had been imparting training in Yama, Niyama, Asana, Pranayama, Samadhi and Kundalini. 'His Hollyness Yogiraj Sharan has given new life to many disgusted and depressed patients'. 'His Hollyness', it was claimed, had successfully cured appendicitis, diabetes, constipation, piles, indigestion, flatulence, loss of appetite, cough, cold, fever, asthma, bronchitis, urinary disorder, 'gouts', paralysis, 'obesity etc'. Every human, irrespective of age and sex, could learn yoga 'through our CORRESPONDENCE COURSE'. Every body could perform these Yogic Kriyas and asanas with the help of pictures 'illustrated in sequence'. 'It is our guarantee that Yoga not only eradicates disease but also keeps the person healthy

77

even in old age.'

'Note: – On successful completion of the course the students will be awarded PRATHAMA (Secondary) certificate by the ashram.'

Delhi, it seemed, specialised in such therapeutic yoga centres. On my way to collect the shirts I met a girl who had just returned from quarters similar to His Hollyness's. She was poring over a large questionnaire. Particulars of diet should be supplied, and of sleep: the number of hours? the sound? respiration? whether noisy or shallow? the stools: frequency? size? mucus and blood/pus content? hard? pasty? knotty? Do you love God and feel His presence even in solitary places where you are tempted to commit sin? was another question posed in this singular paper. Later that day I read in the newspapers that Swami Dhirendra Brahmachari, who ran yet another yoga centre (this one funded by government grants), had been arrested for smuggling aircraft which he employed in his business spraying crops. In the event we stopped neither to sample the hospitality of His Hollyness nor any cures, but left immediately for Allahabad via Agra and the Taj Mahal.

Many people have described the Taj Mahal. All I can say is that its effect on me was miraculous. During the past year an intense uneasiness had set in, a condition which had embedded itself, just as a long illness, or a deep depression, becomes an integral part of you. You cannot remember how it felt before. Every morning when you wake up you are conscious of a general malaise, the source of which you are unable to locate. Neither Delhi nor His Hollyness had done anything to disperse this: indeed if anything they had enhanced my feeling of tension. My mind chattered on: what on earth was I doing? What was I looking for? What if I found nothing to write about? But the moment I laid eyes on the Taj Mahal I became still: my mind shut up. Those lawns inlaid with pools reflecting the white domes and minarets, those curving walls of mellow bricks, those combinations of water, grass, brick and marble were completely harmonious, in the whole and in parts. Everything was exquisite: the marble of the rooms inset with lozenges of mother of pearl and precious stone, their shape curved, polished, leading precisely one from the other in and around. Their harmony was like marvellous music, like aromatic oil soothing the senses. The Taj Mahal breathed life into me and something quickened, something rose up in me that I recognised. A calm glowing feeling, a serenity which comes all too rarely, when you are relaxed, walking in the country perhaps, breathing in the fragrance of flowers, listening to music. At the Taj Mahal I was heartened. I detected a faint stream within myself, a faint current which soothed, comforted and washed away the unease. I moved with new energy and optimism. Even Roy ate less that night and was calm.

We reached Allahabad in thick fog. The main reason for my returning to Allahabad was not Vijay, but Veena Baba, that marvellous veena player. I knew that he returned every year to play at the Mela and I wanted very much to spend some time with him. We stayed at the Tourist Bungalow. Tourist Bungalows differ from place to place; this one, you could say, was erratic. The bathrooms were awash with cold water flowing from every aperture except that which flushed the lavatory. Thankfully we departed by cycle rickshaw for the Mela. To reach the area we had to pass through the wide streets of the Civil Lines – that ghetto to the British Raj with its spacious houses and gardens into which no Indian could penetrate unless permitted. After this came a village, cows and buffalo wallowed, hens ran everywhere and those marvellous pigs grunted along the side of the road, wagging their tails, bristles standing up along their necks like sticklebacks – animated dustbins and sewers.

Now a narrow road traversed some flat marshy land leased out in allotments for growing lentils and vegetables. All this the year before had been a seething mass of people. Presently, it was more or less empty. Suddenly, the way was blocked by a barrier. Here our rickshaw was surrounded by men. 'Botman, botman,' they roared. *Botman?* What on earth could they mean? Some sort of toll? Some sort of ticket? After some days it dawned on me that they were shouting 'Boatman'. Three miles even from the Ganges they were hoping to solicit trade. Soon the road became lined with shops, stalls and temples; on either side trees grew, some inhabited by sadhus, all matted hair and covered with dust – enough to make Roy's heart stir. After a mile or so the route led to the top of a cliff; here the road

79

plunged down a steep hill. At our feet lay a scene resembling that first glimpse of the Kumbh Mela: row upon row of patterned tents, all with flags flying, like some mediaeval war camp, intersected by wide avenues. And far away in the distance the Ganges flowed, glittering blue to join the Yamuna. Microphones blared, music roared and as the evening drew on the moon rose like a great ball, but there were few people. The Mela had hardly begun and Veena Baba had not yet arrived. There was only a sign outside his encampment saying: Sri Swami Parvatikar, Veena Baba, Doctor of Music, All India Radio.

We returned to the town, one of a hundred rickshaws ringing their bells, weaving through the blue winter light, thickened with mist and smoke. Roy's main interest was dinner. We were directed that first evening to the most singular restaurant – Allahabad's smart night spot, El Chico. Unfortunately nothing could have been less chic than ourselves. Roy had only one pair of trousers into which he could fit, and they were being washed, so he was wrapped in his school tartan rug and the Tourist Bungalow blanket, while I looked equally inappropriate in my brown mohair rug and a sari I had forgotten how to tie. Here we were, having travelled thousands of miles to this holy place of pilgrimage, sitting in a huge plastic mausoleum complete with milk shakes, prawn cocktails and music which would not have been out of place in Studio 54, in New York.

Next morning, still enfolded in his school rug and Tourist Bungalow blanket, Roy was a target for all and sundry, begging for money, cigarettes and food. 'Chai baba, chai baba,' they whined. 'I am very hungry today,' wailed one begging sadhu, his forehead plastered in yellow paste, dragging Roy into a tea place and urging him to buy cups of tea. Down the wide alleys to the Ganges other sadhus gave discourses, and holy plays were being acted by brightly-painted actors and actresses; over the pontoon bridge we went and down to the camp of the nagas. There they were again with their hair matted in ringlets, naked except for the occasional G-string or coating of ash – obvious candidates for Roy's admiration. And then we ended up at the maddest tea party imaginable. Back at the top of the hill was a very small camp, marked out by plastic bags, belonging to one who seemed to be a naga, yet was far away from the nagas' camp. He wore a sack loincloth and carried a thing like a hatchet; his eyes burned out of his ash-smeared face, his hair was dressed in matted ringlets and tied up with a piece of tinsel, and his teeth were absolutely black. At the centre of his camp a drain pipe and some iron stakes were stuck in the ground and a fire was burning. Apparently he was suggesting that we join him. Roy accepted with delight. We sat down among several cows, cowpats, flies and other people dressed in sackcloth and ashes.

It soon became clear that our host was an entertainer. He extracted the drain pipe, blew a few blasts down it and croaked some incantations at the top of a cracked voice. Next he stuffed some cigarettes, bidis, cannabis and a dirty old piece of carpet into a clay pipe. He tore up some equally foul red rag, wet it and wrapped it round the stem, illuminated the carpet and passed round the pipe. This was my first experience with a chillum and I would have been only too glad if it had been my last. Roy naturally was expert in smoking the thing, cupping his hands, making a small hole through which he sucked up the smoke through the unsavoury wet rag. When I tried nothing happened at all. Meanwhile more and more people were joining our party. A most beautiful man in a turban, looking like a film star, sat himself exactly behind a small calf which he began caressing, and a fellow looking like a spaniel came and sat by me muttering things. The flies buzzed, the clay pipe cir-culated and, much to the delight of the crowd which had now gathered, the old piece of carpet fell out and smouldered in the middle of my brown rug. 'Shanti, shanti, shanti,' said our host. 'Ticketa, ticketa, ticketa,' which meant apparently, peace, peace, peace, all right, all right, all right. He continued the show. He sang to the harmonium, if you could call such croaking singing, he whistled through his teeth, he passed round paper on which we wrote our names and addresses, and in the corner he told us to mark five rupees. 'Chelas,'* he chor-tled, delighted, passing round the horrible pipe again and again. It turned out we had to hand him the sum we had written in the corner of the paper. The crowd roared. Someone else had joined the group and was acting as a sort of master of

* Disciples.

ceremonies. Our host recited some poetry and imbibed some more pipe. 'Hookah baba!' someone in the crowd said wittily. A soldier appeared with a packet of tea, a pot of water and some bhang.

By now Roy was in a stupor and our host was pretending to the crowd that he was some great yogi. Someone was pressing urgently to meet him. The crowd doubled up again. Next the bhang circulated. Roy for once had come across a narcotic he had never sampled. 'You must take it like a capsule,' instructed the master of ceremonies. Then suddenly he became officious, he was an inspector of taxes, he said, and he inspected our papers to make sure we were not being swindled. The film star collapsed theatrically into a coma against the calf. 'Indian drama!' shouted the host, blowing a few blasts down his drain pipe and then buried it in the fire and used it as bellows. Tea was served and the crowd watched delighted as we ate nuts. We were like chimpanzees at the zoo tea party. Towards sunset our host became quite wild, leaping up and down, shouting, waving his drain pipe at the crowd which was pressing closer and closer for a better view. He pushed their feet off his plastic sacks which he picked up and flapped about. 'You go now,' said the inspector of taxes, not before we had been invited to stop for dinner. As the sun set and the light thickened into the Allahabad night we left accompanied by the man who looked like a spaniel and who seemed determined to become our personal servant. 'I am very poor man,' he kept saying. 'How much that sweater cost? How much that blanket?' eyeing my brown mohair rug. 'I am your servant.' As we left in a rickshaw he leapt in and crouched there on his haunches like a small dog.

Next day we were to meet the Shankacharya. I had placed great importance on this interview. Paul Brunton's meeting with his Shankacharya had been one of the highlights of his trip. His Shankacharya had been reputed to be a healer and to possess prophetic insight. It had been he who had recommended that Paul Brunton should visit Ramana Maharishi at Tiru-vannamalai and had the following night appeared to him in a gold vision floating at the end of the bed. In order that we should be ready and in a suitable frame of mind for this crucial occasion we ordered that breakfast and our kettle of hot water be brought early by the waiter. Nothing appeared. No kettle, no breakfast, no waiter. 'He is not coming today,' said all the other tourists who were sitting on the balcony outside their rooms peering into the thick fog which that day enveloped Allahabad. And, instead, a little boy popped in with a cup of tea purchased from the stall at the end of the road. He was followed by the newspaper vendor and someone who turned out to be a nail-cutter and masseur. Apparently the bedroom is as good a venue for commerce as a railway station.

I was just standing on the bed trying to tie my sari when Vijay entered, together with someone else shouting something. 'The joker has come round to shave you,' said Vijay. 'People don't want to shave themselves, isn't it?' It was neither an auspicious nor romantic meeting. Vijay for a start was nervous and never stopped talking. He was exceedingly put out. He had arranged, he said, for us to stay in the circuit lodge and then in the same breath: 'Why are you not staying at my house? Here there are no foodings: no foodings at all.' A great deal of 'humbug' was going on in Allahabad about which Vijay had much information – information not really appropriate at a time when one was trying to get calm, to say nothing of dressed, before a decisive spiritual interview. Nevertheless we heard it all: someone at the electricity board had stabbed himself, someone else had taken an overdose of sleeping pills and been rushed to hospital, but all the doctors were on strike and the man had died, his infuriated colleagues had disconnected the hospital electricity supply.... He broke off and peered at me: 'Your sari is brooming the floor, isn't it?'

We were eventually driven to our audience in the government jeep, having first negotiated what Vijay declared to be an ill-disciplined group of urchins shambling along eating peanuts but who turned out to be the Allahabad Band celebrating the Republic Day march past. This Shankacharya had a grey beard and huge radiant eyes and received us sitting in what looked like a four-poster bed. What did I want to know? Who were the great mahatmas? the great healers? He was enigmatic. After all, Sai Baba was supposed to perform miracles yet people went and they saw nothing. The great healer came from within. Meditation, he added, was only a gimmick to quieten the mind. What one should do was to make the heart and soul take over, receive the power from within by doing good. And he presented us with a short résumé of his teaching:

1. First see God in all and then treat them as they should be treated.
2. God is present everywhere and therefore do not do anything secretly lest you repent of it in the future.
3. Man should always be cheerful.
4. Meet every circumstance with patience.
5. The state of happiness and sorrow both should be taken in a spirit of drama and detachment.
6. Anger should be totally eliminated, if you are angry for some reason chant God's name at least 108 times and mentally pray for forgiveness of God.
7. Always speak truth. Never tell a lie deliberately.
8. Never speak ill of others. This weakens the power of speech.
9. Think of your motherland as you think of your mother.
10. Love your country as you love yourself.

That was that. No visions. Nothing spectacular. Actually the Shankacharya had given me the directions that I needed: to turn within. But at that stage I could not hear such plain stuff. I wanted to see and feel marvellous things – signs and wonders.

We were hurried away then to Vijay's mother and wife for lunch. This was excellent: wonderful puris, vegetables, hot chapatis with fresh melted ghee. We spent the afternoon 'chit chatting', sitting in Vijay and his wife's bedroom. This was where they lived, sitting cross-legged on their huge bed, drinking whisky and listening to music. We were introduced to the children who were rather like small animals, curling up in a blanket and dropping asleep on their mother's lap whenever they felt tired, and the animals themselves – three small chows which lived on the roof, never leaving the house for fear of disease lurking in the streets. The rest of the household comprised two servants, Vijay's mother ('mummy'), who was sweet and calm, making chutneys and pickles and supervising the cooking, and countless ducks, chickens and geese which lived in the garden. This was a quiet part of the town, far away from the busy centre, and in the street buffalo were milked each evening in that beautiful smoky light before the milk round – which, according to Vijay, is subject to much 'hanky panky': 'watering down, isn't it?'

The situation with Vijay and his family was not so tranquil. Vijay, it seemed to me, had magnified our meeting out of all proportion. He had spent the year announcing at intervals: 'I am going to England.' Rather in the manner of Frank Harris, what he had imagined he now believed. It had become part of him and part of everyone else around him. He and his whole family assumed that I had come all the way to Allahabad solely to be with Vijay. They took it for granted that I should live with them as part of the family. Nor did they question the presence of Roy, accepting that he should come along as well. So there I was, having come to Allahabad on a spiritual quest to see Veena Baba, and there were Vijay and his family supposing I had no other intention than to pass the time in chatter and dalliance. As for Vijay's wife, it seemed to me that she welcomed my appearance as a breath of excitement in her boring life. 'What to do all day?' she would ask. She hated being alone; hated sewing, knitting and cooking, and longed to be out visiting friends, seeing the movies. 'Will you be back in a jiffy?' she would ask Vijay wistfully as he rattled off in the jeep. Vijay, it appeared however, was often out all day and much of the night as well. Altogether it was a most unsatisfactory situation and one with which I had little idea how to deal. I adopted my usual strategy of continuing as though nothing at all were happening.

Later that evening we returned to the Mela, and now Veena Baba had arrived. And there *was* something: there was a magic, in the dimly-lit tent smelling of incense and insecticide, with the photographs of Veena Baba's own guru (who also played the veena and was supposed to be hundreds of years old, living somewhere underground). There was an unmistakable peace in that vibrating music. Occasionally someone would leave, someone else would arrive and the straw would rustle; outside the crows flew past cawing. Now there was no need for words. You sat there in the straw with just an inner flow of peace, harmony, energy, stillness, welling up. It was not unlike my experience at the Taj Mahal. The atmosphere was quite soothing in that tent, the music quite fluid, like waves of delicious water lapping over you.

Even Roy was impressed: Veena Baba looked marvellous.

His hair was matted and bound up in a turban when he played, his eyes were enormous, his presence strong and still. His real name was Swami Parvatikar. He had been born into a rich Brahmin family but he had given up his possessions to devote his life to music. Now he spent his summers in Badrinath playing at the temple there and the rest of the year he wandered. Usually, he maintained silence, but tonight he was breaking it. 'I have been thinking about you very much,' he said to me. So there *was* a rapport. It really had happened. To Vijay he said: 'Speech only leads to trouble. Silence, music is best.' If we returned every day at 1.30 he would play especially for us.

Unfortunately Roy insisted that we stop on the way home at the Hookah Baba's plastic bag compound. The usual crowd was gathered there round the fire and the drain pipe. 'Did I like India?' asked a man in a hat with leather flaps. 'Why?' 'What is your subject?' 'Social history,' Roy put in. 'Social history?' 'What is social history?' 'God?' 'What is God?' 'What is spirituality?' 'What is beauty?' The man in the leather hat was becoming noisy and over-excited. The chillum circulated. ('How are the kicks, Roy?' Vijay wanted to know.) 'Why do you come here?' Leather hat roared meanwhile: 'God is everywhere. We are God manufacturers. The British ruled over us for hundreds of years. We were servants. Politics? What are politics? Bah!' He made such a noise that his guru – who was supposed to be 'a declared genius' and to live opposite under a tree – must have been disturbed. 'I nearly gave him my piece of mind,' Vijay said afterwards. 'Mad! Crazy! you might say.'

Our night was not yet finished. Vijay took us to the Aghori Baba (whom I had met briefly the year before) who lived in his tree further up the road and who was in fact called Pukkhra Baba – Baba who has nothing. What he did have, according to Vijay, were 'powers'. He shifted at night to the burning ghats and employed any spirits that might be lurking around for purposes of his own. He would not speak to most people. But he certainly spoke to Vijay: gabble, gabble, gabble, in a low rasping voice, well-suited to his ghoulish escapades. When not out scouring the ghats for corpses he spent his time crouched over his fire at the bottom of the tree. According to Vijay, a chief of police often visited him by night to discourse. Pukkhra

Baba looked rather like Gibbon's description of the early Christians, unsavoury and extremely dirty. 'Yes,' said Vijay, 'he has to eat slugs, cadavers, isn't it?' Certainly he was neither loving nor compassionate, but on the contrary rather cross, peering angrily through his red-rimmed eyes. 'Go away to a movie show,' he rasped to a small crowd that had gathered to watch us all. 'This is not a circus, you are all ignorant people.' Finally he chased them off with sticks. One man came up: 'I will come and see you again,' he said. 'You will only come if I call you,' Pukkhra Baba growled. Most of the time, however, he and Vijay were gabbling away. 'He is so impressed with you,' Vijay said, 'that you may take a photograph.' Unfortunately we did not have a camera. Well then, what did I want? That Roy should be well? Yes. This Pukkhra Baba would guarantee. But he must not drink alcohol, he must not take narcotics, only tea or coffee with tulsi leaves, pepper, ginger and honey. He smeared ash from his fire on our foreheads and necks and clapped me on the shoulder. 'Now you will be purified,' he said. Unsavoury or not, Pukkhra Baba did have power. There is no doubt at all that a sweet energy surged up inside me, radiant, exhilarating.

We went then to eat marsala dosa and drink espresso coffee by the side of the road. This was the height of fashion in Allahabad – the ideal for a night out was to drive to a roadside café and sit in the car, or on one's motor bike, drinking coffee. It appeared that Pukkhra Baba had given Vijay a recipe – various metals should be purchased and boiled together for both Roy and myself to wear to protect us from the 'Saturday Star' which was against us. 'Saturn,' said Roy crossly, 'not Saturday star.' Roy must also do a pooja with three lingams. But Roy had no intention of doing anything at all. He had had enough. He would not go to the market to get the metals. He had a headache, he said, and must go back to bed. Later, just as I was going to sleep, that energy shot up again. Blissful it felt, again not at all unlike being in love.

That week I went to the Mela as often as I could to hear Swami Parvatikar play. Roy meanwhile had found another so-called holy man, Kass Las Das who, with his wild red eyes and a turban perched on his matted hair, was of suitably outlandish appearance. One could write a book simply on all the different camps at the Mela and their internal politics. One in particular held a fasination for me: the International Centre, as Vijay's mother called it. Its leader was Tiaji, who plainly had an eye for the spectacular. Western disciples attract much attention among the Indians: white devotees, like a white Mercedes, are a mark of status. When Tiaji mounted the dais to make his discourses he was surrounded by his Western devotees carrying candles and flaming dishes. It made a charming scene: the girls wearing long, flowing dresses, the men with their shaved heads and orange robes – they all seemed mysterious and picturesque.

'Guruji' had several Western followers, all of whom he had given Indian names and all of whom were heavily into the 'Indian experience'. There was a ravaged but charming German boy called Shankar with his hair tied back in a pigtail, who was not presentable enough to appear on the dais and who was using the camp more as a hotel than anything else. There was an American with a shaved head and a name like Kamila-nand and there were several rather beautiful girls with long hair who, according to Shankar, were not girls at all but air hostesses having a holiday. An amazing American lady appeared every day to perform her ablutions. Her hair was matted like the nagas' – it had taken four years, she said, to get it like that – and she was wrapped in an orange sack. She did the cooking for a sadhu up the road and her hands were absolutely engrained with filth. Guruji's right-hand man, Ram Das, used to be a fisherman in Hawaii, he ate only fruit – grain he found too heavy and constipating, meat and fish were absolutely forbidden. Ram Das loved the Mela. It was, he said, India in a nutshell. It was all he had ever dreamt of: the camels, the elephants, the bathing. It was all here. Shankar was not too keen on Ram Das. 'He wants to be boss all the time,' he said crossly. 'I don't get on with him, he's confused.' More, I am afraid, out of curiosity than anything else I asked to be taught meditation at the International Centre. A girl called Deva instructed me. First you breathed through alternate nostrils, and then you breathed from the base of the stomach, saying 'so' on the breath in and 'hum' on the breath out. One had to do it first thing in the morning and continue for at least six months.

Meanwhile the situation with Vijay and his family was worsening. Vijay was obsessed by our meeting. He could hear nothing that did not fit in with his illusion. In his mind he had quickened an image of Philippa Pullar which had become his creation and bore no relation to the real one. The Philippa of his imagination was far more satisfactory; acquiescent, yielding, longing only to be transported into his arms. Vijay encapsulated, I saw, the essence of fantasy; more, the essence of insanity. For what is insanity but a degree of fantasy, where the mind, the energy, is focused on delusion? On some concept which has been fabricated by the ego? The line between fantasy, insanity and reality is so thin. Mrs Harvey, Frank Harris, Roy, I, myself, and now Vijay had all hovered over its edge one time or another. 'You must not let me down,' Vijay said. In other words one must do nothing that would shatter his self-made image of protector and lover. It seemed to me that he saw himself as master of a harem, his wife and myself the founder members; who knew where it would end? Having seen the way he treated his one wife I am bound to say that I was not attracted. It occurred to me that this loving family notion was as much part of the Indian conditioning as my own lack of trust was to do with my Western upbringing. The Indian conditioning was more generous and attractive than my own, but it was no more based on reality. They were both an attitude of mind.

I had experienced something like this before. Someone had once made up his mind that he was in love with me and indeed had been marvellous at looking after me all through that curious illness. But the point was it had not been real. The man was intellectually and socially ambitious and he saw himself stepping into Horace's shoes: into his bed and house and 'position' – success would automatically follow. He was outraged when I wanted him to go. It did not fit in with his plans; the future in which he had invested and which he had fabricated had become in his mind reality and he was hurt when I would not accommodate his schemes. In his mind he had signed the contract and settled in. For my own part it had felt wrong from the start – although exceedingly convenient. I did not love him, I liked him for his convenience, his generosity, and he was a good companion and lover. That was all.

Now, just as that had felt wrong, so did the situation with Vijay. My sympathies lay entirely with his poor wife who had been drawn into her husband's fantasies. One night we were watching the marvellous moon: all of us together. 'So romantic,' she sighed. 'You see we both love you'. While she longed for his company, I longed to be left alone. Yet he was always there bristling with nervous energy, battering at me for attention. I was conscious of him hovering, spying, timing my movements. I drove past your bungalow this morning, he would say, and your door was shut. So I knew you would be there for another two hours. Then just as I would be about to set off for the Mela he would appear and insist either on driving me there, hooting and chattering all the way, or worse, carry us off to his family who he said expected us for lunch: 'No, please, it will be very quick really.' And then his wife would be cross and refuse to eat: 'I don't like to be hurried with my food,' she would say. Not only did it make us look horribly rude but also we were then late for Swami Parvatikar. I was becoming paranoid about it.

And how Vijay talked! If there was nothing of obvious interest about which to prattle then he would embark on long recitations: on how the new government was so corrupt, people only using their brains to cheat people; letters not reaching their destinations because people were pulling off the stamps and reselling them, and how the only way to be certain of the mail was to run round to the post office and frank all the letters oneself ... I longed for the silence to be found with Swami Parvatikar, but Vijay talked on and on. One night he had talked so much that neither Roy nor I could take any more. Roy feigned a headache and went to bed, yet Vijay stayed on the balcony talking. His family were expecting us all back to dinner: should he not telephone? No, he said, they don't mind. But they did: they minded very much indeed.

Next day we managed to avoid lunch and arrive in good time for the music, but Swami Parvatikar had that day a particularly flamboyant disciple who kept prostrating himself, jumping up and down, rustling the straw and tweaking the hairs on his chest in time to the music. Afterwards he came rushing out, shouting that we must write down his name and address so that we could send him a tape of the music (that tape-recorder only added to the annoyance since the batteries were always flat, or I would forget to press the right switch). The flamboyant disciple was followed by Vijay's mother who it seemed had also escaped lunch to listen to the music. What happened last night? she wanted to know. They had waited until eleven for Vijay to return with us for dinner. He could have telephoned. Why were we not coming to her house?

The situation was becoming so difficult that we left for a while to visit Ayodiah and Benares. Vijay and Kamilanand provided endless information, all of which proved to be inaccurate. To make the journey from Allahabad one must pass by Faisabad. Everyone's faces grew long at the mention of Faisabad. It was the headquarters of brigands; one would have to stay in the station, it was not safe to go to 'Ayodiah-side' at night. As for the distance, everyone had a different view. Vijay submitted that Faisabad was eighteen kilometres from Ayodiah; that it would cost twenty rupees by tonga; that all the tongas would be waiting to meet the midnight train. Kamilanand remembered there was a set charge from Faisabad to Ayodiah of somewhere between one and a half and three rupees.

In the event, we arrived at Faisabad at midnight. There were no tongas, no brigands – nothing. So we did stay in the station. The waiting room was locked and, when at last the station master was roused and the door opened, four snoring men were revealed, occupying the four benches. So we passed the night lying on the floor outside the lavatory. At six o'clock we set out in a rickshaw along the eight kilometres to Ayodiah, along a ravishing green road, glistening with dew, lined with trees, mosques and minarets. We hurtled down the main street to the river and then were obliged to climb the four miles back again. Kamilanand's memory was faulty; the Tourist Bungalow was not by the bathing ghats at the bottom of the town but right at the top. But it was delightful: set in a large expanse of green, irrigated by water channels and grazed by cows which spent the day coming through the hedge and eating the roses, much to the fury of the manager, who loved his garden. He himself prepared our lunch, while breakfast – the standard Indian breakfast of puris and vegetables – was next morning fetched by bicycle from a stall somewhere nearby.

I had not done my homework on Ayodiah, so the fact that this was the birthplace of Ram meant nothing to me. Even so, it was clear from its calm atmosphere that this was a real place of pilgrimage. It was far more peaceful than Allahabad which is after all a metropolis and with its law courts and university (not to mention its famous power house) draws to it people for reasons that are by no means all spiritual. Ayodiah is a city of ritual and celebration; and since I understood neither the celebration nor the ritual I found it somewhat confusing. We descended again to the river and the bathing ghats. Nearby was an ashram from which emanated beautiful bhajans. I tried to tape them on the awful tape-recorder, which caused the usual crowd to assemble. The world certainly is a stage in India. The Western notion of privacy is quite alien to the Indians. Once, Roy and I stood watching a dog dissecting a carcase by the side of the road while some pigs ate their dinner off the rubbish dump nearby. The crowd gathered to watch us watching the dogs and pigs. 'What are you saying?' they wanted to know. 'What are you watching?' One member of our current audience now hurried us round a corner to where ten people were gathered together under a tree. An old crumpled man was sitting opposite another rather grand fellow who was seated on a wooden throne cutting up fruit. Apparently we had been brought to a famous guru who was about to perform his tapas – or was it japas? This guru has devoted his life to the recitation of God's name.* It is protocol, I knew, to present oneself to the guru – I was learning slowly. So I went and sat before the grand man. There was consternation. The guru was the other, crumpled, fellow. A few leaves and a bit of guava were handed round and then the guru started.

First he recited 'Sita-Ram' deep down in his throat, repeating it five hundred times in a noise rather like a belch. Everyone gathered round and gazed at him with great concentration. For the next five hundred he pitched his voice absolutely treble; then for the next batch he contorted his mouth, pushing his lips out, sucking them in again. We left him no doubt to countless variations on his theme and proceeded back up the hill to the Kanak temple. Here, everyone was also recit-

* The theory is that first you repeat the mantra, later you do it mentally, eventually you become that whose name you reiterate.

ing Sita-Ram – while running round and round an altar. We too ran round and round the altar since people seemed to expect it. We were then given some cotton wool balls on sticks, most beautifully scented, and a saucer of purified water which one put on one's head, and a delicious sweet to eat. I felt I was making progress – although at the less well-endowed temples I was still liable to make mistakes since they gave you sugared liquid to eat instead of sweets and thinking this to be the purified water I put it over my hair.

That evening in Ayodiah was beautiful – again the wonderful thick light, the shops illuminated by hundreds of flickering oil lamps and from the temples the chant of bhajans, the clash of cymbals. All night long they continued, the rhythmic chants: Sita-Ram, Sita-Ram. And the people were so friendly, so generous, so hospitable. Some chartered accountants from Bihar invited us to dinner at a temple – they were there auditing the accounts. 'Come and stay,' they urged. 'Tonight?' 'Tomorrow?' Dinner was delicious, eaten as always with the fingers, sitting on the floor. Before eating we must dedicate the food to the effigies of Ram and Sita and then attend the closing ceremony, arati, at which the plate of flames is flapped around in circles. Here again one is presented with flaming dishes, coloured powder, ash and sugared water, which variously one should sprinkle over one's hair, make marks upon one's face and eat. These effigies of Sita and Ram, the chartered accountant told us, are treated just like human beings. They are woken up, served meals and put to bed. Just as we were leaving a lady emerged from the shadows and indicated that we should follow her. She led us to a holy man who had been standing upright for twenty years. Only two months ago, the lady told us, he had a painful boil on his leg; anyone else would have given up – not he. There he was, sure enough, standing supported by a strange contraption of chains and pulleys which dangled from the ceiling. Seated on the floor surrounding him were six disciples who were cooking over a fire in the middle of the room. We were allowed a glimpse only before being whirled away again, but in that fleeting moment I was not able to detect any great spiritual quality or presence; the man just looked rather exhausted and uncomfortable.

We left next day, not reaching Benares until six in the

93

evening because, as one of the passengers put it, 'a lot of chain pulling has been going on'. It was a holiday and apparently whenever a student fancied getting out of the train he pulled the emergency cord. Thus for quite a lot of the day the train stood motionless in the wonderful lush country. This could never have happened under Mrs Gandhi, said the other passengers. But there you were, if you had a prime minister who didn't observe the laws how could you expect the students to do the same?

Benares had been of great importance to both Yogananda and Paul Brunton. The former had wandered through the labyrinth of streets encountering many holy men who knew instantly and intimately every detail of his biography, while the latter had witnessed many marvels there, he saw dead sparrows quickened by the sun's rays and visited soothsayers. As for us, the priority was to find somewhere to stay. The days of Clark's Hotel were over, my budget only covered more modest establishments. The railway station was less crowded than on my previous visit but as before the area outside the railway station was a seething mass of rickshaws, taxi-drivers and porters touting for custom. Benares runs on commission and one of the most fruitful hunting grounds is the point of arrival. Here all the rickshaw and taxi-drivers catch their prey and carry it off to the hotels, shops and restaurants with which they have special arrangements to receive percentages of any transaction.

Arriving at six meant that the Tourist Bungalow was full and instead we were directed by our rickshaw-driver to the Hotel Relax: one of the most extraordinary establishments in which I have ever stayed. The bedroom was on the ground floor; outside in the street dogs barked, rickshaw-riders rang their bells and children stuck their heads through the window shouting 'hello'. It was no better inside. In the morning most of the inhabitants of Benares seemed to come especially to retch outside the bedroom door, where later I discovered the hotel lavatory was situated (Indian ablutions consist of retching and spitting for about half an hour every morning). The room was adjacent to the front door – grandly referred to by the authorities as the 'main gate' – and all night long this was unlocked, rattled and unfolded by the 'gate-keeper' and locked up again for people passing in or out. Motor bikes switched on at all hours and at six o'clock a piercing machine started up, together with the retching. A notice of rules and regulations for all the guests hung on the wall. 'This hotel is styled in the name of Hotel Relax,' it told us. 'The passengers will show all the room furniture to the Hotel Manager . . . The passengers will have to quit the room for any misconduct.'

'Passengers' was just about the word for it. Clearly the manager had modelled not only his English upon that of railway stations but much of his hotel atmosphere as well. I was just putting my head out of the door one morning to call for a bucket of hot water when I was nearly knocked down by one of the 'passengers' shooting past on a bicycle, down the hall and out of the 'main gate'. The bill was another masterpiece: on the back there was further composition to delight the guests. 'Please do not make any short payment to any represent alive to the Hotel without a proper cash receipt singed by the Manager,' it asked. 'Any wealthy items be handed over to the Manager and shall obtain receipt for that. When you go-out or the room Please switch off the night and fan carefully . . . No out sibers is allowed to go to a customer's room with out the Manager's permission . . . Please avoid any king of eatable materials and drink from a stanger. Thanking for your kind co operation. Manager.'

On our request our rickshaw-driver pedalled us to the banks of the Ganges. 'Everyone is saying "hallo",' he warned. 'Every-one is business man. Don't touch Indian man. I take you every-where, no business man, no commission.' In the evening the Ganges at Benares was marvellously misty and peaceful, with only the sound of crickets. Again a huge load of hay was being rowed down the river, silhouetted against the sky. We slopped along the banks, in and out of gushing streams (composed it seemed of liquid cowpats which poured down the cliffs formed by the carved walls of the maharajah's palaces) and arrived eventually at the burning ghats, blazing orange in the night. Turning away from the Ganges, we plunged into the narrow streets. At once a young man appeared and hailed us. 'We don't need a guide,' Roy told him. The young man was indignant. He was not a guide, he said, he was a Brahmin. Yet these days that is the same thing. Brahmins have to find the means of making a living. They become middle men. This young man was what is called a student guide. Like everyone else in Benares they operate on commission, sometimes collecting as much as fifty per cent of the transactions for themselves. 'Tomorrow,' he said, 'I will take you to Ananda Mai Ma, to the Golden Temple, to the Hindu University . . .' His list for our prospective entertainment was extensive. 'You must watch the sunrise. I'll come to your hotel at six o'clock? No? Eight o'clock then?'

The rickshaw-man was waiting for us to emerge from the maze of narrow streets. 'I told you not to touch Indian man,' he said crossly. 'Tomorrow I come to your hotel at six o'clock?' For all the rest we enjoyed, with the machines, the 'main gate' and the retching, we might as well have spent the night on the ghats. Eleven o'clock in the morning found us being rowed up the Ganges by a little boy of about thirteen, selected, naturally, by our rickshaw-driver. It seemed that I was not destined to meet Ananda Mai Ma. Her ashram is at Benares yet she was away resting and would not be back for some time. So instead the rickshaw-man had arranged this boat trip.

Our rower was no less obsessed by the topic of commission than all the other inhabitants. 'I not cheat anyone,' he assured us. 'I no like cheating. That shop gives twenty-five percent, that shop fifty. Afterwards you come to my house and you hear sitar music?' So we were rowed up the green Ganges, past the washerwomen and men slapping their clothes on the banks, making that resounding ringing sound; past the house boats inhabited by hippies; past buffalo wallowing, past the bathing ghats (where the streams of cowpat flowed); past the crowded main ghat with its umbrellas, people bustling to and fro searching for commission-victims. Drowned cats and puppies were born away on the current, distended like balloons. Then we were back and out of the boat, walking down narrow streets, following the little boy. It is so restless, Benares, yet one feels that if one stayed all sorts of strange things would happen. There is a curious feeling of destiny; here we were being swept along behind meandering cows, chickens, pigs and dogs into this house. We sat on the floor, under a lot of string lamp-shades suspended from the ceiling. Another student guide played the sitar. A goat came in. Tea was brought. The music stopped and then from an inner room saris, sitars, coloured scarves and other produce was brought out to sell. 'You like a small sitar? You like a lampshade? a scarf? a shirt? a skirt?' 'No commission men here,' said the boat boy. 'You come with me to Muslim City. There you buy very nice things.'

On the way back we did stop to buy something – a cheap cotton lunghi – and immediately became entangled with a huge ex-British army major. His name was Joseph Matthews, a black beret was perched on his head and he breathed out fumes of alcohol as a dragon belches out flames. Somehow he raised the wildest fantasies in Roy. 'Will you take me to a brothel?' he asked. That made the major over-excited. 'Is that boy impotent?' he wanted to know. 'Is Ed impotent?' (For some reason he insisted that Roy was called Ed.) Roy was outraged. So was the rickshaw-driver. 'I told you not to touch Indians,' he said crossly. But Joseph Matthews clung like a limpet. He turned up at the Hotel Relax, breaking the rules: 'an out siber' in a 'customer's room', no less, without permission from the Manager. He was furthermore a native of Allahabad and he began to plan how he would return with us. We must go to his house and hear some good English songs. No doubt we were familiar with the old war songs? Pack up your troubles in your old kit bag? No. Smutty songs. Unfortunately the major's own fantasies were stirred. He recited poetry. He told us about the first woman he had wrecked. *Wrecked*? No, not wrecked. Met. 'Fate has thrown us together,' she had said, 'and no matter whether you use me as a treading stone my true love's flame will burn forever.' Yes, he knew most people in Allahabad. Kass Las Das, for example, was a tug. A *tug*? A tuggee? (This was the sect who murdered and robbed people.) But surely the British had stamped them out along with suttee? No, not a tuggee. A thug. Kass Las Das was a thug.

How on earth were we to escape the major? He followed us everywhere. The hour of departure dawned. I scraped back my hair and tucked it into the collar of a white shirt. The major paced up and down the platform peering at people. He came and peered at me – Roy had meanwhile disappeared into the crowd in search of food. Did I know any people going to Allahabad? Was my name Philippa? Did I know anyone by the name of Ed? I waved my hand and dismissed him. But later when we were on the train he came searching all the carriages. In came the ticket collector, followed by the major. "Ah! Ed, here you are! Philippa, you have changed! I know these people, please,' he said to the ticket collector. 'We've never seen him before,' I lied. And he was bustled out, looking hurt. So far our travels round India had consisted of escaping from people. Far from sitting still, being peaceful, one hurtled round like a fox being pursued by a pack of hounds. A vision of our party rose before me. What a crew we could be! His Hollyness, Vijay, the major. I realised now that I had spent much of my life running away. No sooner was I faced with something I did not like than my inclination was to remove myself physically, divert my attention, have a drink, anaesthetise myself. Escape was after all the reason we had left Allahabad in the first place, escape from Vijay and his family.

And in our absence Allahabad had become more 'topsy turvy' than ever. Members of the telephone exchange were engaged in a relayed fast outside the engineer's office and the unfortunate power house was no more orderly: 'gesticulation and shouting seems the order of the day,' observed the local newspaper. The trouble had arisen over paying the bills. The system was certainly singular. On the appointed date a notice appears in the paper alerting the group of consumers who must go that day to the power house to settle their accounts. Unfortunately, the staff is so slow that often people find themselves waiting in queues all day long, thereby missing their own day's work in their offices. This time, riots had ensued.

On top of it all the Tourist Bungalow was full. So we moved to a different hotel – the Villas. Soon afterwards we adjourned to the Indian Coffee House, where two students approached to convey a typically alarming intelligence: all the staff and managers of the hotels in Allahabad, they were pleased to tell us, supplemented their income by stealing and selling the luggage of their customers. 'So please we are now making a suggestion to you: lock up your luggage very tightly.' In fact the Villas was a delightful establishment, more like a family than a hotel, and our luggage was quite safe. Everyone was woken at seven by the cook bringing 'bed-tea'. Did we have any faults to find with the hotel? he would enquire. It was his duty to know. Did we have any complaint? He would try his best to make everything nice for us. And indeed the food was delicious – marsala omelette with onions and chillis for breakfast. The manager took a paternal interest in us. What was our programme? he wanted to know. He had another customer he would like us to meet – a maharajah. At half past eight that evening he and the maharajah would come to collect us. Unfortunately the rooms at the Villas ran over a block of shops – a bookshop with a whole shelf of Barbara Cartland novels and a motor-bike shop whence a frightful noise emanated. The peace that India has to offer is not outward. People jabber and chatter, play transistors and volley ball, blow those noisy little toys that shoot in and out in front of you, throw sheets of corrugated iron on to the streets and incessantly try to sell you things.

That day was a busy one. To begin with I cashed some traveller's cheques – a process which incorporated endless waiting and fiddling about. The bank clerk wanted to know everything. Why was I here? Where was I staying? I asked idly if he knew of a translator. I thought it might be good if I could interview a few people at the Mela. Using Vijay as an interpreter was not on the whole satisfactory since he talked so much one never knew what was going on. As a matter of fact I had made a number of friends – acquaintances rather – at the Mela. One, a beautiful girl who taught Transcendental Meditation, used to come and listen to Swami Parvatikar's music, light his incense and adjust his equipment. That day, both of us spent a lot of time with him. We watched him at his asanas, then we were invited into his tent.

There was the same kind of quality in the surrounding atmosphere as fragrance – in other words it seemed to me that peace was akin to fragrance, that certain men give off a radiation rather as a rose gives off a scent, very subtly filling the air. It was as though one were in some exotic hothouse breathing in odoriferous air. It was very calm, very still, very comfortable. One was so secure with him. It was like being in the presence of a fragrant sun, one could bask in his rays. We have been associated before in a previous life, he said. This was the nearest yet to Yogananda or Paul Brunton. But I was uneasy as to our relationship; self-conscious as how to behave. The notion of reverence and awe is so foreign in the West. I wished I were more musical. I sensed that his path was through the vibrating

99

waves of sound he created. I wished he could teach me an instrument. Meanwhile to be with him was to be refreshed and inspired. His presence had a restorative effect, pulling you into a stream of energy. I felt again a glow verging on love. The feeling engendered in Puttaparthi had been more of a mass energy, here it was intimate. The morning concluded by our receiving bananas and a mantra.

I sat outside his tent and once again I felt that inner current of energy, establishing a marvellous clean feeling of well-being. I waited for Roy who had gone off somewhere. Suddenly a boy dashed up on a bicycle. Roy was at the Transcendental Meditation camp and it appeared that he had been rescued from the clutches of Hookah Baba who had been taking him to the Ganges to murder him! Yes, he would have taken all his clothes, he would have given him herbs, things to eat, so that Roy would have been drowned. Listen! A lot of gabbling was coming over the microphone. Even now a warning was being issued that people must not take food from strangers. Tantrics were abroad. (Tantrics seemed to be the Indian equivalent of bogeymen: if you didn't behave the Tantrics would get you.) Tantrics got you in their power by giving you something to eat. Then they possessed you and then heaven knew what happened. People vanished mysteriously, leaving no trace.

In spite of all the excitement, by eight o'clock that evening I was still basking in the calm that had rested with me from my morning with Swami Parvatikar. I could return to the central current and refresh myself in its stream. At half past eight the manager appeared with a tall dark stranger, who turned out to be not a maharajah at all but a farmer called (like, it seemed, every second person in India) Mr Singh. Mr Singh was in Allahabad to fight a court case: most of his land, he claimed, had been appropriated by Mrs Gandhi's government. Something certainly had upset his nerves. He jiggled his knees about restlessly and drank quantities of whisky. A procession of food kept appearing through the door: potato chops (a delicious dish in a yoghurt sauce), peanuts, crisps, mutton rolls and exquisite little things called poolkas. I sat sewing, basking in my inner tranquillity, while Roy, the manager and Mr Singh talked about cricket and hockey. This did not seem to suit Mr Singh. 'I think you are bored with the conversation,' he kept saying, and I had to turn away from my peace. 'No, no, not at all.'

In the middle of all this the bank clerk entered and helped himself to whisky. He had come to offer his services as interpreter at the Mela. He took over the party entirely. 'Have a little whisky, please,' he said to everyone. 'Help yourself, do.' 'I hope I am not disturbing you.' 'No, no,' the manager and Mr Singh assured him unconvincingly. It grew later and later. Suddenly the manager and Mr Singh stood up (it was only afterwards that I discovered how offended they had been by the arrival of the bank clerk). 'Now we must go,' they said. 'It is dinner time.' But we had supposed all those delicious snacks were dinner, it was impossible to eat more, and besides Roy had collapsed and was asleep. They all left eventually and the evening was over, except that a large plate of cakes was delivered just as we had fallen asleep.

As dawn broke next day a tremendous screeching sounded along the balcony. This was a very old lady, sallow and dessicated, who was supposed to be English. 'All the customers are coming out of their rooms to see what is happening,' exclaimed the cook – all, that is, apart from Roy who was obsessed with some punk song he was 'singing'. The English lady had arrived six months before from Calcutta, on her way to England. But she stayed on. Every Friday morning money arrived by post with which to pay the bill. The furore had begun that morning because the 'customer' in the next-door room had made the mistake of lighting a match in her presence. She was very like Mrs Harvey, this lady. Her voice shot up and down as she ranted and roared – much to the entertainment of everyone. The Villas was the most gregarious hotel I have ever stayed in. To step from one's room on to the veranda was to pass into a perpetual party. 'Good morning, where is your country?' would be followed by invitations: to go to Delhi, to go out to dinner, to go to some town in the north. As for Mr Singh he lurked like a cross giant, forever popping out of his room. 'When will you be returning to this country, please? Are you going to visit the Himalayas? I will show you everything – the Valley of the Flowers, Badrinath. You will stay with me, my wife she will cook all the special dishes. You must promise me you will visit. I have never seen a Western woman before, never have I been so fascinated.' I felt like something in the zoo. What were my plans? Could he also come to the Mela? There would be no drink there, I told him. His enthusiasm dampened. Would I have any time for him? I was going, I explained, to listen to music. Mercifully, he decided against the expedition.

When I returned later that evening, fortified by Swami Parvatikar's music, he was pacing the balcony, his brow darker than ever. 'No, young lady,' he thundered, 'this will not do. I have been waiting for you for three hours.' He had become yet another liability. The English lady was still screeching. She sat facing her window, looking out on to the veranda, shouting through the bars. Demons and dacoits were bothering her, she yelled. Why was the manager allowing them? Mr Singh meanwhile was wheeling in more drinks. He kissed my hand and while Roy was in the bathroom tried to kiss me on the lips. Perhaps he imagined that all Western women were automatically concubines. I longed for bed, certainly – but not with Mr Singh – I longed to bask in my inner current of energy. But it was not to be, we sat there over whisky and chatter and at about eleven o'clock there was a tremendous hooting outside and Vijay, his wife and daughter arrived, very hurt that we had neither informed them of our return nor stayed with them. They sat scowling at Mr Singh, while he sat scowling back in mutual distrust. What a dichotomy! Here were all these people wanting to protect you, provide for you, propel you round their country, pour out drinks and chatter incessantly, while all you wanted was to be away from them all and silent.

The whole thing had become such a liability that we decided to leave the Villas and Allahabad. For one night we escaped, by invitation, to the Lost and Found camp at the Mela. By now I was feeling rather ill from a cold, and spent some of the day dozing on the floor of the tent. It was surprisingly comfortable, a mattress of thick straw, my sleeping bag and brown rug. 'Your nose is cherry red,' Vijay assured me. He kept on appearing to see what I was doing.

There was a parade that day. First came four elephants, carrying actresses, all sparkling and made up, then a number of people beating drums, then a procession of ladies in brightly-coloured saris, all carrying garlanded pots of Ganges water on their heads. The girl from the Transcendental Meditation and I approached Pukkhra Baba. He glared at us through angry little eyes and poured out a stream of what must have been abuse. He would talk, he said, only to the man with the car. And that was that. He turned his back on us and muttered into the fire.

In the evening Roy and I walked with Shankar and a laid-back English boy called Lion (who kept ejaculating, 'far out, man!') to meet Lion's guru, Satcha Baba, who lived about five miles away. We walked away from the din of the Mela, under a brilliant blue sky, over the white sands of the Ganges. Cranes were wandering about, caravans of camels were transporting loads of wood and every so often we would happen across a skull lying in the bleached sand. Caves gashed deep into the cliffs bordering this white river bed. We entered one resounding with high-pitched squeaking – snakes, according to one Indian, who had joined our walking party. High above us were temples surrounded by beautiful gardens, inhabited by sadhus, and a village with sandy streets and white-washed huts, populated by bed-makers who sat outside their houses weaving the bases of their beds out of a hard grass which is smashed flat with hammers.

Shankar told us how he had wanted to sell his watch. As soon as he put the idea out into the ether, people had come flocking up. This idea that you put out thoughts which are immediately collected and returned to you was novel to me. Yet it was not really so foreign. I had been aware, for example, that when you had an idea that seemed new you would often find within the space of a few months an epidemic of articles and books appearing on that subject. It was as though several people had received the idea at the same time.

To reach Satcha Baba we required to be rowed across the Yamuna. His ashram is beautiful, high up above the river, with a garden full of roses and marigolds. For some time we joined about twenty people who were all sitting silent on the floor in front of him. Again there was a stillness. No words were spoken, yet it was invigorating. Coming before a holy, a healthy, a whole presence clearly has an elevating and restorative effect. Again the image of a flower rose up in my mind, or of the sun. These men *radiated* a force which revitalised you.

They could, furthermore, draw you into their own stream of energy and refresh you. Words were superfluous in conveying the basic aspects of energy. Swami Parvatikar used music as an agent for transmitting his power, while this Satcha Baba used silence.

As we left I turned back. Satcha Baba had on his face one of the most benign expressions I have ever seen. He was nodding his head from side to side and gazing out through the door at us, it seemed that he was throwing out his spirit to us, as tangible in its impact as a tennis ball. For my part I glowed with a sense of well-being. We returned through a sunset of incredible beauty, one of many black boats, sliding through water, which had been turned to burnished orange. We sat drinking tea on the outskirts of the Mela, overwhelmed with a feeling of harmony.

For our last night we stayed with Vijay and his family. Vijay collected us, drove us to his house and then for reasons of his own disappeared, staying out until five o'clock the following morning. He looked exhausted, a shade of his former self as he drove us to catch the train for Bombay.

Our next stop was Dadaji, from whose fingers, it is said, emanates a fragrance which adheres to everything he touches. Generally he is to be found in his native city, Calcutta, where he keeps a toy shop. But according to Kamilanand, who it transpired was one of his disciples, he was staying in Bombay. It was a dilemma. Was Kamilanand to be trusted? In any case we decided to go to Bombay. On the train we were subjected to a barrage of questions. How much is a ticket from England? How much is your salary? What is the national income? What is the rate of inflation? What is the rate of income tax? Is there a social security tax? Yet if, in return, you ask an Indian question – directions, for example – either he gives you an inaccurate answer or he just continues to ask questions.

Roy: Is there a telephone here?
Man: Yes, yes, nod, nod. What is your name?
Roy: Roy. May I make a telephone call?
Man: Yes, yes, telephone. What are you learning?
Roy: History. Please may . . .
Man: I too am a student of science.

Roy: ... I make a telephone call?

Man: In which countries have you travelled? And so it would go on.

In Bombay I had been given an introduction to Rahul Singh, the son of Kushwant Singh, editor then of the *Illustrated Times of India*. I had first read of Dadaji in one of his (Kushwant's) articles. Dadaji had drawn his hand through Kushwant Singh's beard and a delicious fragrance had sprung forth. On another occasion he had produced out of thin air a porcelain bottle of whisky. Rahul however was on the whole unenthusiastic, not only about Dadaji, but about any guru. Instead, I should meet a most interesting man who was currently conducting an exposé on the frauds of these so-called Godmen. He had devised some plan to investigate scientifically all these 'miracles' that were being performed, but most of the gurus, Sai Baba included, would not submit to his tests. Now Dadaji? Had he not once been arrested for forgery? Yes, Rahul Singh thought he could distinctly remember the case.

It seemed that Dadaji's circle included a number of scientists. Since it was the scientists who had originally usurped God it was to the scientists that Dadaji was revealing his signs and wonders. 'All these scientists that surround Dadaji, they all have sick minds,' said Kushwant Singh, who had joined us. 'Just speak to them and you'll see.' The P.R. man apparently was Abhi Battacharya, quite a well-known film star; he had been to see Kushwant Singh, and had stood on the balcony and all the passers-by had known who he was. Kushwant Singh showed me the white porcelain bottle materialised for him by Dadaji. Dadaji had asked him to sit down in front of him on the floor and had touched him and all his beard and chest had exuded fragrance. 'You are fond of whisky, aren't you?' Dadaji had asked him. Kushwant Singh had thought he was going to say: 'Well, stop drinking.' Instead this porcelain flask of whisky appeared out of thin air. 'Dreamland whisky,' it said on the bottle. 'Made in the universe. K. Singh.' Dadaji had manifested a watch for him too. Kushwant Singh still had that. He did not know what to make of him at all.

The man in question was staying at Bandra, one of Bombay's suburbs, in a flat by the sea belonging to Abhi Battacharya. Dhows were moving far out on the horizon and away

105

on the right the skyscrapers of Bombay shimmered in the evening light. Inside, photographs of Dadaji hung on the wall, together with another who was called Sri Sri Satya Narayana. Dadaji himself, looking about fifty, although he was over seventy-five, was sitting on a bed dressed in a lunghi and vest, smoking a cigarette. He was shifting next day into the centre of Bombay, so much of his evening was taken up with arrangements. Kamilanand was already there and a number of scientists did indeed make up the company.

There was Mr Pandit, a physicist at the IATA institute, and there was Dr Data who was the director of the solar energy conference which had just been held in Delhi. Dadaji, they informed me, was outside every scientific law. He defied time and place. He was beyond all reason. His manifestations were only to show reality to people – to prove that there is an invisible world that exists under our noses which we are not subtle enough to detect. Only last week Dr Klein of an important Western institution had been brought to him. Dadaji had touched him and from Dr Klein there had emanated the most delicious fragrance. Next, in front of everyone, he had manifested a watch. He had rubbed his finger over its dial erasing the maker's name and had substituted instead by some mysterious means: 'Made in the Universe, Sri Sri Satya Narayana.' For Mrs Klein too he had produced a wonderful fragrance and a golden locket. Dr and Mrs Klein, said the scientists, had fallen speechless at Dadaji's feet.

Meanwhile in the room some people were reading the paper, others chatted. Two ladies arrived and the talk of Dadji's miracles continued. One of the ladies' husbands – head of all the Indian airports no less – had been seized with a heart attack. 'I am going away,' he had said, and was rushed immediately into the intensive care unit. The doctors all looked gloomy. It seemed that her husband was dead. You must ring your relations, the doctors told her. The first person she rang was Dadaji. 'Dead?' he had replied. 'That is absurd. Everything will be all right.' She must go and massage her husband's heart while reciting the mahanam – a special name that Dadaji gives to his disciples upon initiation. On his deathbed her husband saw Dadaji approaching down a long tunnel. He woke up then and recovered.

We drank tea and the lady whose husband had risen from the dead told my fortune. I would marry again, she said – at thirty-two. What age was I now? Forty-two? Ah! She had done the arithmetic wrong. Yes, this was confirmed by her friend. What she had meant was between forty-five and forty-nine. Saturn was going to give me trouble with depressions. But my guru – God – would guide me. After this we entered the room again and there was Dadaji reading papers and smoking another ciga-rette. Out he went again and I was regaled with more stories. Mr Pandit's brother had been a sceptic. He was partial to Lucky Strike cigarettes – a brand which is particularly difficult to get in India. Mr Pandit had taken him to Dadaji, who was sitting as usual in his lunghi and tee-shirt. Suddenly he mani-fested a huge carton of Lucky Strike cigarettes out of the air above him. You could not believe it, said Mr Pandit. Dadaji defies all reason.

Another disciple said he had been sitting in his room enjoy-ing the festival of Holi, with a cigarette and a drink, and gradu-ally his floor and table became crowded with all sorts of articles. He produced some photographs to prove it and there sure enough was a jumble of objects including what seemed to be numerous hair brushes. Dadaji, they said, performs thou-sands of miracles to show sceptics that there are phenomena which transgress all known laws of time and space. His mira-cles have been documented by scientists, doctors, lawyers, judges, journalists, politicians and ministers. He can see and describe events that take place thousands of miles away; he can transmit fragrance to people over long distances. He can halt downpours of rain, manifest fountain pens, wrist watches, sweets and large porcelain dishes. As for his healing, said Mr Pandit, he can cure paralysis, rheumatism, slipped discs, fever, chest pain and cancer. People ring up with a complaint, he asks them to put a glass of water by the telephone, the water is then turned to Charanjal – a healing milky fragrant sub-stance.

Actually, one of Dadaji's main miracles seemed to be with the telephone. Indian telephones are notoriously incompetent. I had the greatest possible difficulty getting through to any-where, yet the few days I was with Dadaji the telephone was constantly ringing, people were calling from all corners of the

107

globe asking for advice, and they appeared to be getting through immediately.

His main theme, it seems, is against gurus. How can another man be your guru? he asks. No human being can ever be a guru. Only God can perform this function. Gurus are crooks, they are after your money. That evening a copy of *The Current* was being passed round in which there was an article claiming that Mahesh Yogi and Saitha Sai Baba were frauds. The author was Sivananda Swami Vishnu, who was known as the Flying Yogi, since he went round with Peter Sellers in an aeroplane dropping leaflets and flowers into the trouble spots of the world. He attacked Mahesh Yogi and his levitation technique (apparently the Mahesh Yogi is teaching people to fly through walls and lift themselves into the air). 'He's doing it all for money,' said the Flying Yogi. 'I'm going after him for fraudulent advertising.' Then he was going after another fraud, Sai Baba: he and Mahesh Yogi had really wrought havoc on the human mind. Sai Baba was doing so much harm with his silly miracles that if someone didn't take action. . . .

By now it was half past eight. Dadaji took me into the adjoining room. He stroked my hair and drew his hand up from my chest. Sure enough a fragrance sprang out (a scent which lingered on my clothes next day and which all the disciples said would return to me again and again when I was apart from Dadaji since time and space meant nothing). Did I believe in God? Did I feel God was separate from me? I must stay in Bombay, he said, and take Roy to him. 'Now Dadaji has blessed you, you can do nothing without his will,' said Mr Pandit. 'You will see, everything will be arranged for you.' and he handed me a pamphlet. Meanwhile Roy had spent his evening consulting a speak your weight machine. Ninety-three kilograms, it had said, 'because of the confidence you inspire you may be chosen to manage large enterprises'.

'A slow but steady awakening is taking place among the non-prejudiced open-minded thinkers that science does not possess the key to the ultimate knowledge, the reality, the truth,' the leaflet (which had been written by someone with a doctorate in chemistry) explained. 'This booklet is meant for all those non-prejudiced, open-minded people ... who possess in their heart, an almost compelling and involuntary urge to fathom the real nature of things: the nature of existence, of God, of the Universe, of Man ... in my association with Dadaji, I have come to the conclusion that the human mind with all its faculties and all its stretches of consciousness is just not able to comprehend, to reach the ultimate reality...'

There is a dimension beyond the consciousness of the human mind wherein lies the secret of existence. Truth pervades the universe: the manifestation of Truth is Divine Consciousness: Truth personified: God.

Dadaji's teaching is that by constant recitation of the mahanam (which is revealed only on initiation) you eventually cross these frontiers of human consciousness. The mahanam is supposed to vibrate through us from the moment of birth, but we forget it. This is, according to Dadaji, the Word of the Old Testament. Sri Sri Satya Narayana is but a manifestation of Dadji's, a symbol of the Truth. It is not Dadaji who performs the miracles, but God. Dadaji asks you to follow him and become a disciple of the Divine, not of himself. The more you follow him, the more tranquillity you get. To follow Dadaji is to be in love with him – you bask in his presence as in the warm rays of the sun. Don't make God a business, he says, make your business God. He does not ask you to give up life: drink or cigarettes. It is not necessary to have solitude, to go to the country, to find God. You simply have to enjoy yourself and remember God; any minute not spent reciting the mahanam is a minute wasted; do your duty, he says, and recite God's name. God is within.

During the next darshan, in an apartment in Walkeshwar Road, Dadaji spent most of the evening discoursing on the equality of men and women, then returned to his theme of haranguing gurus and sadhus. Roy got very fidgety, rolling his eyes up to the ceiling. As far as he was concerned he was missing good eating time. Two people arrived and were taken away to another room with blank pieces of paper for initiation. At the end of the evening Dadaji called me. I know everything, he said. You come every day. So we did, Roy becoming more and more disagreeable. I must say it was hard to detect any benefit. Dadaji would sit discoursing away in Bengali and I would sit staring at him hoping that at any minute he might manifest something – watches, whisky, I was not fussy. Would it happen? Wouldn't it? Would he cure Roy? What would I see? Surely, I reasoned, he knew I was writing a book, surely he would manifest something. He did not. But he certainly had a powerful magnetic presence. Although his meetings were in a sense boring, they were refreshing. You left feeling restored and exhilarated. One evening he touched Roy and the fragrance hung around him for days. Again he touched my forehead and scent sprang from it. Matters were not helped by my relationship with Dadaji – or my lack of it. I was conscious that when I was with him I was playing a role. Since all the Indians wore an air of reverence and awe I aped them, adopting a pose of surrender, falling to my knees and clutching his feet on my departure. Excellent! Dadaji would murmur.

Patience, he preached. Patience is strength. Certainly it was necessary. Roy was at his most difficult. For a start neither of us was enjoying Bombay. It was both expensive and uncomfortable. Ideally I would have liked to have stayed there for as little time as possible. I desired to witness a star performance, a full range of Dadaji's miracles, as quickly as possible, and then move on to somewhere greener.

At least we had removed to Juhu to be away from the city and near to the sea but the only place we could find to stay was a dreadful hotel, modern, plastic, expensive and shoddy. The telephone dangled from one wire in the wall, the door hung lopsided from the cupboard and pigeons nested in the hot water heater, dropping straw down the Western-style lavatory. Indeed the hotel was more like a pigeon loft than anything else; besides perching on the water system about fifty birds lodged in the large black hole which formed the centre of the hotel, through which a lift descended and ascended.

Here Roy's main occupation was eating; daily he grew larger. Sometimes he would cram in as many as eight meals a day, selected from a huge and pretentious menu. Every meal took about an hour to prepare and would arrive pursued by a large cloud of flies.

The menu stretched over eight closely-written pages consisting of sixteen soups including asparagus, 'tomato coconut' and 'cream chicken'; eleven salads; five 'cold sections'; thirteen fish dishes; eighteen chef specialities ('pollo pom', 'pollo Kingston', 'Breast of Chicken Toast', 'Marchal Breast of Chicken stuffed with butter', 'Omelette Pale Mint', 'Chicken Slice with Calary Popularde 72', 'Pollidalla Russian Russiance', 'Popularde Victoria'); then came the sizzlers – 'Sizzling grilled lobster, sizzling vegetable mix grill'; and after that a whole Chinese menu: 'Chinese chopsy' 'chicken chopsy', 'veg chopsy'.

When he was not eating, Roy was singing or rather bellowing punk songs. 'Yeah, yeah, yeah, I wanna be sick on you,' he would roar from the bathroom. Then like a naughty child: 'Did you hear that?' The whole hotel had. Because I wanted him to behave in a certain way he set out to do exactly the opposite, to attract attention, shocking one's own inhibitions by his lack of them. Very effective it was too, and irritating to say the least. Instead of opening up new planes of subtle awareness I was becoming more and more like a nanny or a school matron. I saw, now, how and why nannies, parents and school teachers (to say nothing of the Church and the government) operate on the principle of fear, punishment and reward. This is the easiest and perhaps the only way to control a situation. If you're good you'll get a sweet. If you're naughty you get no sweet and/or a smack; you'll go to hell. I could hear myself just like the children's nanny. No breakfast till you get up/wash/shave. You've got food round your mouth/the carriage/the table; all over the bed/yourself.

I was reading Paul Brunton again. He talks a lot about travelling towards silence and letting the overself well up. I would be sitting there trying to let the overself well up and there would be Roy singing his punk songs, then there would be someone banging on the door to clean the room, someone else to clean the shoes, someone bringing in the laundry. Outside there would be the endless questions. One would be sitting trying to read, meditate even, and up they would come: 'Am I disturbing you?' 'What is your name?' 'What are you learning?' 'From which country are you?' 'Outer Mongolia,' Roy would answer. 'Please?' a puzzled expression would spread over their faces. 'Guess?' 'I don't understand.' 'U.S.S.R.?' 'U.S.A.?' 'Canada?' 'France?' And on the beach little girls would come up and clap their hands. Clap, clap clap. 'Mem Sahib! Mem Sahib!' clap, clap, clap, like tiresome little flies.

There is a story of a boy walking through a field of delicious flowers; his attention is drawn not to their fragrance and beauty but to a piece of litter which is blowing in their midst. This is used as an illustration: what one sees reflects the state of one's mind. I can confidently report that I neither saw nor smelt anything of beauty in Bombay. The train journey for example was like travelling through a malodorous sewer in a tin packed with sardines. And what sardines! As quick as lightning they whipped open your handbag and lifted out your money. In a twinkling, rupees were extracted from a bag cluttered with hair brushes, traveller's cheques and passports. Bombay, according to the papers, was in the grip of crime – groups of people waited at every station ready to snatch briefcases and handbags. Rahul Singh said he had had two pens appropriated from an inner pocket as he was standing by the Taj Mahal. Conditions were not improved by the beggars who work up and down the trains singing, dancing and so on. There was one particularly unpalatable couple, a little girl with her face painted puce, down which yellow mucus flowed unimpeded, mouthed some incantation while her sister, who was in fact quite pretty, rattled some rocks so efficiently that they sounded just like castanets.

The beach at Juhu was extraordinary. Everything was there: charmed snakes, dancing monkeys, hoop-la, camels, horses, drowned cats and cannabis sellers. Most extraordinary perhaps of all was the new Hare Krishna temple – Hare Krishna Land, it is called, like Disney Land. It is a glittering affair with black and white marble floors and silver altars. As for the Hare Krishnas themselves they look no less bizarre here than they do leaping down Oxford Street; the men have the whole of their heads shaved, apart from the small pigtail hanging from their crown, and all the Western ones, both men and women, look curiously unhealthy with their faces as pale as parchment. It seems to be a movement that is attractive to Americans. Hare Krishna Land just then was full of American devotees who spent much of their time at the airport selling enormous volumes of the *Bhagavad Gita*, which is printed in Los Angeles with chocolate-box illustrations. They tried to press a few heavy tomes upon us. The would-be sales girl was rather beautiful with large eyes burning out of her parchment face. 'We are travelling light,' I told her. 'We couldn't possibly carry

112

such a large book.' 'You ought to throw away your bed,' she intoned. 'This book you've got to have.' Although I escaped without the *Bhagavad Gita* she did make me take two magazines.

Next door a most luxurious hotel was being constructed which would be run by the Hare Krishnas and managed by an ex-Army major – white this time – who was already striding about the place shouting out orders in commanding Sandhurst tones. 'Why is this telephone not working?' rang out across the marble floors. Why indeed? No one seemed to answer and the major could be seen picking his way in his smart cavalry twill trousers through the rubble past the pigtailed devotees – a most incongruous sight. The bedrooms appeared sumptuous, all the beds and furniture being in painted lacquer. A shaved head showed us round, mumbling and muttering mantras to himself all the while.

Back in the temple a ceremony was just beginning. Several devotees pranced round banging on drums and cymbals while three shimmering purple curtains were drawn back simultaneously to reveal three silver altars containing Krishna and his consort Radha, looking like fairies on a Christmas tree. Three attendants blew down three huge conch horns, they flapped dishes of fire about in front of the Christmas tree Krishnas, waved huge bunches of plumed things and then fanned them with ravishing peacock feather fans. Two were perfectly in unison, the one on the right was not. Here was a ceremony such as we had witnessed in Ayodiah when the viands were sanctified. We were then presented with a huge leaf of food which Roy followed up by stumping off and treating himself, and a cloud of flies, to prawn cocktail and chicken salad in that dreadful restaurant. The aim of the movement, one of the pig-tailed disciples explained to me, is to bring man back to his original state of consciousness: clear consciousness: Krishna consciousness: a state where all is one. Krishna is realised through the ears and the tongue, not the eyes. Of all the senses the tongue is the most voracious and difficult to control, but simply by chanting 'Hare Krishna, Hare Krishna', the tongue is overcome and mastered.

The humour of the situation struck me. Here were all these shaved heads wearing orange and leaping round banging

113

drums, appearing absolutely extraordinary, in order to drop their individual egos and join into one consciousness. But the more they leap about and try to convince people that we are all one, the more outlandish and different they appear.

As for the magazines they seemed as weird as their authors. One argued that man had never landed on the moon at all. This was endorsed by a Gallup Poll in the *Los Angeles Times* in October 1976. Twenty-eight percent of Americans believed the moon landing to be a fake. Well, the moon landing *was* a fake: it was a colossal hoax on which billions of dollars of public money had been spent. The moon planet is not a lifeless desert at all but a heavenly planet of extraordinary material pleasures on which one may not land without the proper qualifications. What the astronauts had visited is 'not part of our present discussion', but one thing was certain: it was not the moon.

On Sundays there is a public feast in Hare Krishna Land – a performance to attract people, and attract people it certainly did. The food is sanctified as usual but on Sundays the din is colossal – the way to a clear consciousness is apparently through bursting one's ear-drums. All the shaved heads jumped up and down shouting 'Hare Krishna, Hare Rama', while their colleagues fanned the Christmas tree figures. Then hundreds of people were served lunch from buckets – ourselves included – all sitting in long lines on the floor. Roy meanwhile had conducted two interviews. One was with the hall porter at the new hotel who was Portuguese and whose parents had been killed. He was alone, he said, but he had no wish to marry; for five rupees he could sleep with a Nepalese girl. Everyday he made his japas and incanted the required mantras so that he could join the ashram – it was a very good life at the ashram, very easy, free clothes, free sleep, very little work, sing bhajans, eat meals and when he wanted they gave him five rupees and he went into Bombay and slept with the Nepalese girl. 'You have place in England for parents when they are old? Yes? Old people's home? This ashram is the same.'

But another who wished to remain anonymous was less enthusiastic. The whole thing was a racket, he said. It's all run by Americans, for Americans, who would be the only people gullible enough to take this sort of thing seriously. They're worse than Jehovah's witnesses. They oppose the so-called materialistic society, yet they live off it. Look at this ghastly hotel — straight from Sunset Boulevard. Where would they be if they didn't have materialists to pay for it? They are crassly materialistic themselves. They are spiritual materialists and morons to boot.

All in all we ended up staying in Bombay for a week and during that time, apart from the fragrance, I had witnessed nothing marvellous from Dadaji. On the night we were due to leave Bombay I felt bad: uneasy, irritable, frustrated and anxious. I had even less of an idea what I was supposed to be doing or for what I was looking. The small centre of gravity I had established with Swami Parvatikar had gone. I felt I had wasted a week in an expensive city.

That last evening we were invited to dinner with Dadaji's hosts and Kamilanand — not in the flat where Dadaji was staying, but another across the passage. The train time was drawing near and I felt desperate; here we were wasting yet more time by having dinner and still nothing had happened. I must at least ask for the mahanam before I left, Kamilanand said. By the time dinner was finished there was about half an hour before the train and I felt more fit to receive a tranquilliser than anything else. However Dadaji took me to the next-door room and made me kneel on the floor, hands joined together before the photograph of Sri Sri Satayanarayana, and recite the name Ram, with a piece of paper held between my hands. My heart was thundering, it was all such a rush. When I opened my hands nothing had happened. Again, while Dadaji massaged my spine, the performance was repeated. This time on the top of the paper inscribed in very clear red ink was: 'Gopal Govinda'. (Invisible ink, Roy said scornfully afterwards.) One journalist had described his initiation: the words, he said, came thundering down to him. For me there was no thunder apart from my heart.

After reciting them ten times the words vanished, just the plain piece of paper remained. Then Dadaji took a small photograph of Sri Sri Satayanarayana and rubbed it with his thumb. Some Indian script appeared at the bottom, running a little off the lower edge. And wherever he had touched me that fragrance flowed out and stayed with me for several days. That was it: the initiation was over.

So we progressed to Hampi, the ruined City of Victory, Vijayanagar. This was Roy's choice, the scene of some of his mystical experiences. I have always loved ruins and these were some of the most beautiful and romantic I have ever seen. There are marvellous descriptions of the kingdom at the height of its glory written sometime in the sixteenth century by Domingos Paes. Here was a city flowing with abundance and precious stones; its massive walls enclosing palaces and temples. In the bazaars were rubies, diamonds, emeralds and pearls; at its fairs cattle, pigs, fowl, dried fish, citrons, limes, oranges and grapes. It was a city as large and as beautiful as Rome with lakes, groves of palm, mango, orange and lime, conduits rushing with water and streets crowded with elephants; stocked with delicious provisions: partridges, hares, fat mutton, pigeons and pomegranates. The main bazaar had been one of the finest, lined with arcades and ornate houses adorned with intricate balconies. And what feasts there had been! The palaces were festooned with sumptuous stuffs; the wrestlers glistened with oil; the dancing girls decked with glorious jewels, necks laced round with gold and encrusted with diamonds, arms, stomachs and ankles glittering with rubies and pearls. At sundown thousands of torches illuminated equestrian battles, the chargers saddled with exquisite trappings and gilded bridles.

Back in antiquity, Hampi had been the haunt of the gods – the scene of many a mythological tale. Here Ram had killed a devil called Vali, Sita had bathed herself in a holy tank (the marks of her sari are still to be seen upon the ground), and Parvati had done penance in order to win Shiva's love. Today, Hampi offers only the barest of amenities – the floors of caves and temples on which to sleep. At first we stayed at the nearest Tourist Bungalow, which was very superior, fifteen miles away at the Tungabhadra Dam. The Indians are extremely proud of their dams, they are prime tourist attractions. The T.B., as it is called, is one of the marvels of India: such an expanse of water that the other bank is not visible. At sunset a cool breeze blows up and everyone gathers there to stroll along the banks, sniffing the delicious air and watching the sun drop down into the water. It was here at sunset that I had my first experience of dissolving. Dissolving is quite different to disintegration, which is separating, curdling, falling apart: unpleasant and frightening. Dissolving is harmonious, peaceful: melting into an absorbing body – a landscape, for example, a river, a mountain, an animal or another person – so that one loses one's sense of uniqueness and becomes one with it. I had walked by the side of this inland sea in the setting sun and made up my mind to calm myself. I would meditate. I sat down. The air was body temperature, neither too hot, nor too cold. I sat there for perhaps an hour, watching the sun drop down into the water. The absorption was a slow process. Gradually, as my mind became still, the outlines of my body began to grow less firm; by degrees they blended into the air and the land so that I became one with them. And when I left the place by the water, separate once more, I was calm, refreshed, and all my anxiety had gone. It had been absorbed by the air and the water.

The trouble about staying at T.B. was the journey to Hampi. It took ages, bumping along via Hospet, the local town, in crowded buses. One day we received a lift from a sweet and hospitable Brahmin. We must come home with him for breakfast. We must meet his wife, his family – his model family. We must read their school reports. 'This is my son at such and such a grade' and these immaculately-conserved portfolios with titles like 'My school years' were all his photographs and results. Arithmetic: fifty out of fifty; English: fifty out of fifty; teacher's remarks: 'good attendance, keep it up', 'congratulations'. Then: 'This is my eldest daughter who is very clever at zoology.' We must see some perfectly-executed drawings of the custard apple. We must hear tapes of his son singing, his uncle singing and some bhajans from the village temple. Would Roy please sing a national song? To which he obliged not from his punk repertoire but with 'Jerusalem.' 'I am very happy to have you here,' the kind hospitable Brahmin wrote on a bit of paper. Eventually we departed, not without invitations to tea and dinner. Three hours later we were in Hampi and by this time extremely dishevelled, having swum in the river and made love in a cave. I was wrapped only in the crumpled Benares lunghi which by now looked like a mauve rag. Suddenly round the corner we encountered a procession. First a chauffeur carrying a hamper on his head and then, in a polite crocodile the whole model family, arrived for a picnic. 'Come and join us,' they said gallantly. From then on wherever we went we met them: driving in their jeep down narrow paths; visiting remote temples. The more dishevelled we became the more we met them, bumping over remote rocks and boulders, down what seemed to be mere goat tracks.

Shortly after this we moved from T.B. and for three rupees a night stayed in one of those inspection bungalows which was in this case in a converted temple in the nearest village to Hampi. Heaven knew what it was that people inspected in there; perhaps it was the hundreds of cockroaches, or the manager himself, who lived on the other side of the compound and most mornings killed his dinner just outside our window, which then ran round without its head, flapping its wings for quite some time.

From the moment we arrived in Hampi, Roy began to recover, he had lapses certainly, but he became far more energetic, walking long distances every day and swimming in the brown waters of the Tungabhadra River – which used apparently to be the abode of crocodiles. Nowadays Hampi is frequented by other sorts of crocodile: those of schoolchildren being escorted through the ruins by their masters and mistresses who, about every five minutes, trumpet an awful blast on a clarion. All day long, from all over Hampi, one would hear the racket resounding round the old stones.

Hampi is perhaps one of the most beautiful places I have been in and certainly one of the most mysterious. Memories return of fragrant nights, frogs croaking in the streams, seas of cicadas in the moonlight. That moonlight was quite unlike its pale Western reflection. It was as brilliant as neon lighting in which you could see every blade of grass. We were there at full moon and could walk at midnight as though by daylight, through the ruins, whose columns threw thick black shadows. And by day the goats and monkeys jumped through the ruined palaces and women in bright saris stood ankle-deep in the emerald terraces of young rice that grew now in the bazaars. The ruined city stretched over a great area. Red-brown columns and fallen rocks stood out from the lush vegetation, and everywhere hundreds of glittering streams and canals fed by the Tungabhadra Dam rushed through banana, rice and sugar-cane plantations, while herds of buffalo grazed on the river banks. Everywhere were conduits, bath houses, domed elephant stables and temples; everywhere carved columns and inscribed boulders lay toppled and broken. The Vithala temple was specially interesting. Its carved columns were hollow, each column played a note. This was how the music was made for the dancing girls, by tapping the columns with bamboo sticks. Now if one bangs them with the knuckles they ring with different notes, a little like cowbells, some low, some high. And when one presses one's ear to the columns one can feel the vibrations of sound flowing. The sweetest notes were the most popular, their columns were shiny and eroded.

Hippies were everywhere. Hampi is the second stop along the freak's trail – Goa being the first. From behind every rock their chillum coughs wracked the air, bouncing and echoing from the brown stones. Roy displayed an alcoholic's cunning when it came to the chillums which they dispensed so liberally. Whenever he saw a hippy he would engage him in conversation, usually on the subject of rock music. Then he would sit down and wait for the chillum to appear, which undoubtedly it did. Roy's approach to drugs was, you could say, religious. 'It is a modern wave,' I had read somewhere, 'to equate the hallucinatory condition in drugs with mystical experiences.' Wave or not, Roy was the living example of it. Neither joints nor chillums did anything for me however. Sometimes I found the effects distinctly unpleasant, rather more confining than liberating, not unlike that description of old age in the Bible: 'when thou shalt be old, thou shalt stretch forth thy hands and another shalt gird thee and carry thee whither thou wouldest not.'

The hippies were not really my scene. It was not that I felt unsympathetic towards them, at least not consciously. After all we had a lot in common. They were fed up with materialist values; so was I. Their motives were very similar to my own, we were all of us here to extract something from, rather than add anything to, the place. But somehow they presented an unattractive spectacle. They gave the impression of parasites, so languid and laid-back, nibbling away at the energy, sucking at the atmosphere like leeches, even going so far, some of them, as begging in the streets. And they were so incompetent. There was nearly always something wrong with their health: hepatitis, skin diseases, stomach disorders. They lost their money, their passports, their way. Often they just lay round too apathetic to do anything but light up the next joint. As a matter of fact we spent a lot of time with the hippies, lying in the cool shade of the rock temple next to the brown sliding waters of the Tungabhadra River. It was a secret place and difficult to find. You climbed over slippery rocks and round boulders, some of them carved and inscribed, ducked under a toppled column and emerged on this small concealed cliff beach, overhanging the water, which brought to mind the great green greasy Limpopo, but was eminently refreshing. This had been the abode of Roy's guru (or one of them), Gopal Swami, now dead from food poisoning, contracted in Goa. This is where Roy had stayed and where Gopal Swami had dived for fish and cooked it over the fire.

The month of Roy's first visit had been April and very hot. In those days he had been avoiding hippies, they were always begging, he felt, wanting money. One day he had spotted an energetic little figure in flowing robes walking away between two freaks. Later one of these had approached him for 'bread'. Roy gave him five rupees. This great swami, who had done years of Hatha Yoga, lived over there in that cave, the freak told him. Roy saw again the energetic little figure. He was over seventy but seemed possessed by an extraordinary vitality. He had a shock of white hair, a leonine face – very wizened, very canny, very crafty. He was strong, he had authority. He knew something. But his attention was always being diverted by the bunch of hippies encamped there. He hardly took any notice of Roy, it seemed to him, until in the middle of a conversation a strange Dravidian expression came to him. 'Prabhu!' shouted Roy. 'Prabhu!' meaning master. That evening Gopal Swami prepared rice and fish and then came the chillums. He started singing a song during the second chillum, an invocation to the God of the Sun. The song that Roy heard was one of the Vedas, not intoned as a Brahmin would intone it, but sung as the song was originally heard. That Roy knew. It started slowly, developed by stages, gathering strength into a paean of praise – a song of triumph. He did not understand the words, yet perceived something incredibly fine, incredibly intelligent, masterly, virile. Then came the crescendo. The song had been about truth and suddenly as Gopal Swami reached a tonic note it seemed that it became the truth. He threw the tonic note across to Roy, in whom he raised such emotion, such recognition. He had heard it before. He knew it. This was how truth had been inspired by the bards. This was Homer. This man was Homer. This was how Homeric songs had been sung. He felt that the spirit had been thrown into him. The vowels and the consonants had entered into him, overflowed with emotion inside him, striking deep familiar chords. He had never again heard anything so sublime.

At the end of the song the swami had seen his emotion. You stay with me for six months, he had said. Neither had the others ever heard such a song. 'Hey, Swami!' one of the hippies said. 'That mantra really got me going.' It had seemed to Roy that he had been shown some special song and that this hippy was debasing the whole thing. He had not stayed. But the incident gathered importance in his mind. He felt he had missed a great opportunity. He had missed something he would never again be able to find. He had returned after some months to Hampi but by then Gopal Swami was dead. That time he had other experiences. He had gone up to the top of a hill quite far away and the gods had come to him: your heart was golden, they said, but you betrayed the truth. They drew out his soul and deserted him. Cursed, he had eventually returned to England.

So now we lay on that rocky beach, while the hippies puffed their chillums, meditated on the hexagram, lay about naked, played their guitars, and embarked on laid-back conversations about I Ching, T'ai Chi Chuan, Kung Fu, ganja and their health. One golden girl from France was having trouble with her blisters, they had gone septic and were swollen up, yellow with pus; the pain was shooting up her leg, she said. One fair gentle boy was supposed to be working for a well-known auction house, he was to be in the Indian department so he had come to India to study art. He had spent nine months in Benares smoking hashish and had studied no art. He was about to embark on an intensive course of meditation – one of the

121

attractions being that there were strict rules of no smoking, and this was the only way he was going to break the habit. His conversation consisted mainly of dope: Thai stick in London, Colombo grass in Mexico, Acapulco gold in New York and now in Hampi it was opium – a remedy against the dysentery he had just contracted. 'I was stoned before breakfast and I'm still stoned,' he told us all.

Sometimes while we were at the inspection bungalow I would get up early and watch the sunrise from the ruins. It is a wonderful time, that short stretch between dawn and sunrise. Everyone is up and hurrying with their goats, their cows or just themselves to reach their destination before the heat strikes. It is very cool and grey, growing all the time more luminous. The light rises so quickly, daubing the sky with red until the sun suddenly shoots up out of the earth, huge and round. One morning I watched it from the emperor's throne, high above the empty landscape – or it seemed to be an empty landscape, yet within five minutes a man had appeared from nowhere and in all that space came to stand behind the very rock, the very throne, on which I was sitting, and remained there, coughing loudly and spitting.

Before our departure – which I took with deep regret – we came across one of Gopal Swami's friends. Cuppa Baba he was called and a very disloyal friend he turned out to be, telling us at length how Gopal Swami had been only out to cheat the tourists: money, that was all he wanted. Roy met him on the bus in search of laxatives – 'I have not been stool-side for four days,' he was pleased to announce. If we went to his house, built into the ruins of the grand bazaar, next day, he would sing some of Gopal Swami's bhajans, he would, furthermore, take Roy to Gopal Swami's grave. Next day, however, he returned from Hospet, where he had been baking a batch of chillums for the hippies, with indigestion. He sat in a tea-shop rubbing his stomach, rolling his eyes and balancing his cup on top of his head. No, no bhajans. He could sing no bhajans. All he could manage was a cup of curds. He looked quite mad dressed in a sort of matelot jersey, an army great-coat, a dhoti and orange turban and then this cup stuck on top of his head. He slowly ate his curds and then disappared, still rubbing his stomach and rolling his eyes. And that was the last we saw of him.

From Hampi we travelled into the interior, to a remote place of pilgrimage in Andhra Pradesh called Mantralayam. Ever since leaving Swami Parvatikar I had wanted to visit his guru. Not that I knew anything about him except that he was a great veena scholar and said to be three hundred years old, living underground, appearing only to those people who were spiritually mature enough to merit a glimpse – Swami Parvatikar being one of them. Mantralayam is a small village right in the middle of nowhere; you approach it in buses crammed with people, rattling and jolting along mile upon mile of thin road which stretches like a ribbon across brown baking plains. This is no ordinary place. By no means may you not visit it how or when you like; indeed you may not visit it at all unless the guru himself, Ragavendra, wishes it – or so it is believed. Sometimes people try very hard to get there, arriving quite near, but still they fail to reach their destination. The story is that Ragavendra entered his tomb alive in August 1671 and here he will stay for seven hundred years, praying for his disciples. By his grace desires are fulfilled, health is restored, material and spiritual wealth is bestowed. Many pilgrims come for at least three days and will not leave until the saint has appeared to them in their dreams.

I loved Mantralayam. Everyone was so kind, the manager of the ashram, for example, who gave us lunch. 'Are you from the Hare Krishnas?' he asked. The restaurants and tea-shops were excellent, owned and waited upon by devotees. The waiter who brought us our marsala dosa said that Ragavendra was always appearing to him in dreams to guide him; he does nothing without a consultation.

Although I had found Hampi beautiful, it had not been peaceful, what with the hippies and their chillums and underneath its mysterious air had lain a turbulent atmosphere – it is what the hippies call 'a powerful place'. Mantralayam, on the other hand, I felt was soothing and refreshing. And everything, it seemed, was geared for us to be ushered immediately into the morning darshan of Ragavendra. This was rather confusing. All the men must prepare themselves by removing their shirts and draping a towel round their necks. Thus equipped, we arrived in front of a small grille. As usual I had no idea what we were supposed to be doing, or seeing. A small crowd presssd round. He is coming? Yes. Yes. 'Am I good enough to see this man?' Roy wanted to know. Unfortunately neither of us were. We saw nothing at all, except some people running round dusting what seemed to be a seat. Then a plate of flames arrived and we received some of the sugared water prasad, called padoka, which is said to purify the polluted and grant peace, plenty and prosperity. But it was then that I did feel an unmistakable presence. Again it was something that roused in me that delightful current of energy, a stirring, a sort of internal massage. Again I was reminded of waves of fragrance; this energy came over me as delicately as the wafts of lilies and it stayed with me all day.

We had, however, gone about the whole thing in quite the wrong way. We should first have purified ourselves in the Tungabhadra River, which is especially beautiful here, wide, shallow and clear, swirling round islands, deliciously cool in the baking heat. We stayed for hours in and by the rushing creeks. White birds flew low over the water and all round people were washing themselves and their clothes, slapping them on stones, the slaps echoing round and into the distance.

I had been looking forward to going to bed, to see what, if anything, Ragavendra might communicate. I had my pencil and paper ready. But the night did not begin well. This particular Tourist Bungalow had been recommended to us on account of its good furnishings. The man must have been a joker. There was nothing at all in the room but some dirty paper and two mattresses on the floor. We were, moreover, outnumbered several million to one by ants and mosquitoes which made it difficult, indeed impossible, to sleep at all. I spent the night scratching, feeling like the princess and the pea. After a while as I was lying there I did have an experience, not unlike the one a year before on the train when travelling to Benares. I felt myself inflating, blowing up like a balloon, my legs, arms and fingers vanished and there was just this huge balloon filled with a roaring vibrating force. It was most uncomfortable and for much of the time I felt I might suffocate. After a while the balloon subsided.

Sleep came at dawn with, sure enough, a dream. I went into a cake shop in Guildford. There were queues of people all in there buying hot crusty bread and large quantities of sponge cake with chocolate layers. Someone else was with me. 'Now, just you watch,' I said to my companions. 'These bakers are clever. They establish an image by selling hot crusty bread and then they palm off that mass-produced stuff over there.' One of the customers was sitting down drinking a cup of tea. She had long hair with those little hippy plaits in it. She looked up and nodded. Meanwhile the queues of suburban housewives continued buying large quantities of cake. The girl behind the counter had heard what I said. We think this cake is really gorgeous, she said, looking hurt. And they offered me a huge slice, but since I was on a diet the last thing I wanted was to eat it. Try it, she said. So I did. It was as one had supposed, quite moist but synthetic. The girl behind the counter ate hers with evident enjoyment. I was outraged. People were putting their energy into producing and genuinely believing in synthetic things, not real ones. I woke up and laughed. I did not understand the significance of the dream but it struck me as being marvellously humorous. Here I was, somewhere in the interior of India, on a remote pilgrimage to the shrine of a saint supposed to be hundreds of years old and all I could dream of was a cake shop in Guildford.

From Mantralayam we shook and rattled our way by bus and train to a southern beach resort, Mahabalipuram. Much of that trip was spent travelling and quite a lot of it was passed in the main line junction of Guntakal. By now I felt quite familiar with it. Besides being one of the main junctions of India, Guntakal is notable for its team of small boys who work the trains. 'Do you have any stamps, greeting cards, pens, pencils or English coins?' they ask, rushing up and down the corridors – one should travel with a pantechnicon to India, loaded down with old Christmas cards, stamps, foreign currency, rupees, empty tapes and volumes of one's own work for distribution. I must be one of the greatest living experts on Indian railway stations and their facilities. Guntakal's waiting rooms, for example, are excellent, far superior to those of Faisabad. On the whole I enjoyed the railways and even their waiting rooms, but not the buses. They were noisy, bone-shaking boxes on wheels, hurtling hotly through rocks, dust and desert, their klaxons emitting ear-splitting shrieks, scattering pedestrians and animals. Seventy or more people cram into each vehicle with their baggage and vegetables. Beggars add to the crush by squeezing in and working down the aisles with baskets of boiled sweets, crippled children and their own deformities – one lady with no legs managed to manipulate herself expertly through a packed bus and extricate herself as it careered off down the street.

So from Mantralayam we had rattled our way south by bus and train to Mahabalipuram. The purpose of this visit was re-search – of a sort – since I was thinking of writing an article on Indian beach resorts. With its comfortable cheap accommo-dation, its long polished beaches, its dewy mornings, its ravishing nights when the temple stands black against the moonlit sea, its great waves surging in from the Indian ocean, Mahabalipuram is a honeymoon place. I think of orange sunsets, huge rock sculptures, stone lions, rocks, luke-warm seas and sand still warm until long after dark. On those white sands, fishing boats lie with curving wooden bows from which the yards of fishing nets are pulled in by hand. If one passes as the catch is being pulled in one sees the whole heap of fish and crabs writhing, gasping, glittering in the merciless sunlight.

We arrived the morning after the full moon. The place was still packed from the famous lunar festival held there every month. In front of the great ruined temple, stalls were erected; there were bands, processions, snake-charmers and mongeese. Such were the crowds it was difficult to make head or tail of what was going on. Mahabalipuram is also on the hippy trail. The familiar coughs could be heard wracking the cheaper hotels, ricocheting round the small dark cupboards, the apol-ogies of rooms that the hippies inhabited. It is also apparently on the trail for Western religious freaks and parasites. We met Andrew at lunch, where, needless to say, Roy engaged him in conversation. Man has never been able to solve his own prob-lems, was the gist. War was as inevitable as the fall of the dollar. War and its inevitability and then the inevitability of God. I had noticed that he and his companion were ordering all the most luxurious dishes on the menu – not that it was an expensive menu by Western standards but it was a restaurant which also served meat, always more extravagant than idlis, dosas, vegetables and puris. These people had ordered the meat curry, which cost eight rupees. He was an unprepossessing-looking fellow, covered in red boils and pimples. He was here, he told us, on his honeymoon. The poor bride came from New Zealand, her pustular groom from Glasgow. Now, however, they lived and worked in Sri Lanka, with some pop group whose purpose it was to unite everyone in love. 'We want to go round spreading love,' Andrew told us, advancing his supporating chin towards us. He was, he told us, a 'Child of God'. God was constantly visiting him and in a soft voice telling him what to do and where to go. It might even be that he told him to go to a Chinese restaurant or 'to where the sun rises' at which point he was destined to meet a particular person and so on. 'Credit cards, communism, it's all written in the Bible,' said Andrew.. 'The seventh empire is going to come, it's all here. First there's going to be a nuclear war, then communism, then the antichrist who is going to monitor every-one with the credit card system. It's really heavy.' He said, 'It's really heavy,' a great deal.

He had this quiet persistent voice, speaking his words in a sort of monotonous monologue. At last we escaped and retired to our rooms. Almost immediately there was a knock at the door: Andrew and his bride – who never opened her mouth. In they came and settled down comfortably. The ghastly voice droned on and on. There must be a plan, a design, burble, burble, burble. Revelations. Daniel. Certain things must come to pass. It's really heavy, blah, blah, blah. I could not bear any more and left Roy to it. I listened to the waves roaring up the beach and watched two young dogs chasing the crabs, which move like spiders and at the first sign of danger scuttle into their holes; in certain lights the whole beach seems to be moving, darting here and there.

When I returned Andrew was still there. 'God is going to reveal the Truth now,' he was droning. 'In this age. This is a special time. These things are being revealed to people who can see them. Most people shy away from them, refuse to face them. Everything is there, even the credit card system.' (He was obsessed by the credit card system.) 'It says so in the Bible: the antichrist is going to come, probably from Egypt, he's going to monitor everything with the credit card system. It's really heavy.' He changed his tone a little. Could I lend him thirty rupees? they had no money to return to Madras and Roy (who of course did not have any) had agreed to help them. That made me really disagreeable: here was this ghastly spotty fellow, who had been boring us all day long, wanting money which I had no intention of giving him. We would all have been much better off, it seemed to me, if instead of moaning about the credit card system he had used it. What made me all the more disagreeable was that I was so inadequate in dealing with him. Instead of telling him I had no intention of giving him anything at all I crossly gave him five rupees. The result was that he and his silly bride hung about for the rest of the afternoon ringing the door bell and we had to escape through the bushes – running away from the situation as usual instead of facing up and dealing with it authoritatively.

Andrew left behind him a small illustrated leaflet which was even more bizarre than the Hare Krishna's moon theory. This manifesto was by one Moses David and liberally punctuated by exclamation marks. '*What's happening behind the news?!* Tune in on God's views in the news and how it affects *you*. Atomic war, space travel, communism, U.S. destruction, computer zombies, it had all been foretold 1900 years ago!!!!' God, said Moses David, has always commanded his people to 'drop out', to come out of the whore, and this is still his message; to all those caught in the greatest whore of all times – America – HE IS ONLY ALLOWING MAN TO GO SO FAR THEN WHAMMY! Think of that! Fire and brimstone, volcanic rocks a hundred pounds apiece that could batter down whole buildings flat to the ground. 'Whew!' How would you like to be around for something like that? Well, Moses David wouldn't and God's children won't be: 'WE'RE GONNA BE IN SPACE CITY AT THE TIME having a good time feasting and drinking and making love.' According to Moses David the world is divided into Good Guys and Gals who wear flimsy night clothes and have a delicious time and SHITS who smoke cigarettes and have a horrid one. A rather fluffy lady in a short négligée surrounded by stars is depicted as 'God's Gal' while a short-haired trollop smoking a cigarette, sporting a short tight skirt and low-cut top revealing respectively fat buttocks and an ample bust, is the 'System Shit' for whom 'Hellish horrors' are guaranteed. The time will come, Moses David promised,

when no man will be able to BUY OR SELL SAVE THAT
HE HAS THE MARK – the time will come when money will
no longer be used as a medium of exchange. As far as Andrew
and his bride were concerned the time was already here. They
were staying further along the beach in a romantic encampment of straw huts called The Silver Sands. Here they would
eat in the restaurant and then would go round the rest of the
tables telling their fellow guests they had no money and asking
them to pay.

Our informant was another drop-out who was running the
discothèque there. He was saturated with dope and extraordinary experiences. He had met this surfboard performer, he
told us between joints, he could only describe him as an angel.
He was like a grain of sand and the surfboard rider was like a
huge tree. The huge tree sat there shouting at him, but the experience was really cool! Now here we all were sitting having a
conversation. What did it really mean? What could it lead to?
Could it be a platform? What he really wanted to do was to
make a movie – well, not exactly a movie, he'd go round with
his camera shooting things, writing a little maybe. There'd be
him as the central experience. Perhaps he could distribute it to
people who needed his message. Meanwhile here he was being
this disc jockey, putting on music, against which pale Slavic
ladies ate their dinner. What did it all mean? What he really believed in was energy transference. He believed that, if you surrender yourself, laid yourself open to people, their energy and
grace could flow in.

This led Roy to relate one of his experiences. One day in
Hyderabad a wandering fakir had literally projected his spirit
into him. First, for about three hours, he had manipulated him
both physically and mentally. He had taken him into the Sha-
minar, a large and famous domed building, and had seated him
exactly in the centre under the long spike that hung down from
the central point of the dome, so that it pointed directly into
the top of his head. The fakir had blown a conch, put his knee
into the small of Roy's back, handled his vertebrae. He had
taken him out then, given him tea and the inevitable chillums.
He had massaged his spine. Eventually he had laid Roy down
on a red blanket and then a force had shot through his body,
definitely sexual, causing two or more orgasms. But it had

been more than sexual, it had been an energy that had filled him, incorporating every sort of elevating emotion. At the same time he felt so close to this man, so emotionally attached, rather like being in love. And when eventually he had ridden away on his bicycle his whole head had been filled with light.

After all this we returned to our room just as the waiter was bringing in the dinner we had previously ordered. For once Roy was not interested in food, he had had too many joints. And what strong stuff it was! It had had the effect on me that I most disliked, of being taken over. 'Can you feel the cosmic channels flowing through your body?' Roy asked. He made sounds presumably illustrating these occult conduits. 'Weeeeeee Wooooooo!' And just as the waiter was putting down the tray of dinner he made an extraordinary popping sound: 'pop eeek!' The sound of the tray touching the glass set his teeth on edge. After that he sat bolt upright for hours waving his arms and twisting his body, uttering Indian ejaculations and writing pieces of poetry about gods marching through caverns and larks flying into the sunrise: 'a page of territory I never could reach . . .'

Soon after this we bumped and rattled into the interior again, via Guntakal and the small boys, to Puttaparthi and Prasanthi Nilayam. This was to be one of the crucial moments of the trip, the manifestation of the lingam at Shivaratri. But I was foiled again. For the first time in his life Saitha Sai Baba was not at Puttaparthi for Shivaratri. His staff were vague. No, they had no idea where Swami was. Bangalore possibly, perhaps Ooty where he had a new establishment. No, they had no idea where he would be for Shivaratri, only Swami himself could say that. His movements were as bewildering and mysterious as before – this year apparently he had told his devotees that he was going to America for his birthday, everyone had turned up at La Guardia airport and – nothing: Sai Baba had not arrived. Ah! but he had not said *which* year he would arrive, he had explained afterwards.

There we were at the end of a nasty journey and no Sai Baba. There was still plenty of red tape, however: walk in line; don't sit here . . . And plenty of residents who seemed cross, noisy and malodorous. The day was exactly the same as before except there was no darshan, no American devotees and no

Denise. The sand was brushed and combed and sketched into those strange diagrams, the mangy dogs lay about and scratched, the shopkeepers and flower-sellers rose at dawn to sell their wares; the plants were blooming and the beggars were begging. I had not been conscious of the beggars before. Now there seemed to be an epidemic of them: 'Sai Ram,' they whined. 'Sai Ram.' But Puttaparthi was still beautiful with its mauves, oranges and browns and its jasmine bushes. And this time three monkeys could be seen jumping round the ashram.

Roy did not enjoy Puttaparthi. He lapsed. For a start it was against the rules that we should share a cell; accordingly he set out to be as naughty as possible. There was no way in which we could be described as two people in search of the truth, an author and her assistant would not do either; here quite simply was a governess and her unruly charge. 'Encourage good social habits,' one of the notices cautioned us.' This was easier said than done. 'Biggies!' Roy suddenly exclaimed in the bank at the top of his voice – not, luckily, that the inhabitants of Putta-parthi probably knew about biggies. And when we met two South African Indians the conversation was turned immedi-ately to apartheid. Everyone in England, I told them, is horri-fied at apartheid. 'Who says so?' asked Roy. 'Who says everyone is horrified at apartheid? I'm not.' Mercifully he spent quite a lot of his time lying on the floor reading a story by Aldous Huxley about English hypocrisy, neurotic ladies and men who liked young girls. But then he would sally forth to shock and embarrass as many people as possible. 'What a hole!' he shouted along the veranda. In the dining room, where silence was the rule, he announced: 'Spirituality is very middle class.' The tyranny of the middle class trapped him, anything middle class smacked of all the things from which he was trying to escape, and the Abode of Great Peace seemed to him to be wholly middle class.

One of the reasons I had come to Puttaparthi was to tape the bhajans, which are beautiful. 'No. No tape recorder,' said the police ladies at the door. 'No tape recording without permis-sion.' So: 'please may I have permission?' 'No. No permis-sion.' A committee must grant permission and they were all travelling with Baba. So I decided to tape the bhajans without authorisation. The first time nothing happened – the tape-recorder was concealed in my bag and I failed to press the right switch. Next time, however, I surreptitiously managed to achieve a full tape and sneak out with my spoils.

After two nights we set out once more on another horrible bus journey. There were a number of women clustered round the bus stop who resembled more a host of witches than anything else, furnished as they were with sticks, wild straggly hair and one protruding tooth between them. There was also the most repulsive little boy I have ever seen. He beat even spotty Andrew. His lower lip and chin were drawn into his chest by taut sinews which terminated in an oozing growth, barely concealed by his vest; his tongue rolled out of his mouth and a fungus sprouted all over his head. Every so often he would shake his head and wet spray would fly into the air. But his hands were rather beautiful, he held them out towards Roy who was, needless to say, surrounded by this unpalatable crew. It was a relief to board the bone-shaking bus.

Since Sai Baba was not, as it were, at home we intended to pass Shivaratri with his double: Neelakantha Tathaji. The similarity between the two seemed too close for coincidence: the orange robes, the Afro hair-styles, the miracles, the white Mercedes, even the names of the ashrams are alike, Prasanthi Nilayam changes only to Prasanthi Mandir (The Temple of Great Peace). There is a booklet about Neelakantha Tathaji that achieves its most lyrical passages when it describes Prasanthi Mandir which, 'situated in midst of beautiful natural landscape appears to the pilgrims like heaven on earth, the tall mountain tops of the Neelakantha ranges in the west and north and the mango groves in the south, the green carpet stretching beyond bring peace and solace to the troubled mind. The lush crops in the field present a pleasing spectacle, the atmosphere and water have a healing quality. . . .'

Now the atmosphere at Prasanthi Mandir may be many things and the last thing I want to do is to appear ungrateful for the kindness and hospitality that we received therein, but by no stretch of the imagination could the surroundings be said to be composed of 'lush crops', nor do they appear like 'heaven on earth', or not anyway in March. Prasanthi Mandir is situated right in the middle of the baking brown plains that surround Mantralayam. We had in fact been there before, after our visit to Mantralayam, but Tathaji had been away. Halfway between Adoni and Mantralayam an arch is stuck down incongruously in the desert – this is the entrance. The drive leads about a mile from the main road through brown sand – which by night slithers with snakes, pythons as thick as your arm, we were assured. Now, Tathaji was still away, but he was returning that night. Meanwhile we must rest. No one else had arrived yet.

According to the same booklet, Tathaji is worshipped by his followers as a great saint. He was born a peasant and for years was a very poor fellow, marrying at fourteen and working with oxen. He received his realisation when he was twenty-three, apparently as a result of the constant recitation of his mother's mantra: 'Aum Namah Shivaya.' He had battered his head against a pillar and told God that if he did not appear he would commit suicide. So Shiva did appear. Now he is fifty-three and has three sons and a daughter. He began teaching when he was thirty-seven and believes in group prayer, group recitation of his mother's mantra. There is an illustration in the booklet of Tathaji singing in his temple with a live cobra erected beside him. He is said to have performed many marvels: healed disease and blindness; transformed foliage into statues of the goddess Saraswati; manifested figures of the goddess Laxmi; travelled twenty-three miles on an empty petrol tank. He has the ability of being in several different places at once. Flooded rivers have been said to divide permitting his car to pass. He, himself, has been observed entering a trance and departing from his body, which has astonished its beholders by emitting a shining blue light. Like Sai Baba he claims to be an avatar: God come down on earth 'for the protection of the good, for the destruction of the wicked, for the establishment of dharma, I am born age after age....' Unlike Sai Baba, however, he is totally available to his disciples, advising them on everything down to the most trivial details. Nothing is private and we were shown everything: Tathaji's bedroom, bathroom, kitchen, swing chair and library, whose subjects ranged from Bertrand Russell to kundalini. All round the walls were instructions: Maintain silence; Hook the fish of desire with the rod of abstinence; Love not pleasure but God.

In other respects Prasanthi Mandir was but a shadow of the giant plaster pavilions of Prasanthi Nilayam. Here, there was only a small compound containing the library, temple, Tathaji's house and a few huts. Nearby was the old traveller's lodge for the village of Omnagar, which had now been purchased by some devotee and donated, along with the electricity supply and some bags of cement, for the benefit of pilgrims. It was a long, low bungalow, four rooms and a bathroom all leading one into the other like a passage. There was no such thing as privacy, the doors were kept open and everyone walked in and out. The place was managed by a caretaker, a very old man with sparkling eyes, who kept offering us mugs of (healing) water, his wife, who turned out to be the cook, their son and their baby. They showed us proudly round the premises. One room contained nothing but a grand gold chair and another only a bed on which two young boys lay asleep like the little princes. In our room the furniture consisted of a wooden bed, with no mattress ('no mosquito net either,' snapped Roy), a tin chair and a very smart carpet which was brought in by the caretaker. They were very proud of that carpet which was a bit like a piled Aubusson, deep red with patterns. The worst thing one could do was to walk on it with one's shoes – this was deeply insulting.

After the carpet, one of the little princes entered. 'Good morning, I am Baba's son.' Everyone walked in and out of the room rolling and unrolling carpets, bringing incense, together with photographs of Tathaji and books about him. Our room seemed to be the ashram headquarters, and incredibly hot it was too, there being no fan.

Roy was in a bad mood and getting worse. He had a new ruse which was to lie with his lunghi gaping wide open and his legs apart. It is not hard to imagine what aspect he presented to the company. The cook appeared and, as I understood it, wondered if we would like tea. Yes, I said greedily. But instead of tea she brought the baby which lay on the floor and screeched. 'What are they doing in our room?' asked Roy in a loud and cross voice. To divert everyone's attention I gave the cook a melon I had bought that morning. She started chopping it up with a grass-hook. 'Please tell her,' I said to Tathaji's son, who was sitting quietly in the corner, 'that this is a present for her and her family.' 'Yes, yes, I have told her.' It took a long time to cut up the melon with the grass-hook, the baby screeching and Roy exclaiming in a loud and rather hollow voice, 'What a ghastly baby!', the heat beating down. When eventually she had finished, the baby was given some, which made it scream even more. She handed the plate to us. 'No, please, it is for you.' 'Why don't you want this melon?' asked Tathaji's son. At last everyone disappeared, looking bewildered and unhappy.

As evening advanced, birds flew, curling and uncurling in formation like wreaths of smoke. A wedding started up in the village, music blared out through the microphones. The sun went down, the rocks turned mauve, the bright green of the rice fields lit up and for a moment the surroundings lived up to their description. And then it was dark and the night filled with the noise of frogs, cicadas and mosquitoes. We ate dinner outside the kitchen door while the baby swung underneath the table in a hammock made from a blanket, grizzling while its brother rocked it.

One might imagine that in such a remote place one would enjoy a peaceful night. But, the more remote a place in India, the noisier it is, with its dogs, drums, bhajans and babies. Never have I spent such disturbed nights as those at Prasanthi Mandir. It was so hot that no one slept inside; everyone lay down in a row on mattresses along the veranda. We had just settled down for the night – having been joined by a fat man – when the caretaker, the cook, the little boy and the baby all arrived, shouting to make Tathaji's son – who had settled down peacefully in the only room with a fan – come out and sleep on the balcony. About an hour later Tathaji returned in his white Mercedes. You could see the lights sweeping up the python-infested road, and then as we all lay out like corpses the drums started up for the village wedding and beat all night. Somehow I got to sleep but something with little feet ran over me and woke me with a start. 'A frog, a frog,' shouted the caretaker and lit a smoking oil-lamp. The dogs barked, the drums beat, the baby moaned and the fat man snored. At last I slept again and dreamt of Horace who was promoting a new literary club where you could stay till seven in the morning. It would have been preferable to our veranda, there was no question of staying there until seven in the morning. Before dawn, bhajans started blaring out on the microphone, waking the baby which started to moan again. The sun rose over the ashram and we all got up.

Next day, with the return of Tathaji, preparation for Shivaratri began in earnest. First Tathaji and his wife started off the relay bhajans. All through the week of Shivaratri teams of seven people chanting 'Aum Namah Shivaya' and clashing cymbals walk by day and night in relays round and round a table holding a brass snake, a head of Shiva and what looked like a drying-up cloth wrapped round something. 'Come to me,' Tathaji says, 'and I will recharge the batteries of your soul.' The theory is that running round and round that table, day and night, conjures up some restorative psychic force. All through the day disciples arrived. One man had come from Hyderabad, only for a few hours, just to see Tathaji, whom he had never met before. He was glittering with joy and optimism. Yes, he had had darshan, had prasad. He had received something he must keep with him always. He had told Tathaji of some of his problems and from today there would be no more problems, there was no question of it. Everything would happen automatically. I could see how comforting such a faith could be. Roy meanwhile had discovered the village, with its thatched huts, sandy streets and small tea shop in which we drank endless cups of tea and ate the odd upma – a delicious dish of semolina and vegetables.

The people were sweet and rather shy; in fact, of the inhabitants, we saw mostly children – the most beautiful little girls with flowers in their hair and large lustrous eyes, made all the larger and more lustrous by the addition of kohl. Only one other white person, it seemed, had ever before set foot in Prasanthi Mandir and he must have taught all the inhabitants to shake hands. It was a sort of party piece which for some reason they thought marvellously funny. When he was not shaking hands Roy was absorbed by cricket. There was no possibility here of his getting a paper so he was obsessed with the score of the test match. 'What's the score?' he kept asking the newly-arrived devotees. 'Do you know the cricket score?' 'Do you have a newspaper?' 'Where can I get a newspaper?'

Tathaji's disciples seemed mostly to be government officials, civil servants, doctors and so on. There was one who was said to be a famous tennis star who entered into complicated negotiations with Roy. He would send him silks and satins if Roy dispatched to him a certain sort of tennis racquet. All the disciples talked a lot of Tathaji's miracles. To see one, said the government official, one must be with him a lot. He cannot just produce things like that. He feels he wants to give something to someone but he does not know what it is going to be until it mysteriously turns up in his hand. I must, as a friend, get Roy to sing his relay of bhajans, said the government official. 'He is very obstinate,' I explained. 'Obstacle? I can't understand your pronounciation.' 'He's very naughty.' 'Naughty? I don't understand.' 'Stubborn.' 'Stubborn. . . ?'

One extremely pretty girl from Bombay was there with her baby. She had been planning, she said, to see Sai Baba, but then Tathaji, she had heard, was coming to Bombay. Why, a friend asked, did she not go and meet him? He had all the powers of Sai Baba without the crowds. So she did and she was so impressed that she and her husband became his disciples at once: all sorts of strange things had happened ever since. For example, her husband, a doctor, had temporarily handed his dispensary to a locum. Suddenly at three o'clock in the morning Tathaji appeared. 'Hurry' he said, 'to your dispensary and see what's the matter.' The doctor was not keen – it being three in the morning – besides he was frightened. 'Don't be frightened,' said Tathaji. 'I am with you.' So off he went. And there sure enough were all the doors and windows which had been left wide open by the locum.

Clearly Tathaji is a great comfort to his disciples. For myself I found him gentle and unassuming but I did not experience any particular strength or peace emanating from him. But he was a sweet man, he even composed a prayer especially for Roy and myself and, thereafter, whenever he saw us he would burst into song. 'Oh my God! Neelakantha bless us!' he would chant, in a special lilting rhythm.

Certainly his disciples are all extremely proud of him. 'This place really has something,' said one lady happily. It certainly had excruciating nights. For the next night was worse than ever. Indians seem able to survive on no sleep at all. The cook, her son and the caretaker discoursed until midnight – the caretaker apparently had something wrong with his feet and nose, a topic of absorbing and noisy interest to them all. Tathaji's son and his little friend also conversed and when at last they

137

stopped it was time for their nocturnal turn round the table. Roy too was awake. 'When did the deb season start?' he wanted to know. Then it was time for everyone to come back and leave on all the lights and then the baby woke up and screeched and then the sun rose . . .

Next day we escaped to Mantralayam to swim again in the Tungabhadra river. It was so hot waiting for the bus that people were squatting in the narrow fingers of shade afforded by the triumphal archway to Prasanthi Mandir. Since all the strips were occupied and the bus was not due for an hour we walked along the road a little way to two trees we could see on the horizon. But what trees! Full, we discovered, of decaying corpses of animals, goats or some such cadavers, whose stench filled the air. So we hitched instead a lift from a lorry. This, it seems, is a commonplace thing to do, you pay the driver three rupees or so and either you cram into the cab with a host of others or you rattle about the back with his load. Mantralayam and the Tungabhadra were as refreshing and as peaceful as before, the waiters as charming and the idlis and dosas as delicious, and we were sorry to return to the babble of Prasanthi Mandir on the eve of Shivaratri.

What a whirl of activity it all was! And what a din! No one, said one of Tathaji's disciples, has any sleep that night, no sleep, no food. As the day advanced into evening everyone rushed here and there from one source of din to the next. It was not at all clear what the programme was. In the centre of the compound a village dance was in progress. A circle of men and women danced round and round while, in the middle, a village band played fiddles and drums. One moment all the disciples would be in the library singing bhajans to Tathaji, swaying gently in his swinging chair, the next everyone would be rushing off to see how the relay bhajans were getting on, or hurrying off to some celebration in the temple (and wherever I went I was pursued by the same small group wanting to recite 'poetry' into my tape-recorder and then hear the sound of their own voices played back). There was constant speculation about what would happen, constant histories about what had happened in the past. Once, a disciple told me, as we all dashed along to the temple for the approaching climax, once they were all sitting here at this time doing pooja and six cobras came in;

Tathaji told a lady to pick one up and wear it round her neck, and he did the same. What happened then? Nothing. They had all slithered out again. One man said that this year's ceremony would be concluded by Tathaji producing amrit from his finger-tips, mixing it with milk and distributing it. Another said that he would heat a pot of water just by his presence, indeed he was going to boil it, yet another said that like Sai Baba he would produce a lingam from his throat. I was in a constant state of dither lest I was missing some marvel. Snakes might be invading the temple just as I was inspecting the library for boiling water; amrit might be oozing from Tathaji's extremities while I was scanning the dance area. In the confusion I saw nothing, or nothing that I could distinguish. No snakes, nothing manifested at midnight, apart from Roy wanting two rupees for a cup of coffee.

At about two in the morning the excitement began to lessen. Bundles appeared all over the compound and those who were keeping a vigil settled down to pass the night with a good 'chit chat'. 'What countries have you visited? Tell us something of your experiences? Tell us something of the economic situation in the countries you have been in. What country would you choose to settle in? Etcetera, etcetera. Underneath the platform where Tathaji had sat during some stage of the evening's proceedings were three toads; suddenly, without blinking their enormous eyes, one or another of them would shoot out a long tongue and scoop up a passing mosquito or ant.

Finally there was a concluding ceremony, at which we as Westerners must give a speech. This was delivered most excellently by Roy and no doubt recorded for posterity in the ashram's annals: appreciation shown by Western devotees. But the point was that we had received kindness and hospitality for which there was no question of money changing hands. And surprisingly, even after those fitful nights, those days of chattering and chanting in all that heat, I did feel refreshed, full of energy, even. Before we could leave we must attend a farewell feast held in Tathaji's house; then we must ask for Tathaji's permission to leave. Yes, we could leave but we must return for his birthday on 8 August and if we could not we must get a group of Westerners and send them instead. I liked to think of some of my friends coming here for their holidays and clattering round and round that table in the heat of the plain . . .

Now it was nearing the end of our journey and back we went
south, via Guntakal and the small boys, to Tiruvannamalai
and the ashram of Ramana Maharishi. I found Tiruvannamalai
to be as peaceful a place as it is possible to find in India. A large
South Indian temple rises up out of its midst, while Arunachala, the red hill, soars high behind the town and can be seen
for miles around. When Paul Brunton came here in the 1930s
the hill and the outskirts of Tiruvannamalai were entirely
covered in jungle, inhabited by monkeys, snakes, peacocks and
chipmunks – those lovely little striped squirrels. Now the
jungle has gone, cut down to make houses, and the outskirts of
Tiruvannamalai are rather like a glorified garden suburb.
Nevertheless the place manages to conserve some of its wild
aspect. Cows and pigs roam the sandy streets, monkeys popu-
late the roofs of the temples, peacocks utter their strange
echoing cries and there is still very little motorised traffic.

The ashram lies about two miles outside Tiruvannamalai, a
green and beautiful place well shaded by trees, next to a large
cistern, of which there are many in the area, looking rather like
inverted pyramids with steps leading down their sides to the
water collected in the apex. Ramana Maharishi had loved
animals, the striped chipmunks had nested in his bed, peacocks and his special cow had eaten from his hand. Above all he
had loved the hill; older even than the Himalayas, Arunachala
is a remnant of the vanished continent of Lemuria and is cited
in one of the ancient texts, the Skanana Purana, as the heart of
the world, the abode of Shiva. For centuries it has been held as
a sacred place. It is, Ramana Maharishi told Paul Brunton, inhabited by hosts of spirits of varying grades, culminating in
those of great sages. People often have psychic experiences
here, one woman heard strange music emanating from the
depths of the hill which, when recorded, turned out to be classical.

It is said that Arunachala is even now the home of countless
sadhus who live unseen in secret valleys, for this is such a large
and mysterious hill that, even with the jungle gone, one can
wander for a lifetime and still not be familiar with its ways. As
the sun was setting I walked that first evening a little way up

the lower slopes; from there you can look down on the green trees of the ashram. It was an idyllic sight, with a woman in a blue dress feeding the peacocks which were balancing on the white balustrades and towers of the temple. Flocks of emerald parrots flew against the brilliant sky. Further away, encircled like a saucer by a range of hills, was the bright green of paddy fields, in which the waters of countless lakes and cisterns glittered, reflecting the azure of the sky; nearer in the foreground, floating it seemed high above the plains, was a hill surmounted by what appeared to be a castle. The familiar slap of clothes being washed echoed up from the valley, together with the occasional hoot of a lorry or a bus. And then, gradually couples began to climb up the hill to sit facing the sinking sun, reciting prayers and mantras in beautiful lilting Sanskrit. On the plains, goats were being driven home from their pastures, a small wind blew up, my neighbours on the hill fell to their chanting with renewed vigour and away on the horizon the plains filled up with mist.

The ashram itself is composed of several buildings – dining rooms, libraries, men's quarters, a temple, a tomb wherein Ramana Maharishi lies buried; and at the back of the garden are other tombs where sadhus, one of them English, and special animals and birds are interred. The meditation hall, where Ramana Maharishi received Paul Brunton, is a delicious place, dark, cool, shining and peaceful. The sofa where he used to lie – and where the squirrels used to nest – now supports a large photograph upon it. As I sat there I recognised again that purifying current of energy, it was like being polished inside so that all the tensions and unease were wiped away.

There was one particular disciple of Ramana Maharishi's whom I was anxious to meet: Sadhu Om, the author of *The Path of Shri Ramana*, who, as it turned out, lived close by the ashram. He was aged fifty-six, rather small and toothy, with hardly any hair and a most surprising voice – high and strident. But it was his singing voice which was the most curious of all, very strong, clear, high and beautiful, just as I imagined a castrato's voice must have been. Indeed his voice had not changed at all from when he was aged six or seven. He allowed me to record his rendering of one of Ramana Maharishi's hymns. 'The Marital Garland of Letters'* is a hymn in one hundred and eight stanzas to Arunachala, a love song in much the same vein as 'The Spiritual Canticle' of St John of the Cross and 'The Song of Solomon' in the Bible. Arunachala is for Ramana Maharishi the symbol of God, the beloved, the absorbing body into which he dissolved.

'O Arunachala, you root out the ego of those who think of you at heart;

Stay firmly in my mind, O Arunachala, so that it may not elude you and wander elsewhere.

Reveal your true beauty, O Arunachala, so that the fickle mind is prevented from wandering in the streets and is stilled by your Presence.

Is it manliness, O Arunachala, if you fail now to embrace me and destroy my maidenhood?

When those robbers, the five senses, enter my mind, are you not present there at home to keep them out?

As a magnet draws iron, draw me to yourself, O Arunachala; hold me fast, be one with me.

Ocean of compassion manifesting as a mountain, have mercy on me, give me your grace, O Arunachala.

O Arunachala, you who stand and shine before me in the form of my guru, destroy utterly my faults, cure me and convert me, and as your servant govern me.

Ripe fruit in my hand, O Arunachala, let me drink in your true sweetness and be mad with joy.

Sun whose bright rays envelop the whole world, O Arunachala, make my heart-lotus blossom.

Arunachala, O moon of grace, with your rays as with cool fingers, touch my heart and open the nectal mouth within.

Remove this cloth, expose me naked and then clothe me with your loving grace, O Arunachala.

* Written in Tamil and translated by Ramana Kendra.

Reveal to me true formative knowledge so that I may give up this delusive worldly knowledge.

Unless you join me, O Arunachala, this body will melt away in a river of tears and I shall die.

O my lord Arunachala, let me by your grace merge in your true being where only the pure and the mind-free merge.

To you as to my only God I came, O Arunachala, and me you have totally destroyed.

Embracing me till there is no you or I, give me the state of one eternal bliss, O Arunachala.

When I melted away and merged in you, my refuge, you stood there naked, O Arunachala.

My mind is now fragrant like a blossom. Add your perfect fragrance to it and make it infinite, O Arunachala.

As snow in water melts, let me dissolve in love in you who is all love, O Arunachala.'

Sadhu Om's life is now devoted to interpreting his guru's work, which he does with the help of a large strong lady with shingled hair, probably of German origin. Every day, either in the early morning or the evening when the sun has lost its heat, he follows his guru's instructions and walks the eight miles round the hill. The rest of the day is divided between devotional duties and his writing. He tried his best to explain his theme.

Everyone in the world, said Sadhu Om, is striving to enjoy himself, striving for happiness. As a man grows he accumulates round him his sources of pleasure – food, clothes, possessions, wives, children. All through history, effort has gone to acquiring objects of satisfaction with which to delight the senses. Yet peace can only be reached when the mind is in a state of quiescence. Happiness is nothing but a state of quiescence when the mind is still and the inner sense of well-being surges up. It is true that the state of quiescence may come fleetingly through the senses – eating something very good, listening to music, seeing something very beautiful – but it does not last. The mind starts up again and all that happens is that the senses become satiated. So, in the long run, indulging the senses is a waste of time: in other words all through history human effort has gone purely into wasting time. This has happened because people believe that happiness comes from external things; that the body is the Self; that 'I' am the body, that 'I' am Mr So and So. But to identify with the body, with what one thinks or feels, is only misidentification: this is ego-consciousness, and the source of all misidentification comes from the ego-consciousness. In truth the 'I' is the only reality; the spirit; the self-consciousness. What has happened is that, in the course of time, truth has been rendered lifeless by the incorrect explanations of bookworms who have mastered the letter but who do not know the reality.

Let us suppose, said Sadhu Om, that a broken piece of mirror is lying in open space on the ground in full sunshine. The sunlight striking on that piece of mirror is reflected on to the wall of a dark room nearby. The ray from the mirror to the inside wall of the dark room is a reflected ray of the sun which makes it possible for a man in the dark room to see the objects inside the room. The reflection on the wall is the same shape as the piece of mirror but the direct sunlight – the source – in the open space outside the room is boundless and of no specific space. The self-consciousness, the 'I' consciousness, is like the direct sunlight in the open space while the ego-consciousness is like the reflected rays stretching from the mirror to the inner wall of the room. Like the all-pervading direct sunlight which is boundless the self-consciousness has no adjuncts of form. Just as the reflected ray takes on the limitations of size and shape of the mirror, the ego-consciousness assumes the limitations of the body. Just as one recognises objects in the dark room through the aid of the reflected beam, the body and the world are recognised only by the ego and the mind.

Let us now suppose that the man in the dark room stops observing the objects in the room and is possessed by the longing to see the source whence the rays come. To know this he should fix his eyes on the very spot where the beam strikes the wall and then follow the ray of light. What does he see then? The sun! But what he sees now is not the real sun but just a reflection of it. Not only that. It appears to him that the sun is lying on a certain spot on the ground outside the room.

He can even say that the particular spot on which the sun is seen lying is so many feet to the right or left. But does the sun really lie on the ground in that particular spot? Of course not. If the person wants to see the real sun what should he do? He must keep his eyes fixed to the reflected beam and without moving the eyes to either side follow it to its source. He must break out of the dark room and into the sunlight.

In the same way a man may find the source of his being, his self-consciousness, by Ramana Maharishi's method of self-inquiry, by keeping his attention fixed upon the beam of the 'I' consciousness deep within himself. Self-enquiry: who am I? is the only way. Take for example: I am Philippa Pullar. Who is the 'I'? The 'I' has no body. The 'I' is the reality. As soon as you put something into the second and third persons – for example: 'I am Philippa Pullar' – you get something manifested by the ego. By repeatedly practising 'Who am I'?, the strength of mind to abide in its source is increased. The power of attention in self-enquiry is diverted from the second and third persons, from the Philippa Pullar, and directed towards the first – the 'I'. It is now in the nature of *Being*. So long as the attention is directed outwards to the second and third person, or the world, it is mind and intellect; when the attention turns to the first person, the Self, it is no longer mind or intellect, it is consciousness. Thus the mind and intellect are only useful for examining external affairs of the world, they are useless for turning inwards and examining the Self. The awareness, 'I am', is common to one and all; it is pure consciousness, pure knowledge of one's self and not of anything external. When the 'I am' is mixed with an attribute – i.e. 'I am a man' – it becomes mixed consciousness. All you have to do is to practise remaining quiescent with the awareness of the 'I' consciousness while waking from sleep; the 'I' consciousness shoots up to the brain like a flash of lightning, from the brain the consciousness spreads through the body along the nerves – electric energy, pure and free. The annihilation of the ego is liberation. So you must turn inwards, start your self-enquiry, though in the beginning countless thoughts will rise up one after the other, like waves of the ocean. But they will all be destroyed as self-attention grows.

Ramana Maharishi has written the following stanza on the

145

Self:

'When, forgetting the Self, one thinks
That the body is oneself and goes
Through innumerable births
And in the end remembers and becomes
The Self, know this is only like
Awaking from a dream wherein
One has wandered over all the world.'

The realisation of truth is the same for both Indians and Europeans, Ramana Maharishi told Paul Brunton. Admittedly, the way may be harder for those who are engrossed in a worldly life, but even then you can and must conquer. The current induced through meditation can be kept up by habit. Then you can perform your work and activities within the current itself. There will be no break, no difference between meditation and external activities. If you meditate on this question 'Who am I'?, if you begin to perceive that neither the body nor the brain nor the desires are really you, then the very attitude of enquiry will eventually draw the answer out of the depths of your own being, it will come to you of its own accord as a deep realisation.

I had not made much sense out of Sadhu Om's books before and I was not able to make much sense of all this now. One hears only what one is ready to hear. My attention was like a butterfly, captivated still by sensual blossoms, to say nothing of mundane ones. As for Roy, he was not at all impressed by Sadhu Om. With his lack of hair and toothy academic manner he did not fit Roy's vision of a virile hirsute guru, puffing out clouds of dope. 'Castrated!' he muttered darkly and would have none of him. He was, however, enjoying himself. Tiruvannamalai, Arunachala and Ramana Maharishi between them attract a number of Westerners, some of them seekers, some of them spectators and plenty of them hippies, who come because it is one of those 'powerful places' in which to sit, smoking joints, many of them becoming so apathetic that they cannot conjure the necessary energy to leave. Roy was particularly pleased with two Americans called Bill and Susie who practised Hatha Yoga. Susie had plenty of opinions with which he

146

returned. Susie said, for example, that meditation had quite the opposite effect to what it was meant to have: it made you more egocentric rather than less. Susie said also that all Indian men were impotent.

Besides Susie and Bill there were plenty of hirsute swamis lurking around Tiruvannamalai. One was called Ram Suraj Kumar – God child – whose photograph we had seen on our first day, stuck up in the tonga which had drawn us to the ashram. He was shaggy enough for Roy's taste. His hair was dressed with a piece of tinsel and he lived with his dog – Sai Baba, no less – at the top of a flight of steps quite near the temple. He referred to himself as 'this poor beggar' – this was certainly an accurate description of his occupation which he performed with much charm and panache.

'What do you know about God, Baba?' Roy asked.

'Nothing, my friend. I am a dirty sinner. It could be my father's wish that a dirty sinner like me will have to live for thousands of years. If my father wants me damned, I don't mind.'

'Is Sai Baba a vegetarian?'

'Oh no, he will go after any old bone, then he will leave this poor beggar's side and crack, crack, crack, he will make an awful noise.'

A Scandinavian girl called Christine joined the group. She looked pale and unhealthy, wore a crumpled white sari and spent most of her time meditating. She settled herself at the top of the steps opposite the God child and at once seemed to nod off into a trance. All the time people kept bringing offerings, food, cups of tea and hundreds of cigarettes which 'this poor beggar' chain-smoked, cupped in his hand as though he were inhaling a chillum. Often he would break off to laugh hysterically, so much so that once all the cigarettes flew from his fingers. He had rather a sweet way of saying yes: yes, yes, very clipped. And if something struck him as strange he made a long-drawn-out sound: oooooh!

'We saw your photograph in the tonga, Baba,' Roy continued.

'All propaganda to enable this poor beggar to eat without working, ha! ha! ha!'

'Is this a good town?'

'This poor beggar can get food easily. It must be a good town.' For years apparently he had wandered, spending much time in Badrinath.

'Many sadhus in Badrinath, Baba?'

'This poor beggar did not see them. Very cold and this poor beggar had no clothes, no food.'

'What good English you speak.'

'A lot of meaningless old words, meaningless dirty old words just put together.'

'Susie says that either people are born enlightened, or they are not and there is nothing you can do. There is no system. No technique. It is just God.'

'Oooooooh! Roy: you are so wise! I wish I was as wise as you!'

'It's not me, it's Susie.'

'Oooooooh! Roy: you and Susie are so wise!'

Christine knew of another singular fellow, Poonis Baba who, it is said, had been dug up accidentally by some villagers. He had been lying buried in the ground. The villagers had taken him and built a beautiful house into which he refused to go, staying where he was, more or less in the middle of the road entirely without eating. Some said that he was one hundred and fifty years old, others that he was seven hundred. The custom is to take him a packet of cigarettes from which he will extract one, smoking it to show that he has taken over your karma. So we jolted off in a bus through the coconut palms and rice fields to his remote village where he lives in a tiny hut built above the pavement just opposite the bus shelter. Certainly Poonis Baba was a very old man, he was crouched in his hut in front of the fire, puffing at cigarettes, while a queue of visitors filed past extending/their packets in return for which he applied ash to their faces. Three very small and pretty kittens draped themselves meanwhile over his chair. When Christine visits Poonis Baba she sits opposite in the bus shelter – meditating.

We spent about a week in Tiruvannamalai. For one rupee a day it is possible to rent a room in one of the houses near the ashram. It was a bit like a garden city suburb here, all carved out of what used to be jungle. Houses with their own gardens and wells lead off wide sandy lanes hedged with purple bougainvillaea whose petals lie on the yellow sand like exotic magenta butterflies. The owners of these houses let most of their rooms to Westerners, retaining only a small portion for their own use. Facilities are of the barest minimum: large bare rooms with the well for washing. Our room gave on to the veranda where the family would congregate and gabble away most of the night. The other occupants seemed to be laid-back rock and roll singers. They lived in quiet disorder, sighing laid-back sighs, sitting around smoking dope, discussing the really groovy things one could do: Kung Fu, acupuncture, going to Nepal: you name it, they discussed it. I remembered Kushwant Singh remarking that you could not communicate with many of these Americans who came to India; they wore a glazed expression in their eyes and you could not get on the same wavelength with them at all. Poor things, this lot seemed to be decidedly seedy, suffering from skin diseases, elephantiasis and for all one knew leprosy (there was plenty of it about), and their noses were peeling and their skins a dirty blotched brown – even the dog was under the weather, having lost a leg.

The social centre was the banana stand where everyone congregated to drink tea, eat bananas and discuss groovy things. There was Liz who was usually so stoned and laid-back you could not hear a word she said, another rather plump girl, probably Norwegian, played the guitar, and Bima, a fat American from the Bronx, with some guru in Andra Pradesh who was now his mother, said things like 'there's a lot of energy in Goa and I lost my centre'. The plump girl said she was really relaxing here but she'd got so fragmented that she couldn't get it together to go back. 'I'm going to Bombay to see Maharaj,' she told us, 'perhaps he'll give me a buzz to stay.'

Maharaj was apparently the closest thing you could get these days to a living realised person. Someone called Arthur recommended him to us. Arthur was a German who lived alone, quite far away. He seemed to have a certain authority. 'It's no good doing anything unless it is whole-hearted,' he said one evening at the banana stand. One must select a guru, a discipline, and follow it whole-heartedly. Otherwise one was just playing mind games; that way nothing changed, one just mouthed things. What one needed was literally a change of heart, a basic change from within, otherwise one remained exactly the same: bored; looking for diversions and escape.

Very near the banana stand another of Ramana Maharishi's disciples lived. She too had published a book, *Sages, Saints and Arunachala Ramana*, and it was with her that my friend on the train had been staying. Ma Taleyarka was from a rich Parsee family who had thought her quite mad moving to Tiruvannamalai and building herself a house in the jungle – even now she has three snakes living in her garden. 'I have only association with religious people,' she says, and sooner or later most pilgrims to Ramana Maharishi find their way to her house where they are received warmly. Christine was often there, so was Susie. Ma Taleyarka loves to regale her guests with stories of her own and her guests' religious experiences. One lady was sitting at the table when it was seen that she seemed to be nodding off, just as lunch was being served. No, she was not asleep. She was having a vision of Ma in the company of Jesus Christ.

Poor Ma Taleyarka, though, was plainly not in the pink. She was nearly blind and had suffered much illness in her life. Her aim was to cherish an intense love for humanity but it seemed to me that she illustrated the dichotomy in us all. She wanted to be generous and loving, she longed to love people, yet through her efforts she over-extended herself, became imbalanced and suffered heart attacks and cancer. She wanted to give, wanted to be generous, and instead she found herself feeling resentful, exploited, persecuted and paranoid. 'My house is yours,' she said to me. 'This is your house now; whenever you want you can come and stay here; you are mine.' And again all my lack of trust came into play. I could not quite believe it. And as for poor Ma Taleyarka she believed that people were stealing from her. Her maid, she said, had had a duplicate key cut. The manager of the ashram too, he had embezzled a whole gift (pound notes, as I understood it) which he sold on the black market in Bangalore. And even as I was sitting there a man arrived to regale her with how the criminal case was proceeding.

She was a member of the 'So you've come' brigade. All her life unknown sadhus and saints would come up to her. 'So you've come, my child,' they would say, and assure her that she was protected and blessed by countless saints and sages. Cobras would coil themselves in her sandals and sit behind her chair with their hoods spread out. She had been visited by Krishna and Buddha and had been cured miraculously, by Ramana Maharishi himself, of one of her cancerous growths shortly before she was due to have it removed surgically. She had travelled all over India with Ananda Mai Ma and out of the blue had been summoned by telegram to Puttaparthi by Sai Baba who had extracted her from a crowd of over a thousand to tell her exactly what had been going on at the Tiruvannamali ashram (against whose administration Ma Taleyarka seemed to be at war) and what new obstructions were being directed towards her. 'You need not be afraid, I will be with you,' Sai Baba had said, giving her a signed photograph. She believes thoughts are powerful forces. She has only to think of something and it happens: there she was, thinking about her servant yesterday, and here he was today coming through the door. 'How dare you come to see me just when I am thinking of you,' she greeted him.

The ashram has a well-stocked library. I lay in the heat of the afternoon outside the meditation hall, which was closed in the middle of the day, reading a book by Major Chadwick – another of Ramana Maharishi's disciples. This had something about a crazy American who bought a party of his fellow countrymen to India to penetrate the centre of the Himalayas: you descended in a lift and there behind sealed doors were all the masters, including Christ, sitting waiting.

Just as I was reading this, a party, an educational tour, arrived, rather like those at Hampi, except that this time there was no trumpet, just a lot of boys and girls and their schoolmistresses, who all proceeded to lie on the ground and go to sleep. After about half an hour they woke up again and all came trooping over to find out what I was doing. What was this book? What was it about? Who? Ramana Maharishi? It was clear they had no idea what they were doing here. It was simply a nice place for a picnic. Afterwards they were going on to see a dam.

Very often I felt lulled by a great calm like a velvet eiderdown coming down to soothe me. I would lie there in the heat and after Major Chadwick I read John Blofeld's beautiful book

151

on Buddhism, full of colours and fragrances, as refreshing as the Tungabhadra River at Mantralayam. It was ironic: there I was in that beautiful spiritual place reading of someone else's mystical experiences, rather than enjoying my own. It was doubly ironic since my whole purpose in coming to India was not for information received through the mind, but for first-hand experience. Again and again, I found it reiterated: the Self, the truth, the reality, cannot be found in books. You must find it for yourself, in your self. All you need to do is to keep quiet. Peace is your real nature. If you remove all the thoughts from your mind peace will come. Liberation is your nature. The very fact that you wish for liberation shows that freedom from bondage is your real nature. Liberation is *from* the person: not *of* the person.

Ramana Maharishi always advised his followers to circum-navigate the hill, which must be done either in the early morning before the sun grows hot or in the evening, preferably without shoes, in a clockwise direction. To walk anti-clockwise is positively dangerous, Sadhu Om had explained; those bogeymen, the Tantrics, are, according to him, trying to get you to do precisely this and draw you into their power. As you walk, you come to different magnetic fields which affect you variously at different stages. During my stay at Tiruvannama-lai I walked round the hill three times: twice with Roy, once alone; twice in the early morning, once in the evening. It felt different each time. It was a strange walk along that circular road, bordered by miniature temples and shrines, stone bulls and cisterns; with always the hill on your right, rearing up in strange silhouettes, bumps and crags. I could feel the attrac-tion, a strange and subtle force. Right over the other side, opposite to Tiruvannamalai, is a small village surrounded by rice fields, spiked with coconut palms; in the centre is a temple, similar to but smaller than that of Tiruvannamalai. As we approached at sunset the sinking sun bathed everything in a golden glow before vanishing into the liquid green paddy fields. Unfortunately the inhabitants were a noisy and unpleas-ant bunch: they followed us in hordes for quite a long way throwing stones and shouting: 'What is your name?'

I did feel the attraction from the hill. I did feel the peace in that shining meditation hall and a current of inner energy. But

152

my precarious attention was always being drawn outwards, particularly to the uncomfortable atmosphere in our lodgings. One evening, about five or six days after we had moved in everyone as usual was smoking dope and playing guitars. They were doing a lot of that particular laughing that hippies do: they would all be sitting there quite quietly and suddenly they would all burst into laughter. Ha! Ha! Ha! Stoned again! they would sigh. That night everything was made the more uncomfortable because the family was clearing out the well and there was nowhere to wash. I lay in the sweaty heat under the mosquito net which was precariously supported by nails that kept giving way precipitating it hotly on to my face. The floor seemed unbearably hard and Roy was particularly restless, running in and out with cups of coffee, fruit and joints.

Suddenly my discomfort and uneasiness became too much. At midnight I departed, followed reluctantly by Roy. The plump girl was amazed. 'You are leaving tonight? That's very sudden, isn't it. Why are you running? Can't you cope?' She had seen a lot of strange things, but she'd never seen a stranger one than this... All I could say was that she hadn't seen much. But she was perspicacious. I was running as usual. Instead of dealing with the dope and the atmosphere I was running. But what a relief it was to leave that place and those people! They seemed again so unhealthy, so incompetent, so enervating, so *dreary*.

Halfway to the town we were given a lift in a hand-drawn cart by three men who presented us with juicy pieces of sugar-cane to suck. The hotel, built into the temple wall, was a simple row of rooms giving on to the inevitable communal balcony. It was – at three o'clock in the morning – full up. So we spent the rest of the night with our baggage, sleeping outside the front door, adjacent to the dry cleaners, which in the circumstances was handy since our clothes got filthy. The hotel watchman squatted next to my head talking to a friend: not polite hushed voices but, as Ma Taleyarka would say, loud, from the bazaar. At dawn three cows walked past and crunched up some of the sugar-cane which was covered with squashed banana and a host of ants. A family of monkeys, their tails erected like cats', patrolled the roofs opposite, and then two small puppies appeared out of a hole in the wall and bounced

153

bravely at a much larger dog. There was never a dull moment in that road. Some pigs appeared and consumed the rest of the ants and the sugar-cane, the nightwatchman was joined by three immaculate friends and the puppies narrowly missed being squashed by a bullock cart. Soon a group of small boys gathered to marvel at this scene of two Western bodies lying in the gutter absolutely filthy. We all waited together until the doors of the hotel rattled open and we were able to wash, change and have breakfast.

That morning I was escorted on an expedition by Ma Taleyarka. Since she believed the manager of the ashram to be a robber she was bequeathing all her belongings to a convent. This had been recently constructed, all in seven months, and all on charity, the mother superior said, as she dished out home-made ginger cake. The nuns were a refreshing antidote to the hippies. They radiated warmth and energy. 'Such work,' said Ma Taleyarka. 'Coolies: they are working from morning to evening.'

A high wall ran for about six yards, fortified by glass, and then stopped: run out of money, explained Ma Taleyarka: they must get some more money and finish the wall. As it was, anyone could come in and rob them. Two days before a large poisonous snake came in. This reminded Ma Talayarka of another case of trespass. 'You know my house is all locked up, well, someone came in there and stole my watch . . .'

I was shown round the convent rather like the Queen. 'Stand up, children, and say, good morning, Miss,' said the nun. And there were all the little children so clean and tidy and pretty with their white shirts and ties. 'See the children here,' said Ma Taleyarka. 'Such good discipline – not like the municipal schools. No wha, wha, wha here!' Instead, it was ba! ba! ba! They sang and recited 'Ba ba black sheep', 'Little boy blue' and 'Mary had a little lamb'. English was the first language taught here, Tamil the second. On the blackboard some of the exercises could be seen inscribed. 'What are called deserts?' 'What are natural vegetation?' 'This is my class,' said the nun proudly as we stepped through a door to inspect another immaculate and delightful group. 'A very naughty set.' The naughty set burst into a song about God's love: so deep, so round, so tall, miming it as they went along.

Next morning we rose at four o'clock to ascend the hill before the heat of the day – as we opened the door the family of monkeys was just passing along the balcony wall. According to Sadhu Om, people lie in wait for unsuspecting travellers as they make their way upwards. It was not clear whether they anticipated your money or your life and it was not clear either who these predators were: dacoits, the dreaded Tantrics, or distillers, who are said to ply their illicit trade in secret caves. In any case we saw no one. A narrow winding path leads up from Tiruvannamalai to the summit. We climbed past the first cave in which Ramana Maharishi had lived, shaded by trees and watered by a cool spring gushing out from the hill, containing the tomb of a great yogi from the past; then higher, to his second abode, a small house near a grove of trees where again the same stream flowed out into a wide pool. Here women bathe on their way home after a day spent on the hillside cutting grass, carrying it down in the evening for their animals, loaded down so heavily that they look like walking haystacks. But in that early morning there was no one. Stones sparkled with crystal in the rising sun and lines of crows perched on the rocks following the contours of the hill. As we reached the higher slopes women were already cutting grass and everywhere there were coloured butterflies, some brownish with white spots, others blue, others again green and yellow. And all the way up eagles circled round the hill. At the summit is a flat plateau, black and oily from the fat which feeds the great beacon lit each December and burning for weeks commemorating the occasion when Shiva appeared here in the form of a spouting flame. Up here the eagles swooped down upon us with a rush of wings, tremendous birds with great curved beaks and gold plumage. And down below the world lay stretched out in geometric patterns, tiny squares of bright green, spiked with palm trees, temples, cisterns, gocalums. Now there were no people, no obstacles, no little girls who shouted, no stones to hurt your feet, no hippies with their dope: they were all invisible. The only reality was Roy, myself and the huge swooping eagles, perched up high above the world on this extraordinary hill.

I would like to have stayed at Tiruvannamalai but now it was nearly time to return to England – via Goa. The journey there was long, hot and tedious, involving several changes, and we arrived at Londa at six in the evening to discover that the train for Goa would not be arriving until crack of dawn next day – half-past three in the morning. How we passed the intervening hours is a study in how one diverts and deludes oneself. Roy, together with a policeman, crossed the railway lines, entered a goods truck and vanished across the junction, returning about half an hour later with a bottle and a half of arak which we and an Irish girl, encountered in the waiting room, proceeded to swallow, chasing it with the inevitable joints. It was the perfect example of how alcohol, to say nothing of narcotics, can delude you into supposing you are having a marvellous time, when the truth is that were you sober you would see that you were having an absolutely pointless, excruciatingly boring time with someone with whom you have nothing at all in common except the alcohol. And were you not drunk and stoned out of your mind you would not be talking to them at all. The Irish girl, who was a clothes dealer, talked about chicks – all the chicks she had met along the way (and they had not been too well spoken, most of them) could only talk about their boyfriends and the joint they were smoking. She could talk about the clothes she picked up in the markets, while we at the end of the evening could not talk at all. I can just remember the horrified faces of the other occupants of the carriage as at last we staggered on to the train. Hippies! They shuddered. 'They've been smoking and drinking, isn't it? Very unhealthy!' They were right. Next day I had an appalling hangover and when the headache and the sickness had subsided the mind took over, whirling, chattering, diverting, distracting, exhausting.

Goa is much larger than I had imagined. To travel from the main town to any of the beaches entails jolting through palms and ricefields for hours in the usual hot buses, crammed with about a hundred people. Along the way we could glimpse small girls in coloured dresses, some with babies on their laps, swinging from trees on the long roots of banyan trees. Kolva is a beautiful beach, with a fringe of palm forest along its edge through which the wind makes a strange hissing as though it were raining; and crows fly so low that they send up small whirls of sand with their wings. Waves roll in from the Arabian

156

sea up the long white sands, gentler here than at Mahabalipu-ram and just as warm. And here were the same fishing boats curved and black in the night against the sea; the same spider crabs scuttling into their holes, and other crabs too with strange startled faces. But there is one notable and unfortunate difference between Kolva and Mahabalipuram which lies in the stench of fish – everywhere it is laid out to dry. They fish here with snakes as bait so that at sunset there are half-eaten snakes and empty skins littering the water's edge.

One day we went sight-seeing to Anjuna beach – the hippy beach. It involved a long hot journey by bus and motor bike. There is no doubt that Anjuna is beautiful, marvellous brown rocks all along the beach and a palm forest which contains a large village. On the day that we arrived there had been a mass exodus, the hippies had left that morning on the freak bus for the Poona rock festival; from there they would move north to the Himalayas, rather like the swallows, they had left Goa for another year. The scene resembled a battlefield after the armies have decamped. Western litter lay about, dirty cotton wool and other unsavoury pharmaceutical deposits, tins and paper. There were a few casualties too who had missed the bus. 'I'm only a freak,' one told us, looking like a refugee with a skin disease. He had been here for about four months having driven out in a mini-van. Were there a lot of drugs about? Roy wanted to know. Yeah! People were always coming up to sell you a trip, but they weren't good quality trips – the acid wasn't pure. They had had a party last week, all the freaks had come, they had seen where the cupboards were and they had pinched everything.

By comparison with Anjuna, Kolvar is a funny mixture: no freaks here but hundreds of nearly naked fishermen, burnt black, and a few white people like ourselves doing our best to char ourselves as dark. Some middle-aged fat Indian couples swam, or rather stood in the waves, fully clothed, holding hands, and an aimable pair of Western ladies of a certain age ate prawns and walked along the beach as the sun sank into the sea. I was reading as usual: Iris Murdoch. She was fascinated by the good life, by being good, by virtue. How does one become good? she was asking. It seemed so totally incompatible with living an ordinary life. I too was becoming increasingly bewildered by the duality. How was turning the attention inwards, conjuring up the Self as advocated by Ramana Maharishi, compatible with directing it outwards to the guru, to this paternal ideal fellow whose guidance one sought? Just as I was writing this and pondering over what seemed to be insurmountable difficulties, a sort of mad revolutionary with a peculiarly scarred forehead appeared. Was I meditating? Not exactly. Was I writing? Foolishly (would I never learn?) I said yes. Ah! he too was a writer, of sorts, although he did not accept any payment for *his* articles. He had even written a comparative study on the behaviour of the Germans and the Indians. With the Indians he was disgusted, with their physique and behaviour. Everywhere there were Indian children all quiet and well behaved, going off to school with their books, while German children were playing about in the trees yelling. The Indian children sounded infinitely preferable, although judging from the group of young scholars who had arrived that lunchtime to picnic on the beach it did not seem to be uniform behaviour. The revolutionary went on grumbling. You couldn't see anyone walking on his hands along the beach for example, why not? he'd like to know. His theory was that it was due to the climate and the diet. How, the revolutionary wanted to know, was Indian ever going to be powerful? With six hundred and sixty million people she should be one of the most powerful nations in the world, but where, he asked, were the Newtons? The Einsteins? Where were the gymnasts? Yoga? Pooh! he dismissed that. What about sport? Cricket? Roy suggested, having just wandered up. No. He dismissed that too, cricket was not at all an active sport. The trouble was that Indians were not a revolting people: look at China, they had revolted. Now they were all right.

Our journey from Goa to Bombay encapsulated all the trials of travelling by rail across India. First of all the train would hardly move. It stopped, started, groaned to a halt and at last limped into Londa. The trouble, we discovered, was that our coal was wet and the train could not get up steam. Next the engine sprang a leak and we missed the connection at Miraj where we were obliged to remove to a special boogie which was on its last wheels. The taps and levers were so rusted they would not turn on and there were gaping holes in the floors and walls. Here we waited in a malodorous siding. To pass the time we went for lunch in the restaurant which was full of hippies looking as though they were in the final stages of decomposition. One couple shuffled over and sat at our table. They were filthy dirty, ragged and covered in boils and pustules. In this condition they were on their way to the rock festival at Poona but had missed it, preferring to take a trip rather than the train. First of all they had swallowed speed, then a pyramid, then a purple something or other. Well, the man's trip had not been rational. It was too intense – know what he meant? Could he interest us in some of the commodities he had on offer? Afghan grass and some of this purple whatever it was. Mercifully the food arrived and they shuffled off.

Hippies give a very bad impression, said our travelling companion (who was from the State Bank of India). They are spoiling Goa, polluting it. They are smugglers also. The Hare Krishnas are the worst. Singapore has banned them, won't let them in at all. All smugglers. What were they smuggling, Roy wanted to know. Opium, it seemed, though the man from the State Bank of India did not know its English name. And there was another mysterious substance, a clear liquid which laid you flat in a minute. Was that like opium? But the man from the State Bank of India became quite huffy. He didn't know anything about these things, he said.

We arrived in Bombay for the festival of Holi – the occasion at which the hairbrushes had manifested in front of Dadaji's disciple. From an outsider's point of view it is hard to find much enjoyment in the celebration, at least not for those much above the age of eight. Everyone goes round splashed in coloured dye. For little boys it must be a paradise, their faces and clothes are as gaudy as clowns, their fingers red, green and blue. Driving along in our taxi, balloons full of coloured water kept coming in through the window and spattering us, the final straw being when a carload of people struck up with 'High, High Hippy, Hippy, High!' when they saw Roy and me. Next day we read in the papers that some of the coloured powder was poisoned and several children had ended up in hospital. Several other people – not children – ended up face downwards in malodorous puddles from the surfeit of bhang that so many people enjoy on this merry day.

We stopped in Bombay just long enough to visit Albert's Sri Nisargadetta Maharaj. He lives in one of the poorest quarters of Bombay, in a narrow lane above the bidi shop in which he makes his living. He is quite plain about his realisation. 'It so happened that I trusted my guru,' he said. 'I did what he said for three years and I achieved my realisation. He told me that I am nothing but myself and I believed him.' For a while Maharaj had abandoned his family and his bidis to wander in the Himalayas, but eventually he returned to his household. Now he was eighty-four and totally unpretentious. It was only later that I realised the value of the visit. At the time I was confused by his teaching, which seemed nothing but verbiage. As for his meditation sessions, they were like bedlam.

Sri Nisargadetta Maharaj receives in a long low room which has been constructed by making a platform under the ceiling of the bidi shop. It is furnished with vases of flowers, bundles of incense smoking like so many fragrant bonfires, and photographs of holy men each freshly adorned every morning with red spots on their foreheads. Here every day at eight o'clock Maharaj supervises meditation. When Roy and I arrived it seemed more like a railway station than a time of contemplation. One lady was rubbing a wooden dish with a wax preparation, chatting the while in voice like a corncrake's – a long conversation in Marathi punctuated by cackles of laughter. Maharaj meanwhile was wandering round blowing his nose loudly, doing the dusting. Gradually the room filled up with lines of seated disciples – including Albert, hot from Tiruvannamalai. A interpreter arrived and read from the Vedas. Then there were some noisy bhajans, cymbals clashed and reverberated round the room, conches were blown, bells were clanged.

An hour later comes Maharaj's darshan and through his interpreters he encourages people to ask questions. Why have you come, he asks newcomers. Who are you? The person will then give his name. This is not the correct answer. One is misidentifying. One is not the body at all. Indeed his teaching endorses Ramana Maharishi's. Roy was the main subject that day, he embarked on the saga of his mystical experiences: this spirit has taken him down a valley and made him have a bath, others had arrived and the voice of God has sounded. Maharaj dismissed all this. We have all had experiences like that, he said. You are merely obsessed with yourself. Fascinated. But who are you?

Later we went to the flat of an American couple, Rudi and his wife, who were staying in Bombay for three months. Rudi reminded me of my acid-trip companion. He was cantakerous and verbose. It did not appear that their time in Bombay was doing either of them much good. Both enjoyed a catalogue of ailments. Rudi had a bad liver, piles, and seven large jars of vitamin supplements from Illinois Health Stores; his wife was visited by bed bugs and a frightful allergy. Each morning before going to Maharaj they engaged in two hours of exercises. Rudi seemed to me to turn the next darshan into a chat show, wasting the time by asking tiresome convoluted questions like 'having forgotten, is forgetfulness achieved?' – all of which had to be translated by Maharaj's interpreter. She plainly was fed up with wasting hers and Maharaj's energy in transposing such nonsense and herself tried to offer Rudi some advice. This did not please him at all. 'Has anyone got the switch?' he asked rudely.

Maharaj then was angry. 'You all cool down,' he said via the interpreter. No one should return for five days, not even for meditation. Before we left I was able to have a few words with him. I had sat there for three days, I told him, and I was totally confused, bewildered. 'Very possibly,' Maharaj commented drily. 'Go and be still: just be still. Leave your mind alone: ask yourself who you are,' and he recommended two volumes of his dialogues – *I am That*.

The night we left India there seemed to be a mass evacuation of Hare Krishnas. One hundred and ninety of them were flying with mountains of tin trunks to Los Angeles. 'Whatever do they hold?' I asked, recalling the man from the State Bank of India and his theory that whey were all smugglers. 'Things for the temple,' one Hare Krishna replied vaguely. 'All our clothes for a year,' said another. 'However are they supported?' wondered an Indian suspiciously.

International flights from Bombay leave at unearthly hours of the morning. This one departed at 4.30. The Hare Krishnas, however, were like a cabaret keeping everyone entertained as they paced round and round reciting their mantras. Some were fat, some were thin, one was like a pink pig, another wore a balaclava, and all of them combined to present one of the maddest floor shows I have ever seen as they blabbered and jumped en masse round the airport. One American tourist had a hypothesis with which he was delighted: they were a screen, the Hare Krishnas, for either a spy ring, a terrorist gang, or they would be an international betting school mouthing to each other the racing results.

But it was Sai Baba who had the last laugh. In the confusion I had registered through the zip bag which held my tape-recorder and tapes. The tape-recorder and all the tapes – Swami Parvatikar, Sadhu Om's rendering of 'The Marital Garland of Letters' and the forbidden bhajans at Puttaparthi – they were all stolen.

PART III

Back in England my attitude towards spirituality remained unchanged: it was still some sort of exotic phenomenon, illuminated by full moons, redolent with fragrant oils; it was separate from Christianity and totally incompatible with London.

'Be still,' Maharaj had said, 'just being still means you are free from the obsession with what next. When you are not in a hurry and the mind is free from anxieties it becomes quiet and in the silence something may be heard.' Immobility and silence are not inactive. The flower fills the space with perfume, the candle with light: they do nothing, yet they change everything by their mere presence. Between the banks of pain and pleasure the river of life flows. It is only when the mind refuses to flow with life and gets stuck at the banks that it becomes a problem. Accept. Let come what comes and go what goes. Desire not, fear not, observe the actual as it is. Stand aware and unconcerned. Watch events come and go.'

I had returned with his two volumes, *I am That*. The first thing I read was the translator's introduction. He himself had stopped reading books, just as he had stopped arguing and discussing; books, he said, caused obstruction to knowledge. You had to still the mind, be quiet, dwell in the spirit. Actually, these two volumes only endorsed Ramana Maharishi's teaching, but much of it took a long time to sink in. It was so alien to the bulk of my training, to my Western upbringing. To hear that you were not the body and that the world was not real still seemed to be double Dutch. Nevertheless there was much here that did resound from the past. And gradually much of this teaching was assimilated so that it became as much part of the furniture of my mind as my previous instruction had been. And since this teaching is in a sense a milestone I give here a synopsis of it – or part of it – in as concise a form as possible:

Man is two things: body and spirit: gross and subtle. But while he is alive his body attracts his attention so completely that he forgets his subtle being, and the secret world to which his spirit belongs becomes lost in a world of empirical objects, earthly desires and delusions. So it is that man believes that he is the body, that he has been born and will die, that he has parents and duties. He learns to like what others like and fear what others fear. He becomes a creature of heredity, living by memories and habits.

The world's only purpose is to perpetuate and expand consciousness. Man's only reason for being in the world is to become aware of himself as a spiritual being and to liberate himself from the gross body which is a shell imprisoning him. Anything that does not work towards this liberation, this subtle expansion of consciousness, is a waste of time. Yet most human beings spend their lives and their energy in building mental and material prisons for themselves, and through their conscious efforts to liberate themselves they reinforce the walls of their separate identities. Although human beings are alive, they are also in a sense dead, insensitive, unaware, unalert. They vegetate in a dream state gathering experiences and enriching their memories.

So where has man gone wrong? It is because he knows himself only through his mind and his five senses. He believes himself to be what these suggest. Since he has no direct knowledge, he can have only ideas. And, because he has no inkling of reality, of what is truth, no inkling of what is real and what is illusion, he pursues false aims, he aims at empty targets. He chases after happiness and pleasure because this is the only thing he knows.

By its very nature the mind of man separates, divides, opposes, creates analysis. It craves formulations and definitions, squeezes reality into shapes and of everything requires an idea. Without ideas and thoughts the mind of man does not

164

exist. Yet thoughts are dust originating in memory, not insight. Thoughts are never original, the only way to originality is through inspiration: literally by breaking through to the unconscious with the conscious mind. The mind of man should be a tool, an instrument, by which its operator may express the creative energy within him, instead it is generally a dominating master. Its domination comes because man is fascinated by his thoughts and his ideas. Its power comes because man trusts it. It is the only thing he knows to trust; the only agent through which he believes he will acquire knowledge.

True knowledge can come only through direct experience. Nothing of value can come from outside. Once a man is inwardly integrated outer knowledge comes spontaneously. Schools, universities, the entire system of modern education, teaches a man to cram as though memory were knowledge. But memory is parroting: knowing the letter and the word but with nothing of any real significance. Like the mind, memory is a good servant but a bad master, effectively preventing real discovery. What is remembered is never real, it is coloured, shaped, changed, made agreeable or disagreeable, exaggerated, toned down or dismissed altogether. If what man hears is not to his liking, not a recognisable part of what he believes to be himself, he discards it. He does not hear.

Although some of this was confusing there was much that I could salute from my bygone experience. That the body was a shell imprisoning the inner spirit: how well I knew that! That the purpose in life was to liberate yourself came as no surprise either: that is what I had been after all my life, though I had been trying to get *out* rather than *in*. And direct experience? Was this not what I sought in India? Had I not felt that I required experience that could come from no book, no mind? And that parroted knowledge, that paper information with which in the past I had wrestled, trying to arrange it in logical order, and which then refused to be retrieved from my memory: I knew about that too. I knew also about perceiving the world as though through a veil, being unalert, unaware.

'It is in peace and silence that you grow,' Maharaj said. 'Keep quiet therefore. Watch what comes to the surface of the mind. Reject the known, welcome the unknown, reject that in its turn. Go deep into the sense of "I am". Deepen and broaden your awareness of yourself. Open yourself to a spiritual stream in which your spirit can refresh and restore itself. Keep the "I am" steady in the focus of consciousness, the only clue you have, your certainty of being. Be with it, play with it, ponder over it, delve deeply into it, until the shell of ignorance breaks open and you emerge into reality. When the mind is quiet it reflects reality. When it is motionless through and through it dissolves and only reality remains. You need not seek anything at all. All will come to you naturally, effortlessly. To find yourself you need not take a single step.'

There I had been, stepping all over India, and what had I found? Each time I had arrived at a new place and sat down in front of a new person I had hoped I would see something extraordinary, or at least some sign: eyeballs dangling from sockets, snakes, diamonds emerging from thin air – anything would have been acceptable. But, as it was, the spoils had been none too good: an orange and a few handfuls of ash one year, some wafts of fragrance and some red writing in an unknown tongue the next. As for myself there had certainly been no explosions, no spiritual trances, ecstasies or metamorphosis. Yet there had been glimpses of that internal energy I now supposed to be reality, or at least a reflection of reality. At the Taj Mahal, with Swami Parvatikar, at Mantralayam and Tiruvannamalai my mind had been still, I had been conscious of that inner current. It was the same feeling that can come while one is quiet, listening to music perhaps; starting slowly, a feeling of peace, growing stronger, sweeping away unease.

I wanted now to be still, to open myself to that spiritual stream. I found myself unwilling to return to my previous life, to mix with people who had no spiritual bent. I could see that below many of my previous pursuits there were subtle undertones. Was it not a longing for communication that lay beneath many of those long and hollow dinners in pursuit of happiness, a fear of loneliness and isolation? Yet on so many of those evenings there had seemed little communication in the real sense, so many people not listening, looking for an opportunity to sparkle, to perform, to establish, as Maharaj said, the walls of their separate identities.

As for my erstwhile friends, I could see that not only were

most of them embarrassed by my new direction, they considered it a bore. There was, however, one aspect of my journey which was to them a topic of absorbing interest. How much poverty had I seen in India? What about the dirt? The spectre of dirt and material insecurity haunted them. People sleeping in the streets, lack of possessions and lavatories, no roof over the head, all these were too awful to be imagined. They went on a lot about human dignity, on the assumption that material wealth automatically bestowed that quality. Yet one of the most undignified and pathetic people I knew just then happened to be a millionairess. She longed to be invited everywhere, but such was her neurosis that she rattled with tablets and brimmed over with alcohol and on the occasions that she did go out it was in such a drugged and inebriated condition you could not hear a word she said. This would not have mattered except that, late at night, she buttonholed you, and before collapsing into a coma she would command your attention with an unintelligible, often ill-humoured, flow of verbiage.

As a matter of fact I had indeed been struck by poverty, but not in India. In England I had again been shocked by the spiritual want that I felt everywhere. It struck me how much healthier were so many of the Indian attitudes. Our refusal to face death tied closely in my mind with the horrible approach to our animals: on the one hand the sentimental slush over our 'pets', on the other the callous way that millions of food animals are crammed out of sight in factories. And if the living hens, pigs and calves are invisible their death is more so. Shut away in impenetrable slaughter houses the beasts re-emerge wrapped in polythene, prettily packaged in cardboard. Eat more, people are urged, consume more: it is your right to eat roast beef, roast chicken, roast pork, just as it is your right to drive a car, own a washing machine, a deep-freeze and a colour television. It seemed to me that resentment, greed, obesity and unhappiness were more evident than human dignity.

At this juncture I paid a visit to the Festival of Mind and Body at Olympia – the Ideal God Exhibition, as someone called it. Bernard Levin wrote about it afterwards: it was the strangest fair he had ever been to, he said, but what it demonstrated was that all over Europe there were hundreds, thousands, of people for whom the materialistic values of the Western world simply would not do. They might be blessed with material comforts and happy families (and a good measure no doubt of human dignity) but there was a hole inside these people and however much food and drink they poured into it, however many well-balanced children and loyal friends they paraded round its edge, the void ached. Here at Olympia he saw a huge range of suggestions as to what one might do to make one's life better. How one might grow to one's full potential was the overall theme.

The Festival of Mind and Body, it seemed to me, was rather like India: you could see anything here you wanted to see. One person might survey the scene and see gathered together crowds of serious responsible people searching for ways in which to pursue a gentler, more compassionate way of life, another might see a load of cranks, cosmic lunatics, vegetarians and their cucumber-eating cats. It was a bit like a giant kaleidoscope, every time you looked you came up with a different aspect. The goodies versus the baddies, for example: the goodies wanting this more responsible way of life and the baddies wanting to sell them commercial produce at a profit. Us versus Them: Them signifying the establishment, a great cohesive structure crushing the small individual forces, a giant production line turning innocent beings to robots.

That aspect was one that fitted very nicely with my own views – my own conditioning – I could sit comfortably back and salute it. Here was everything imaginable to do with the alternative society – to say nothing of the commodities that opportunists over the past ten years had fabricated to cash in on the rebellion against factory farming, pesticides, insecticides and orthodox medicine. Everything now must be 'natural', everything for health, unpolluted by modern technology. What a range of 'health food' there was, what a lot of herbal cosmetics and remedies! And then there were all the idealists who longed to escape the pressures and restrictions of modern life and return to the land and self-sufficiency – an idyll of vegetable-growing, goat-keeping, cheese-making, bread-baking, spinning, weaving and so on. There were also plenty of spectacular side-shows, such occult diversions as faith healing, pyramids of energy, tarot cards, dowsing, fortune-telling and aura-photography. Quite a number of well-known gurus were here. One elderly couple from Croydon watched bewildered as a group of devotees performed arati, rotating the flaming dish in front of their guru's photograph. Ah yes! the couple nodded one to the other: they're meditating. Meditation was for them some exotic word signifying incomprehensible actions.

The Hare Krishnas were banging and crashing away in a corner, selling yoga trousers and giving cookery lectures, while in front of a stand promoting the Flying Yogi, Sivananda Swami Vishnu (author of that article in *The Current* attacking Mahesh Yogi and Sai Baba), a man stood on his head. Perhaps most conspicuous of all were Rajneesh's disciples in orange. Bernard Levin had been very taken with their propaganda. 'We have a wide range of meditation and group techniques to support your quest,' he had repeated. '*Your* quest, note.' He had been impressed by that, feeling that it showed a lack of pressure. What he failed to mention was the price of these techniques. All of them were at a price. One of the dialogues in *I am That* seemed interesting here:

'Another difficulty one comes across quite often ... with Westerners is that to them everything is experience – as they want to experience food, drink, women, art, travels, so do they want to experience yoga, realisation and liberation. To them it is just another experience to be had for a price. They imagine such experiences can be purchased and they bargain about the cost. When one guru quotes too high in terms of time and effort, they go to another who offers installment terms, apparently very easy, but beset with unfulfillable conditions ... naturally there is vast cheating going on at all levels and the results are nil.'

There was, too, an undercurrent to the festival, an orgiastic undercurrent of mysteries and midsummer madness. Here was the hippy world again, the drop-out world of tipi settlements and festivals at the summer solstice, where liberation meant sex, drugs and music, where everything was free – or it was supposed to be free, but like everything else in this world it had its price. Free festivals meant that the organisers sold a lot of

dope to pay for overheads, like food, which they then distributed as 'free'. As a matter of fact this was a world to which some
of my younger son's friends belonged; with their hair plaited
and wearing earrings they spent much of the summer going
along to these 'free' festivals and reading hippy magazines
(which I was interested to see reflected all the neuroses of the
materialistic society: Rona, the heroine of one story, missed
out because she didn't have orgasms). The magazines were a
strange mixture of lust and idealism. To be 'Kool' you had to
make love, play the guitar, smoke dope, swallow blues, speed
and acid and rave. It was like India all over again: sit down and
blast your mind with noise, have a joint, a trip. It was a
mixture of orgiastic celebration and spiritual yearning which
can best be seen reflected in the mixture of dubious verse.

> Bodies lie together
> Sweating in their joy
> Giving thanks together
> For their final joy
>
> Lust unbridled flowing
> Thru the sultry night
> Both the partners knowing
> Loving is alright!

and:

> There's a change in the air
> We must help each other
> To become aware
> Respect the birds and respect the bees
> And let the planet breathe with lots of trees
> Leave the fishes in the deep blue sea
> They too must be free
> We must find ourselves
> Before we can find each other
> Help your sister
> And help your brother
> There will be confusion
> And confused people may kill

170

But let no intrusion
Keep you from being still
So we'll sit and gaze into the skies
And feel the warmth of the rising sun
And after a while we may realise
That we are all one.

The next highlight of that cold wet summer was the appearance of Dadaji and Abhi Battacharya in Neasden. They were en route for a grand tour of Europe and America, staying with a disciple. Already there had been a drama. Against Dadaji's advice his hostess had driven off on a shopping expedition together with the lady whom Dadaji had imported to prepare his meals. They had collided with some long poles which were protruding from the back of a lorry. Later the hostess could remember nothing about the incident except someone, she supposed it was the ambulance man, exclaiming: 'They must be dead, nobody could survive this.' Nevertheless there they were in hospital, broken, it is true, but patched up with plaster and alive. When I arrived Dadaji was at the hospital, visiting, and the small room was filled with Indians enjoying a tape of Dadaji singing. Suddenly the peace was interrupted by a singular white lady. She was short and fat with plump blotchy arms and legs, protruding veins and frizzled hair standing up on end like a terrier's. She believed in Sai Baba, she announced. This was met by stony stares. No good, said Dadaji's disciples. 'We don't believe in him.' No good? she was astonished. No good! Well, in any case, she too was a faith healer. And she went round the assembled company trying out her powers. She went first to a doctor from Ilford who was sunk in meditation.

'Can you feel tingling?' she asked him several times. 'Can you feel heat?'

'No, nothing,' he said impatiently.

'I hope you'll feel better soon. Do you feel better?'

'No, nothing.'

Plainly he was irritated by her. She stood there, her blotchy little arms held over his head, then over his stomach. At last he diverted his attention.

'When did you first feel these powers?' he asked politely.

'When my dog died. Before, I had no belief. My mother's house was chapel; we had no faith, when we died we believed we got into the grave and that was that. But after my dog was married. . . .'

'*Married*?'

'Buried – he came back. Before, I had no spiritual faith at all. Not like Peggy Mason.'

'Perry Mason?'

'*Peggy* Mason.'

'I see,' said the doctor (who like all of us was clearly none the wiser as to the identity of this obscure Peggy Mason), and returned to his meditation.

Next she tried a very old lady, who was sitting all muffled up in a jersey, her head covered in a sari, rather like a parrot which had been put to bed. Her would-be healer snapped open and shut her bag, fidgeted about and wrote down some recipes for the old lady who was to concoct some ointment from mutton fat, suet and olive oil.

'You must get the fat with little veins running through it,' she caroled.

'I can't think how they're communicating,' said the old lady's daughter. 'Mummy speaks no English.'

Dadaji meanwhile was singing the Song of Truth and according to those who knew about these things the doctor from Ilford was getting a Presence – or he definitely would have done had it not been for the fat white lady snapping open and shut her bag.

To assist Dadaji with his tour, his right-hand man had flown in from California. Harvey Freeman (which is not his baptised name, but a symbolic indication of his liberated state) drinks no alcohol, eats no meat and has done just about everything. In the States he had been some sort of orthodox priest; he had worked with hypnotists, psychiatrists and mental illness, was the author of several spiritual books and had in the past been something of a guru himself. He had travelled extensively in India and his meeting with Dadaji smacked definitely of the 'so you've come' school. He had had no intention whatsoever of visiting Calcutta, yet somehow he found himself irresistibly compelled thither. Soon a man arrived at his hotel. 'Dadaji is waiting to see you,' said he. 'I don't know any Dadaji. I'm not interested in any gurus or babas,' Harvey Freeman had replied. All the same he found himself going round to see Dadaji who greeted him with the familiar words: 'Ah! my son, I have been waiting for you for so long.' From that moment Harvey Freeman never looked back. It is like having a love affair, he told me. When he is apart from Dadaji he longs for his soothing presence in which to bask. Dadaji is his sun; while the mahanam is beyond everything. All things happen for him automatically, he does not have to do or to worry about anything. Last October, for example, he was again compelled to go to India. But on arriving at Delhi it was discovered that his visa was out of order. No. It was not possible for him to proceed to Calcutta. But how could it be impossible when it had been Dadaji who had called him? Sure enough, ten minutes later, he was receiving V.I.P. treatment (from the man whom Dadaji had raised from the dead and who ran all the airports) and everything was arranged. As for material needs he owns a chain of organic pizza parlours somewhere in the States – money flows in as he needs it. According to a spiritualist friend, he was in his last life a holy man, a sadhu in India, he wore the clothes, had all the trappings yet he had no faith, now he has none of the trappings, only the belief.

Dadaji's speciality, as I knew from my time in Bombay, is scientists. It was now revealed to me by Abhi Battacharya in Neasden that he is also interested in all brands of successful people, particularly writers and journalists. Certain people were ordained to come to Dadaji on this trip – already he had been to Germany where he had met some 'top-most' man, some chancellor or other. Clearly what he was interested in, in Europe, was publicity. He wanted to meet people who would give his arrival the maximum weight and coverage.

I had imagined that when we met again there would be some kind of rapport, some éclat of recognition. But Dadaji did not remember me at all. It was only when it was revealed that I was a writer, a journalist, that he turned his attention to me. He peered at me, into me, for some time, then: 'very simple,' he announced to the assembled company. 'She is very simple.' Whether this was a term of approbation or not I had no way of knowing, however from then on I received preferential treatment. If ever I wanted to return to India I must write to Dadaji and he would arrange everything, no question of payment. I would be met, escorted, protected, cared for – everything. Was I saying the mahanam? (I was not.) Did I want to know how *he* (Dadaji refers to God as he) smelt? Then he took me upstairs and touched me as he had done in India and immediately that delicious fragrance sprang out, lingering on my head, my throat, my clothes for days. There was no denying it: I felt wonderful, exhilarated, and so secure. 'Don't worry,' everyone said as I left, 'no harm can come to you. Dadaji will look after you.' Even the bus conductor was affected by my state. 'Been on the booze then?' he asked. 'You've been out enjoying yourself somewhere, haven't you?'

Dadaji stayed about a week and during that time I went several times to Neasden and saw quite a lot of Harvey Freeman. We went to the theatre together and he came to my house. I enjoyed being with him, he radiated energy and it felt so harmonious, united as we were under the umbrella of Dadaji's attention. We were plugged in together to the same stream of energy. It was in a sense the same sort of enjoyment that I noticed people shared together standing on the common watching their dogs dash round with the sheer exuberance that dogs have. Their owners would be gathered together focusing on their dogs' energy and for a short while they would plug in to the same source and, united, could communicate within this flow. This is what disciples can do: join together, communicate within their teacher's stream of energy. It was an invigorating sensation and I continued to feel marvellous. Yet when I was actually with Dadaji I was still uncertain how to behave. I felt overwhelmed and exhilarated by his presence, yet I did not feel any bond and I was self-conscious as to my behaviour. As before, in India, I aped everyone else, adopting again the role of surrender, falling reverentially to my knees, speaking breathlessly. And indeed I was overwhelmed. It was not so much what went on during these evenings at Neasden, but this exhilarating force that I felt emanating from Dadaji. His English I found very hard to understand. I caught rather little of what he said. Once I took some water for him to treat. He passed his hand over the bottle, whose stopper as far as I could see was screwed tightly on, the water turned cloudy and when the top was removed it was quite fragrant – Charanjal – and it stayed like that for a year.

What Dadaji wanted was to come to my house whither I would invite a select gathering of journalists and eminent men for whose admiration he would perform a pooja. It was however impossible in the time. Bernard Levin, for example, who might have been interested, was away for his holiday. I could not get Bernard Levin but I did get Horace, who was by this time not only a 'name' but almost a public figure.

Summer had at last arrived. We sat in the garden while roses cascaded through the trees and I explained that God's agent, if not God Himself, had arrived in Neasden. As illustration I produced the photographs of Dadaji taken with Dr Klein. 'God seems to be wearing a skirt,' observed Horace. Indeed the photographs were marvellously comic. Dadaji so benign and Dr Klein looking so bewildered. 'Where are the fellow's shoes?' Horace wanted to know. 'What? You take your *shoes* off?'

In retrospect it seems to me that what most astonished Horace about his trip to Neasden was my reverential pose of surrender which was quite outside the behaviour he had known from me in the past. Nor would he have saluted Harvey Freeman's 'laissez faire' attitude towards life and money; he had never liked what he saw as lack of responsibility in the hippies' approach to life and this would seem to him to smack of the same, while the notion of everything happening automatically would go strictly against his own meticulously planned, budgeted schemes. Dadaji, on meeting him, peered at Horace for a long time in silence. 'He's putting you through the computer,' Harvey had explained. 'You're very lovely,' Dadaji had pronounced in tones of moving sincerity. 'You have a very beautiful soul. You are a very brilliant scholar in this world.' It seemed to me Horace bridled a little. 'Do you believe in God? Do you believe it is you who is writing?' It was a ridiculous scene. There was Horace being elegantly, politely eloquent; as though he were addressing a literary society, he explained his beliefs in God and how his work was his meditation, while Dadaji's English seemed to grow sparser and he looked to me for translation. 'Is that true?' he asked once, but I had not followed the conversation. I felt rather like those early days at school. I had no idea what was going on. I was conscious only of this overwhelming magnetic presence before me. 'Why have

175

you come?' Dadaji asked Horace: out of all the millions of people that could have come before him how was it that Horace had come? Perhaps he was going to say that he had been waiting for him for years, but Horace spoilt it by saying he had come out of curiosity. The interview concluded by Horace disappearing upstairs with Dadaji and descending after a while in a cloud of fragrance; like Dr Klein he was photographed sitting on the bed beside Dadaji, then he hurried odoriferously away to a dinner engagement.

He missed the pooja which took place upstairs in the bedroom. One person remained, sitting there on the floor, while Dadaji and everyone else squeezed downstairs into the sitting room. It was rather hard to know what was supposed to be going on, but I gathered that after half an hour the bedroom would be awash with fragrant waters while the disciple and the photograph of Sri Sri Satyanarayana would ooze with amrit. I was the first person to be called upstairs to witness these marvels. There was no doubt that a remarkably heavy fragrance hung about the room, but otherwise in the dim light I could see very little, only a few damp stains on the floor in the corner. But perhaps the conditions were not ideal since the disciple's bedroom was fitted with a wall-to-wall carpet, of which only a little had been pulled back. Besides, a queue of people was pressing in behind me so that I may not be doing the performance justice.

Soon after this, Dadaji, Abhi Battacharya and Harvey departed for America. On the day that Dadaji leaves England, Harvey had announced to Horace, it is going to be cold and wet – Dadaji had said so. But the departure day dawned fine and as their aeroplane rose into the sky the sun burned down hotly.

Having been to India, it seemed that one was now on some sort of spiritual mailing list. Soon after this a circular came from something called Spiràl, which, under the direction of someone called Sat Prem, was holding a workshop in Devon; it was, apparently, something to do with Nisagadetta Maharaj. The workshop took place near Dartmoor in a mill house, which was overseen by yet another ex-army officer, a disciple this time of Rajneesh: he presented a weird spectacle, sporting an army manner and moustache above orange robes and a medalla from which the large face of Rajneesh peered out. He, along with five or six others, all equally orange, lived in the mill house while Sat Prem and his group, who were mostly Dutch or German and suffering from flu, camped in the barn. Sat Prem, it seemed, had a knack for sizing you up at once, finding in a second your weak points. I forget what he said to me: whatever it was I agreed. 'Don't agree,' he snapped. 'You're playing games.' As for Roy, who had accompanied me, he was pronounced to be a little boy of four, misunderstood, wanting love, full of anger and frustration. Sat Prem explained that what he himself was doing was working with energy, which is exactly what Christ was doing – indeed like Christ he expects to be assassinated within five years since energy is very volatile and depending on how you are moving it can explode and blow you up. But where the Christian Church is a business selling grace and salvation Sat Prem is merely selling people to themselves. He never plans anything, he just does what seems to be appropriate.

After dinner therefore it seemed appropriate that we all repair to the barn with a bone, a stone and a stick. There we must sit in a circle round four lighted candles and visualise all our fantasies and anger and pour them into our stones, which we held cupped in our palms, while breathing in a certain way. Most people very soon fell into fits, roaring and shouting. The man next to me coughed, spat and was eventually sick over my skirt. The noise was indescribable. After we had sat roaring and spitting for about an hour we all had to think of a number and then walk the equivalent amount of steps (two hundred in my case) and bury the bone, the stone and the stick where we ended up. Some people must have envisaged thousands, they vanished into the woods and it was quite a long time before our next exercise could begin. This was to massage a partner – who was selected by the same sort of principle as a Paul Jones. This was no ordinary massage but a strange sort of subtle air mani- pulation, while mustering lovely thoughts. I sat there imagin- ing all the lovely things I could – fragrant Rosamundi roses in a blue porcelain vase, cats purring in front of a cosy fire – and my partner burst into tears.

Bed was on the floor in the barn; downstairs, rock music played loudly and the Rajneesh disciples danced. Rajneesh's policies do not include privacy – privacy is inhibiting, as apparently are clothes, so everyone lay round naked, playing the flute and the guitar, and there were no locks on any of the doors. With about forty people trying to use the lavatories the results can be imagined. There you would be sitting, and in would troop a whole crowd. 'Hallo. What's your name?' – just as though you were at a cocktail party. 'I'm Narine, I'm Fritz, I'm Ma Prem Kokila, mind if we brush our teeth?'

Next morning the sun was shining and everyone had to be up at seven because the barn was to be used for a session of dynamic meditation. Music was put on at ear-splitting level and everyone started to 'cathart', which meant that everyone puffed and banged and thumped, supposedly expelling their aggression. Soon, most people started roaring and bellowing again. Then, after a pause, everyone was supposed to jump up and down, but since the floor was shaky they were encouraged to thrust out their pelvises and say 'Ho' instead. It was an extraordinary scene: seven in the morning and a barn full of naked people shouting 'Ho' somewhere in the depths of Devon. In Poona, I was told, Rajneesh has special underground chambers for 'catharting' but here there was nothing underground about it and just after the session had finished the postman arrived.

After breakfast there was T'ai Chi centring, which was quite calm, swaying through the air, cutting it with the hand, then a humming meditation, employing the body like a channel to let out all the aggression and draw in new clean energy. This reduced two ladies to a fit of hysterics. Relaxing into it, they were, Sat Prem explained: excellent! It seemed quite common for someone for no apparent reason to collapse suddenly into a fit of violent sobbing – 'relaxing into it,' Sat Prem would explain again.

The country around was a joy, some of the best in South Devon: tiny lush lanes with every sort of wild flower, foxgloves, cow-parsley and scented orchids. It had everything, marvellous woods through which a clear river flowed, humped-back bridges, bridle- and foot-paths. If it had not been for Sat Prem and his workshop I could have happily stayed there for ages. But after all Sat Prem was the reason I had come. He wore about him an air of authority. I felt that he *knew* something. There were two girls with Indian names who took some of the courses, and they too seemed surrounded with an aura of mystery and authority. Sat Prem was perfectly open about himself. It's all a big joke, he kept on saying. What is the point of it all? To find yourself: to gain an appreciation of body and consciousness. But (and here he became confidential) it takes a lifetime – lifetimes probably. A session, an encounter group like this, will do no more than to break the ice. Some years ago he had recognised the need to be with a master, he was getting into some 'big psychic spaces', he would walk into a room and know all about everyone there. It was so easy. He had never been able to understand why or how people were so dumb and unaware.

Originally he had left for India to see Sai Baba but en route for the South he had arrived in Poona and from there he had never looked back. Now he was everything: shaman, mindreader, clairvoyant, astral traveller. What Rajneesh does, according to Sat Prem, is to make fun of everything, make everyone appear ridiculous. This is why he dresses his sannyasins in orange and gives them Indian names and identities (Sat Prem, for example, means truth and love, which he should live up to) and encourages them to provoke themselves and everyone else. Nothing is forbidden, everything is to be enjoyed. It turned out that the local people in South Devon disliked this abandoned behaviour just as much as the inhabitants of Poona do: the ex-army officer and his orange household had been banned from the nearest pub.

At dinner Sat Prem devised a new ruse. Did anyone want to make love? Yes? Three women put up their hands. All right, they could select ten partners and write their names in order of preference. The experiment would start that night with number one and they should use it as a new sort of meditation. So, that night, into the barn came the 'meditators'. Certainly, it was hardly less noisy than the dynamic meditation had been: chatter, chatter, chatter in Dutch and German accents and then unspeakable squelching noises. 'Can you be quieter?' I snapped, exasperated. 'This is a room for everyone,' said a guttural Dutch voice. 'Yes, exactly, and I'm trying to get to sleep. Don't inconvenience others by your experiment.' (Matron was with us again.) 'No,' said the guttural voice. 'This is *your* experiment.' 'It certainly is not. I didn't choose to go to bed with *you.*' The conversation was developing into a schoolboy banter. The squelching noises resumed, died down, there was a moment of fitful sleep and then they all sat up and had cigarettes. That was when I moved downstairs. It must by then have been three o'clock and there was Roy (with whom I was not supposed to communicate throughout the duration of our stay) sitting reading *The Magus* – sitting reading about orgies while they were going on all about him. Eventually I slept in the dining room with a lesbian in a sleeping bag next to me, and the only good thing that could be said was that everyone was too exhausted to get up for dynamic meditation next morning.

Never had I felt worse: furious, uneasy, neurotic and exhausted. 'Excellent!' said Sat Prem. Get out the emotions, feel them, recognise them, ventilate them because they will always be there, this is the human condition. Like sun there will be happiness: like rain unhappiness. You must learn to recognise them: here is the sun, here is the rain, here is anger, here is happiness. Your biggest responsibility is to remember yourself. Live on undisturbed with the emotions recorded in the background. You must not be caught up in your emotions. It is bad management to dissipate energy. You must not be involved: it will all happen anyway. Live on with the force flowing through you like a river. Being unrealised, said Sat Prem, is such a drag, it's like trying to paint a picture blindfolded. And off he went to view a farmhouse in Cornwall which was on the market for £80,000.

We thankfully made our escape: shaman, clairvoyant, whatever else Sat Prem might be, he was also absolutely exhausting. Roy and I had to snatch some sleep in a ditch on Dartmoor before proceeding to stay with some friends who were electrified by our descriptions. Whatever is the point of it all? they wanted to know. Is it to lead a happier, a better life?

After this it would be hard to say that I was leading a happier or a better life. That summer was more like the dark night of the soul. Like Iris Murdoch I felt that spiritual life was incompatible with ordinary life; that it was impossible to pursue a spiritual life surrounded by what Sai Baba would call wordly people. I longed to turn inwards and connect up with that current of energy. I realised that there would always be distractions; that no sooner had I got rid of one disturbance than the next would be there. The only way indeed was to be uninvolved. But how? Dissipating your energy, Sat Prem said, is bad management. I knew I dissipated my energy – my energy and how other people dissipated it was my neurosis that summer – but I could see no way of not doing so. 'I could see you,' Harvey Freeman had said, 'sitting on the sofa, at the same time you were in the kitchen, out in the garden, upstairs. All your energy was being dissipated. What you need is a channel, a pipe.' I knew that was true, but again how on earth was this to happen?

At the time I was reading Hermann Hesse's – *Siddhartha* – in which I found a marvellous peace reflected. In London it was impossible to listen to the river or the sea, only those awful trains and aeroplanes rushing by. But here again it was reiterated: one must establish one's inner sanctuary, one's inner stillness, and listen to that. There one would be, trying to listen to one's inner stillness early in the morning, trying to be silent and still, and the telephone would ring: some drunk ex-lover ringing from New York, just in from Studio 54 and looking through his telephone numbers to see who he could call. . . . No matter how much I tried, my equilibrium depended on external things; again and again people would shatter the ghosts of my tranquillity. The more I heard we were all one consciousness, the more I longed to be by myself. I felt I was not whole enough that summer to be with people. I did not even like them, let alone love them; as I tried to turn inwards, I felt they were wrenching me out again. I felt uneasy, that I was wasting time; that the small portion of peace I had managed to establish would vanish.

They fell roughly into two types, these people, and although most felt irritated, threatened even, by my quest, some seemed to me to use it as a vicarious source of entertainment for themselves. There were the sceptical ones. After those endless bottles of wine, inevitably the conversation would turn. 'We are all one,' I would parrot, trying to recall Maharaj. 'It is only our egos which make us suppose we are different.' 'Nonsense,' they would chorus, as confident in their own sense of uniqueness as I was uncertain of my knowledge. 'We don't have time

181

for all that tosh. Eternity, evolution, you use these terms, these are what you believe in, we don't. We don't believe in these things, just as we don't believe in reincarnation or the life hereafter.' They were on the whole successful, these people, their time strictly regimented to appointments and work schedules, so that every moment of the day was as far as possible organised. 'Well, I don't have time for you,' I would wail, and burst into tears. Horace was one of the more irritated. 'So a mind is unimportant then?' he would bristle. 'You don't receive enlightenment through the mind,' I would recite. 'Could this be put forward by someone with no mind as a camouflage?' he would want to know. I felt absolutely exhausted after these evenings, the pointlessness, the uselessness, of words to convince either them or myself. I felt my own inadequacy, trapped in the prison of my body and the cul de sac of my mind. I knew that, if I waited, eventually what I needed would come to me, I was more or less firm in this belief, but after an evening with a party of sceptics my confidence would be quite disintegrated. In that climate I found I was always being diverted, always in a state of panic and resentment. I felt as though poison were coursing through me. As for my own mind and memory, neither of these was functioning properly. It had always been an effort for me to retrieve information, now it was virtually impossible. My mind refused to concentrate, it would go blank. It would neither work to retrieve information nor would it be silent. When I did not want it to work, it jabbered away.

Regarding the other type; these were the gregarious party ones who could not pause in their whirl to know whether they were sceptical or not. Their main concern was with my withdrawal from society. This was only a phase I was going through. I'd been through it before and I'd go through it again. But wouldn't I feel very cut off? Cut off from what? I wanted to know. On the contrary I was trying to join up – with reality. And I would explain that hitherto my life had been lived in a fantasy world, rushing out every night to parties, filling myself up with anaesthetics in order to jabber away the night, ending so drunk that I would go to bed with anyone. And then it would be their turn to feel uneasy, since some had been those ending up with me in bed. 'Now look here: we think you're exaggerating,' they'd say. 'We don't think what you're saying is

182

true.'

It seemed to me that life was like a long road and much of it was spent jumping up and down, waving and shouting on the same spot, getting nowhere. That is how it felt after those evenings, as though we had all been jumping up and down, not knowing where to go, gesticulating, ending up exactly as we had started, only more exhausted. All that food, all that wine, all that sitting round the table. What for?

Meanwhile, Sat Prem arrived to stay in his orange robes. He drew up in a large white Jaguar, towing behind him a speedboat called Bass. It had not after all seemed appropriate to buy the farm in Cornwall, instead he had purchased a yacht, which was even now being sailed through the Bay of Biscay to Portugal. He and his disciples would soon follow, he travelling with his girl friend in the white Jaguar, his disciples in a luxury coach. Those that could not fit into the yacht were going to live in a glass bubble and meditate in a balloon.

Quite a few people came round to view Sat Prem – it was all part of the entertainment. And he, with his knack of finding what he called the chink in the armour, produced in us all varying degrees of unease. In a flash he pinpointed our fears, our neuroses, and exposed our so-called selfless actions for the self-interested operations they were.

'The vicar' came to consult him on his lost vitality. In a second 'Mr Sap,' as he called him, had analysed him. How had his mother treated him at the age of eight? Was she warm with him? She was not, but one of his nurses, who had been very ugly, had lured him into bed assuring him that he and his parts would soon develop. Fears, said Sat Prem, you must go back into your fears. Why didn't he come to Portugal? My dear, 'the vicar' couldn't possibly do that, the parish needed him. He had to say mass, only the other day someone had broken in and stolen the chalice.

One of my most beautiful friends came to meet him, too. Frigid, said Sat Prem. She was frigid. Look at how she was sitting with her legs crossed. Was it his aim to help people? she rejoined. What do *you* do to help people? he turned the question back to her. Well, every day she tried to do something to help someone: today she had given the old lady opposite a glass of wine. That's not helping her, said Sat Prem, that's encouraging her to be an alcoholic. Next she had mailed a whole lot of papers to an old man in Australia. What you're doing, said Sat Prem, is preparing against your old age. You are frightened of growing old and dying and you're preparing for it.

In Horace he detected the same sort of spectre. For him he used the analogy of clothes. When one is growing, or expecting to grow, one buys a suit of clothes which is too big for one. Horace buys clothes exactly the right size. It's safer that way; that way he knows where he is. He makes life comfortable and secure for himself, writing about these dependable dead people; he likes being alone, yet dreads isolation, so he surrounds himself with the dead.

Turning his attentions to myself he saw me trying endless apparel, first this dress, discarding it, trying the next, dissipating my energy in trying on clothes. As for my armour Sat Prem pierced it directly. He turned to my younger son. Now, what you are looking for, he told him, is a hero, someone to lead you. Your energy is being dissipated by your mother – she is a neurotic, pressured by her mother – you're going to fall into the same trap if you don't break out of it now. I was speechless. My son's energy being dissipated by *me*! It was quite the other way round, I felt. It was absolutely unfair. I writhed with anger and unease. The scene was made more ghastly by my current research into mediaeval Christmas dishes for an American magazine. As Sat Prem stirred the shit (as he inelegantly put it), I stirred my plum pottage; every night we sat down to a mediaeval collation. We are all one, Sat Prem would explain, gingerly tasting the Christmas pye, or whatever it happened to be. We are all one consciousness; our difficulty comes when our individual egos pretend to be separate and prevent us from joining the cosmic consciousness.

Every day Sat Prem dressed in his orange, but I noticed that when he was telephoning he would give a plain name – J. Bell. There was a lot of telephoning. He had discovered this new hydraulic machine which worked on nothing at all and supplied boundless energy and which he was planning to sell to the Israeli government. It had to be a government rather than an individual since an individual, he thought, would be liable to be assassinated by Shell or B.P. But first of all he had to get it patented, and find a patent lawyer. So his discourses would be interrupted by the telephone: lawyers, hydraulic experts or people with Indian names.

Sat Prem's aim was apparently to recreate innocence. Education is destroying innocence. People in the West tend to be intellectual, to operate through their minds and, from about the age of three, to fall out of touch with their emotions. So what he was trying to do was to balance a person, put him back in touch with his sentiments. He was, he told us as he conveyed a bubbling spoonful of dark spiced brew to his lips, he was the absolute 'I am'. He had complete control over his mind and his body – with which he did not identify at all. Although J. Bell and Sat Prem still existed with all their neuroses, they were nothing to do with him: he was simply an instrument through which the force worked – something was working through him, guiding him and giving him powers.

At this point someone called Mahonta (which means Saint) arrived to stay the night, dressed in deepest orange. Saint lived up to his name, treating Sat Prem like a lovable rogue, who it seemed had appropriated three thousand of his pounds in some carpet venture. Both of them seemed delighted, chuckling over the memory. Sat Prem returned to his theme: what he was doing was being a fisherman, he went out and hooked people, pulling them into his boat so that they could die and be reborn. All gurus used devices to hook their disciples. Sai Baba manifested jewels, Dadaji fragrance and whisky, while he, Sat Prem, had a yacht. It was show business. They hooked their disciples, who must surrender, die and be reborn. It was the death process, the killing of ignorance. Of course people were frightened; they were terrified of death; their egos were terrified to die. That with which one identified, one's religion, one's education, everything must go, since it was all part of the structure of the ego. The more highly developed the intellect the more unattractive was the notion that everyone was the same, since an intellectual spends his life preparing, then reinforcing, his own sense of individual uniqueness.

Sat Prem's therapy, it seemed to me, had a horrible curdling effect. His purpose may well have been to balance people but all I can say is that he left me feeling totally unhinged. I was bogged down in my neuroses instead of being lifted out of them. I was reading Hesse's *Steppenwolf*. Steppenwolf angry, red-eyed, laughing; leering at the bourgeois who was trying to make himself comfortable, give himself peace of mind, settle himself down, surround himself with possessions. I saw how I was completely bourgeoise, tricking myself into little games in order to try to live peacefully and comfortably, passing the time agreeably with little diversions. I saw how it had manoeuvred me into a trap. Here I was in this house, surrounded by my cats, my plants, my garden, my home-made pot pourri and furniture polish, all of which I loved, yet all of which in their turn worried me, they all had to be looked after and protected from burglars, they had to be sustained. The rates had to be paid, so did the other expenses.

I went off with Roy to do a travel piece on Ireland for the American magazine, which involved a great deal of rushing about, eating and drinking. Ireland had never seemed so beautiful, blue and glittering in the September sunshine, yet when I returned I felt worse than ever. The house seemed always filthy and I appeared to do nothing but clean it and juggle round the bills. Each anxiety took me into a mental compartment and locked the door behind me so that I became trapped. I was back again in the familiar pattern, prey to palpitations, asthma and inertia. Two things enhanced all this. One was the death of my favourite cat. No matter how much I tried to witness the workings of my mind I was still overwhelmed by a storm of grief, sentimentality and memories. This was her chair; this was where she would stand on her hind legs on the edge of the bath in the mornings, rubbing, anticipating her breakfast. Soft, warm, sweet-smelling cat, who growled when people rang the doorbell, who purred so softly, who walked behind the pillows in the morning, who snorted when her food was put down, blowing down her nose. She would come in bellowing when she caught a mouse, yelling out, expecting an answer. After tea she liked to sleep on my stomach, flattening her ears when she was stroked. O most intelligent cat, how can I bear to be without you! My attention would be briefly diverted but the ache would linger on, drawing my mind back once more through the channels: no more big fat cat looking like a tea cosy perched under the table, no more Lucy snuggling into my brown mohair rug from Harrods.

The other – and just as bad – was the publication of the illustrated book about debutantes. Sat Prem had talked a lot about books. There are some like *Siddhartha* and *Steppenwolf* which can change their reader's consciousness, where the author is possessed with a real knowledge which through his pages he can convey democratically to his readers. Then some books are excellent works of entertainment, exploiting perhaps certain qualities, innocence, virginity, love, the struggle between good and evil as enacted in murder, detective and science fiction. Many, however, are written by those with nothing to impart to their readers but received opinions. Many again are simply collections of regurgitated verbiage. Such a book, I have no hesitation in saying, was *Gilded Butterflies*. Several interviews were arranged for the radio and so forth. Sometimes the talk would go well, more often it would not. I would be crippled by tension, my mind would go blank and refuse to retrieve the information I required. Often you hear of people's astral bodies projecting themselves outside their physical ones. I felt this had happened to my mind; when I wanted it, it seemed to be floating like a bubble somewhere above me. It was as fickle, as perverse, as ever, sailing off when you needed it, and then when you did want it to go away it settled down for a good chat – rather like the Indians – and assaulted you with ideas.

Everything reflected back to me my disintegrated state. For example I went as a surrogate mother to a function at Westminster which was celebrated by a service in the Abbey. It should have been refreshing, bracing, with the singing and the candle-light, yet the whole thing seemed most depressing. Even the headmaster, who only a year before had been such a fount of strength and optimism, gave an address which turned out to be without hope. Man was going to destroy himself, that seemed certain. Everywhere was destruction and war. The only hope was somehow to find God. All he could wish was that the young people would walk out that night saying: 'I don't know that my redeemer liveth, but I hope so.'

PART IV

It was in this unhappy condition that I went to a seminar held
by the Sahaja Yogis at Easthampstead Park. This had once
been an Elizabethan hunting lodge, now it was hired out for
weekend courses to Scottish dancing groups, Baptists, Electricity Board trainees, lady gymnasts and now Sahaja Yogis.
The weather was perfect for a spiritual seminar. Everything
material was lost that first morning and enveloped in a thick
mysterious mist. The grass was drenched in autumn dew and
the branches of huge trees loomed dimly out of white fog. The
air was still, silent, and a strange feeling of insubstantiality
hung round with the fog. At about eleven the sun broke
through, turning the mist into pink gauze, gradually clearing it
away to leave behind a radiantly gold October day.

We had risen at six to meditate. This was not so much meditating as 'taking vibrations'. We must sit with our hands extended towards the photograph of Her Holiness Mataji
Nirmala Devi – the guru. Gradually, but only very gradually,
the tension and unease flowed out of me and I felt traces of
peace seeping through, as enveloping and silent as the white
mist outside. An energy began to course through me, coming
up through the hands and the arms, the air began to feel like
waves of electricity rushing up my fingers and arms while
outside it pulsated round the body like soft feather cushions.

By the end of the weekend of meditation, lectures and a visit
on Sunday from Mataji herself, I felt euphoric.

The Sahaja Yoga technique appeared totally different to
anything I had previously come across. The human frame was

to be used as an instrument for harnessing nervous energy. A chart hung on the wall showing this squatting figure whose inside was looped up with coloured lines representing the channels through which nervous energy flows. The human body, it seems, is constructed in a series of conduits for conducting the vital airs. As briefly as possible the theory of Sahaja Yoga is as follows.

Inside every human being there is a primordial force which guides all evolution and which has transformed the amoeba through various stages into a human being. This evolutionary force is known in Sahaja Yoga as kundalini. It is for rousing and harnessing the kundalini that the human body is created. It is an instrument, a computer, waiting to be connected to the source of supply in order that it may evolve to a higher stage of consciousness: this is its only purpose in life. The nervous system is created simply for channelling this vital energy.

The gross body consists of various conduits and organs which are governed in the spinal chord and the brain by their subtle counterparts, called chakras. These chakras control the organs of the physical body as well as the neuro-endocrinal system. Each chakra controls its organ, gland and plexus and in turn each chakra is controlled by a goddess and her consort. According to Sahaja Yoga we are cornucopias of gods and goddesses and when we behave in a bad way the gods and goddesses may leave their seats; so that gradually one becomes more and more insensitive, more and more gross. This is what is meant when it says in the Bible that the wages of sin are death: it is the death of the vibratory system and the chakras.

In the human body there are three main channels (nadis) through which the energy circulates. They control complex interconnected sets of smaller channels within the whole body. The three energy channels together with the seven chakras manifest the autonomic and the central nervous system as well as the specific function of the two hemispheres of the brain: the ego-dominated part of the brain (left hemisphere) is connected with the right-side sympathetic nervous system (pingala nadi) while the super-ego-dominated part of the brain (right hemi-

sphere) is united with the left-side sympathetic nervous system (ida nadi). Within the spinal column we have the subtle central channel known as sushumna; the gross manifestation of this channel is called the parasympathetic nervous system. On the right side of this we have the channel known as pingala nadi which corresponds to the right-side sympathetic nervous system. On the left side we have the ida nadi which corresponds to the left-side sympathetic nervous system. Placed on the central channel we find the seven centres (chakras) which control our physical, emotional, mental and spiritual bodies. The chakras are expressed as plexuses and sub-plexuses outside the chord.

The activities of the parasympathetic aim at conserving, restoring and balancing the energy while the activities of the sympathetic prepare the body to dissipate the energy – the sympathetic is the medium by which we programme ourselves and are programmed. The parasympathetic channel has a gap at the navel, so that whenever we make a conscious effort towards an action we move on to the outside sympathetic systems. When we gain some control over our sympathetic nervous system we also acquire a corresponding degree of control over the subsequent course of our lives. Until this happens, and so long as the sushumna remains closed, the energy crosses from left to right and back again in endless elliptic movement between action and reaction.

When our attention passes on to the right side we are involved in thought, planning and organisation. When this channel is overstressed the ego becomes inflated and accounts among other things for mental restlessness and exhaustion. When the attention passes to the left it becomes involved in feelings, the past and recollection; when overstressed the super-ego is inflated and the subject becomes over-emotional. It usually happens that when one side of the sympathetic nervous system is drained the opposite side will be affected, falling prey to the perpetual pendulum movement of psychic energy. Ultimately, the subject may end up possessed: when the super-ego is inflated the subject may be threatened by psychic intruders, while with inflation of the other side the subject becomes possessed by his

190

own ego and victim of self-deception and delusion.

Either way, if we move too much from the centre we become imbalanced. By over-activating one, or several, of our chakras, our nervous energy becomes blocked and injurious hormones are released into the system; ultimately we may develop diseases, diabetes perhaps, heart attacks, cancer. With the latter case, the chakra continues emitting energy but if not regulated by the parasympathetic system this becomes destructive and starts the mutation and proliferation of cancerous cells.

How can we overcome this endless swing between action and reaction, between the ego and the super-ego, so that attention can be turned to the self? Sahaja Yoga says it can be done by channelling the energy, the kundalini, up the parasympathetic, the sushumna. In the past this has been difficult. Now it is believed that Mataji has the power to raise the kundalini within us. This is because such powerful electro-magnetic vibrations flow from her person that they have the power to ignite the force in others.

The signal that the kundalini has risen is to feel in the hands a cool breeze, which emanates from the presence of Mataji herself. Subtle vibrations, electro-magnetic waves flow automatically from everyone and everything although hitherto we have not been aware of these. From a divine, an integrated person, we receive cool vibrations, from a sick or a mad person hot ones. So as soon as we feel this cool breeze the theory is that the kundalini has risen, we are 'realised' – linked up to the mains. The human microcosmic computer is connected to the cosmic programme. The information starts flowing through the nervous system in the form of vibrations.

Now the theory is, we have an absolute standard of reference. Any question may be put to the cool breeze test. In other words we are supposed to be able to enjoy a dialogue with the divine. 'Yes' is indicated by a cool flow, 'no' is burning; tingling, heat. Furthermore we are now supposed to be able to treat others. We may use the hands as a multi-purpose transmitter of energy. It is believed that the hand is linked with the central-

191

psychosomatic system, each of the fingers sending forth and receiving different vibrations from the corresponding chakras; thus by extending the hands we may feel upon the fingers how and where another person is malfunctioning and by massaging symbolically the energy up his spine we may not only balance and correct his faults but raise up his energy so that he himself receives realisation.

Through the awakening of the kundalini one stands, it seems, upon the brink of a new life of subtle perceptions and awareness. The theory is that once aroused the force begins working, stabilising, restoring, illuminating the system. As the subtle centres are threaded together the organs of the body and the mind begin to work harmoniously like the instrumentation of a great orchestra. Stability of attention is achieved and a certain objectivity in life which removes obsessive worries and habits. People have been cured of drug and alcoholic addiction, mental and other serious diseases including cancer. The curative technique operates through the subtle integrated network of the endrocrine glands, yet healing is not the objective – only a by-product. Physical and mental ailments come in the way of man's evolution and have to be cured. After self-realisation the individual becomes a channel for the primordial energy, which he can now use for healing and balancing not only himself but other people. He is now part of the collective consciousness.

I have given this résumé in order that the technique may be understood as well as possible, but at the time all this was by no means clear. There was, for example, very little to read at all: *The Advent* by Gregoire de Kalbermatten, from which much of this detail is drawn, was not yet published. Indeed it was asserted positively that one did not have to know anything intellectually about Sahaja Yoga; the less one knew intellectually the better. What one had to have was the experience.

So I found the weekend bewildering yet eminently soothing, uplifting and more: I returned to London restored, euphoric, determined to commit myself to Sahaja Yoga. I realised that I must practice what the guru preached or I would continue to stagnate, grumbling about other people exhausting me. It was not, I must say, that I felt that Sahaja Yoga was better than anything else; certainly it made me calm, refreshed and exhilarated, but then so had the presence of Swami Parvatikar and Dadaji. Indeed it would be true to say that the actual presence of Dadaji (and, as I remembered it, that of Sai Baba) was more magnetic, more powerful than that of Mataji herself. The point was that Mataji was available. 'I will explain everything to you,' she kept saying. 'Everything.'

I had as a matter of fact been attending Mataji's lectures at Caxton Hall (whence she was driven in the regulation white Mercedes) in a somewhat fragmentary way all through the summer. I had even taken my youngest son who had been pronounced 'born realised'. Her Holiness Mataji Nirmala Devi, the advertisement in *Time Out* ran, had granted Self-Realisation to millions of people.

The first meeting I attended struck me as crazier than anything I had seen in India. For a start Caxton Hall itself was so comic. The Model Soldier Society was in concert in the York Room, the Darby and Joan Club somewhere else, the Blood Transfusion Unit was in the main hall, while Sahaja Yoga was in the Kent Room. Roy and I had in fact arrived right in the middle of the meeting so the procedure was hard to follow. Several people were standing up waving their arms and twirling them about (this was the symbolic message up the patient's back). 'I'm working on him,' one would say to another. 'It's stuck at the heart.' 'Can you feel anything?' they would ask the patient. 'Cool breeze?' 'Tingling?' Certainly I felt something: a violent and painful shaking in the right arm. 'That must stop,' said Mataji, who had swept down from the platform. 'How many gurus have you been to?' 'Oh God!' According to her, most gurus are bad. Such a lot of damage they do – they take your money – dreadful fellows! See this lady? She, it seemed, had been burnt by one (a highly esteemed saint, according to Roy, a Sikh with a large following), now she could not stop crying and being depressed. And see this mad little boy of eight? He had been to one guru and the guru had taken away his power of speech. See, all he could do was to rush around Caxton Hall roaring like a bull. Her disciples went down the front row of the audience inspecting their necks for medallas and lockets; these they cleared away with expressions of extreme disgust. 'Guru shopping ugh!' spluttered Mataji indignantly. You don't know, you are so naïve, you don't know

193

the befuddling ways of these fellows. She came to Roy. There were, she said, black spots all over his face. Black spots? Blackheads? You could see that Roy was not pleased. No. Not blackheads – devils. Roy was possessed. At this he embarked on Gopal Swami. Mataji was not impressed. The stranger the name, the more outlandish the appearance, the more you go for them, she cried – remarks which though perspicacious were not to Roy's liking. His face grew dark. He had already had his kundalini raised, he told her, referring to his experience at Hyderabad. Kundalini? He had? No, no, that was quite impossible! Now he must co-operate a little, he must follow the treatment she was going to prescribe. He must bring seven limes and seven chillis next week and she would vibrate them, and then all the devils, the negativity, would go into them. This was her brand of exorcism. Christ used pigs; she used vegetarian techniques. They would all be thrown, devils and all, into the Thames and washed away out to sea.

But next week Roy was not co-operative. Finally, very disagreeably, he went and sat through Mataji's lecture reading a book. Today Mataji was talking about the ego – Mr E.G.O., she called it – how 'he' deludes us into misidentification. Matter is our trouble, its only purpose is to give us joy, but we are all bogged down in it and instead of joy we receive anxiety, worry and pressures. We should think only of joy, not of what something costs. Unless something has a price we undervalue it; unless something is a business we fail to take it seriously. Money is the end seal of respectability, the criterion of seriousness. Obviously if a thing is incompetent, if a thing does not work, then it can give no joy. One should have efficient things, a car, for example, should certainly work but it should not be a status symbol. One should surround oneself with things that give good vibrations, not with plastic. Thoughts are like bubbles on the sea; on the surface the tide goes backwards and forwards; deep down on the ocean bed everything is still. Thinking is a disease. Too much thinking, too much looking about, over-stimulates the liver; if the liver is bad the attention is all over the place, one is unable to concentrate. Too much thinking, like too much physical effort, also affects the heart; too much thinking and the brain goes. We should be like flowers, they do not think, they blossom. We must simplify our lives. To know the truth we must experience it. We must pass through the experience. Otherwise how will we know what is what? So now we must all go into meditation. All of us new people in the front with our hands extended towards her. We should close our eyes. We should be quite comfortable and relaxed. Soon we would feel cool in our hands, we would not have a thought in our minds, we would be quite thoughtless, quite aware – thoughtlessly aware. Thoughtless awareness is the first step towards merging with the universal unconscious. Now all the realised ones should step to the front and work upon us. A feeling of well-being stole over me and there was cool in the hands, to say nothing of the feet – I should add that this was not too curious, since the night was chilly. I could see that a cool breeze is a positive asset in the stifling heat of India, but in draughty Caxton Hall it was something else. Nevertheless a soothing feeling did creep over me. Meanwhile all the disciples were standing in their strange postures. 'Better? Do you feel better?' 'Right heart!' one would exclaim. 'Vishuddi!' 'Are you a great thinker?' one asked me. 'A writer,' I said. 'Oh dear, oh dear! an intellectual!' cried Mataji. 'They are the worst! Books are no good. What one has to have is real knowledge. The mind can only move in a linear direction, isn't it? A really learned man must be religious. Unless he has experienced reality, God, his knowledge will be shallow, superficial. Intellectual competiveness in the West makes things very difficult. You waste your energy so much, all of you. Your bodies should be like a channel, a flute, through which the divine energy flows.

Before realisation, Mataji explained, one is only a dummy, nothing can go right with a vacuum at the centre. As soon as one connects up to the system one has a centre upon which to start working. In the heart resides the spirit through which the connection is made – she, Mataji, is the connection, we are the wires, the transformers of energy from the source. We must cleanse, cleanse, cleanse so that we can plug into God.

Mataji had been that week to a healing conference in Tunbridge Wells. There she had seen a lot of people – acupuncturists, faith healers. They were very nice people, no doubt, but they were not 'realised.' How then could they heal people? How could priests teach about Christ without realisation, without being linked to God? Where was their authority? Going to a theological college, passing exams, does not give them real authority. Only kundalini, real experience, real knowledge, is the thing. It is a physical force which *has* to rise eventually.

Certainly something was on the move inside me. There was a feeling of choking, stifling, of catching in the throat, then something ran up one side of the neck and behind the sinuses. Roy meanwhile, in spite of the cold night, was sitting there beside me feeling hot, indeed pouring with sweat and looking furious. A small dark man had started on him. 'Do you get on with your parents?' he asked. 'Yes,' said Roy and launched into Gopal Swami. 'Forget it,' said the small dark man aggressively. 'If you can't forget it, go away, you're wasting your time here. What are you going to do? Are you going?' Up came Mataji. 'How are you feeling? Better?' 'He has a dead guru,' said the small man darkly.'I know, I know,' said Mataji. 'Now you must co-operate a little,' she said, stamping her foot and clicking her finger. All round were these people waving their arms. One started to gasp. 'Yes, I know, you feel very insecure, don't you?' 'No,' said Roy. When she moved away he snatched up his lemons and chillis (which I had bought at some expense at the local delicatessen) and left. I was irrationally upset. There I had been sitting one minute with this feeling of harmony – albeit somewhat choking harmony – and the next it was disintegrated. To be so upset that someone refused to put seven lemons and seven chillis under his mattress was crazy.Yet I had this fear, this disintegrated feeling, curdling, falling apart, Next someone showed me what seemed to me to be a spell. You protected your aura by waving your hands over your head seven times. If someone bothered you, you wrote their name down on the floor, encircled it seven times and banged it with the heel of the left shoe 108 times. When eventually we got home Roy emptied the chillis and the lemons into the fruit basket. That was that, he said, he was not going again. And he did not.

But I continued to attend Caxton Hall (when I was not with Dadaji in Neasden or Sat Prem in Devon). Sometimes I would feel cool and would come away as though I had enjoyed a spiritual emetic – an esoteric dose of bran. On other occasions there would be nothing. Do you feel the vibrations? they would ask,

196

and I would experience only heat, sweat, puffiness and great pressure in the head, as though it were going to blow off. And when I extended my hands towards others nothing happened at all. The explanation for this was that my vishuddi had been so damaged by bad living that it had deadened all the nerves of the arms and the fingers, which it controlled, so I could not be aware of anyone else's blocks. Indeed I felt extremely silly standing there. The strength, after all, of the technique lay in the experience; unless you felt the energy and the vibrations working within you, Sahaja Yoga simply appeared a bit madder than any other technique. Like myself people were often so blocked, so insensitive, that they received very little, if any, experience at all. It was ironic: it seemed you were 're-alised' without realising it. 'I've got realisation just because I've got a cool breeze in my hands,' one boy had scoffed.

Human beings have grown so insensitive in this Kali Yoga, Mataji would say, they are like cats without whiskers, blunder-ing about all over the place: as men have grown more civilised and urban they have lost much of their sensitivity and in-tuition. So far as my own realisation went, I must confess that I thought very little of it. I still had my preconceived notion of realisation, as understood from Paul Brunton. It would cer-tainly be some sort of sensation, perhaps an explosion of light, a spiritual trance, some sort of brilliant illumination resulting in total transformation, a flooding of instant wisdom. As it was, I hardly felt anything. There was, however, a Sahaja Yogic explanation for this. Hitherto realisation had been very difficult; one had to spend a whole life preparing for it; one withdrew from society, cleansing, purifying each chakra in turn, establishing it, so that when realisation came it was very strong, very powerful, lasting. Now people came out of order, crippled; their health, their emotions, their minds crippled by cigarettes, alcohol and bad living. It was no wonder, said the Sahaja Yogis, that the experience is so diluted.

Sometimes my crew of curiosity-seekers would accompany me to the meetings. Like myself they would be riveted by the extraordinary aspect of the scene. Subtle, you must become more subtle, Mataji would counsel: you must concentrate on the subtle – this is so subtle you have no idea. Alas! my com-panions and I often did have no idea, our attention was con-

197

stantly diverted by the gross and the superficial. Some complained that Mataji was too exotic for them, too foreign, that the technique was alien to Western culture, others found her too middle class – not exotic enough. Some found her irrational and disliked the way she criticised the other gurus. This she did on every possible occasion. They are devils, she said, their aims are to mess up seekers, spoil their chance of evolution. They are psychic gangsters, pirates, who employ occult devices to damage the delicate human vibratory system. Look how they will never explain their methods: you can't understand it, they say, it is beyond understanding. They are employing all occult devices: hypnotism, magnetism, autosuggestion, spirit possession, thought implantations. There is no end to the astonishing devices with which these gurus befuddle their disciples. She knew of one lady, the sister of a friend of hers, who had been hypnotised by a famous guru into giving her all her money. He appeared to her in a dream and asked for all her diamonds. This same guru (who preaches the pure life) often appears to his disciples in dreams and makes violent love to them; five ladies, Mataji had heard, are employed to bathe him in milk and honey. Police files are full of people who have mysteriously vanished without trace, believed murdered by these terrible thugs. Ravana, Rasputin, Hitler, Herod, you name the horrible person and there he is reincarnated as a modern guru. Christ himself has pointed out in the Bible that false prophets would come, misleading many, that they would claim to be messiahs, declare to be God, producing many signs and wonders. Well, they are all thugs. Ask the vibrations: you will see. Down, one by one, all my heroes were struck, not even poor Yogananda passed muster, and the only relatively modern guru whom Mataji could countenance was Ramana Maharishi.

She would surely have thrown a fit if she had seen Sat Prem. I had in fact taken him to meet her but at the time she was incapacitated by some operation she had had on her ear (the result, seemingly, of everyone's bad vibrations), and we were received by one of her disciples who had had a distinctly glazed look on his face and spoke in a funny stilted way, rather like a robot.

'I hope that's not a picture of Rajneesh you have round your neck,' he said. 'He's an awful man.'

'I quite agree with you,' said Sat Prem.

'Then why do you allow yourself to wear it?'

'I'm not responsible for what I wear,' said Sat Prem.

'Pardon?'

'No. This body is wearing this medalla in order to provoke. Some people, you, for example, are provoked. Some are attracted, some people don't see it at all.'

'Well, why do you allow yourself to wear it?'

Sat Prem changed the subject. 'How long have you been with Mataji?'

'Four years.'

'You seem very tight.'

'Pardon?'

'You seem very tense.'

'I've found the truth.'

'You've found what?'

'The truth. It's obvious that Mataji is the truth. She's the reincarnation of God.'

'We're all reincarnations of God,' Sat Prem said dryly. 'What kind of sickness does Mataji have?'

'Something to do with her inner ear. Since she's had her operation the weather has cleared marvellously.'

'Ah! That was the work I was doing in Devon with that stone,' said Sat Prem, looking across at me. 'Now I'd like to be very quiet and give Mataji some energy for five minutes.' He breathed heavily for a while. 'Now in about three days time Mataji will ask for a glass of water and she will be quite restored to health.'

Outside he gave me a large wink. 'You take these people too seriously,' he said. 'Never judge a guru by his disciples. But the energy was good there: Mataji's energy is good.'

If we are to believe Sahaja Yoga our energy is all too often appropriated by sorcerers and spirits. We are victims of a cosmic struggle; of a plot devised by the satanic forces to overcome the world. Unbeknown to us our psyches are nothing but cosmic battlegrounds for the forces of good versus those of evil. And here we encounter those bogey-men again: the Tantrics. According to Sahaja Yoga, all the ancient demons are Tantric sorcerers who yesterday were reincarnated as Herod, Rasputin and Co. and today are gurus and false prophets.

They are everywhere, these sorcerers, penetrating the media, the world of show business, the arts and publicity, diverting the attention towards sex and pornography, The permissive society is nothing but an opus of these sorcerers who have had the devilish notion to present sexual degradation as a tool for spiritual growth, to confuse sexual perversion with spiritual enlightenment. Just as, in India, they have taken over art, carving lust and passion all over the temples, insulting the gods in their sanctuaries, so they profane the human body (which is after all only a temple of God), doing whatever is possible to insult the deities and to spoil the nadis and chakras therein. If the seeker falls into the Tantrika trap the attention of God ultimately recedes and the satanic guru may then introduce a spirit (known in the Sahaja Yogic vernacular as a 'boot,' presumably after the Sanskrit 'bhuta') into a chakra – this is called initiation. The entity acts like a parasite on the nervous system, sucking the host's energy so that he becomes debilitated, his attention is disintegrated and he confuses the effect of spirit possession with spiritual awakening.

The atmosphere around us is, according to Sahaja Yoga, a bank of spirits, which are filed either in the sub- or the supraconscious ready to be inserted into our psyches. On the left side in the collective subconscious are those weak souls who have ended up overwhelmed by conditioning and bad habits; on the right side are the domineering shades who have overdone their physical, mental and ambitious activities. Through occult practices the sorcerers have acquired the means to overpower and control all these 'boots', depraved and otherwise, and inoculate them into the psyches of their victims, always matching a corresponding spirit to its subject, the weak receiving the weak, the imperious entertaining the spirit of some general perhaps, some dictating executive, so that the imbalance may be further exaggerated.*

* Sahaja Yogic theory is that Hitler was the medium for right-sided spirits. His mentor Karl Hanshoffer when a general in the First World War exhibited clairvoyant powers and was in close contact with Tibetan tantric sets who were working on the pingala nadi. The core of the Nazi secret doctrine was the preparation of a super race which would welcome on earth the Luciferian advent of outside powers that were supra-conscious demons. During his first phase, Hitler used supra-conscious powers for his political ascent but he was overpowered and the forces of evil used him instead. As he spoke his

The techniques of these sorcerers are, it seems various. They may use brain-washing devices and meditations. They may draw the victim's consciousness into drugs, alcohol and perverted sex. They may introduce the entity through food, thus implanting it into the nabhi (stomach) chakra. They may attack the heart and the vishuddi (throat) by talismans and necklaces. Direct contact is not necessary. Often pictures and statues are used; as the attention of the human being is drawn into the symbol the spirit may be sucked from the sub- or the supra-consciousness to enter into the psyche. Mantras are a favourite vehicle. The guru will give the disciple a secret mantra: 'Rama', perhaps, 'Krishna', 'Aim', 'Rim', 'Klim', and then they give the same name to the spirit they are controlling. As the disciple goes on chanting the name the spirit, controlled by the sorcerer, enters into the psyche and settles down in the vacant area of the body. The disciple then may lose his reasoning, his critical sense and discrimination; his moral codes and understanding may go and he can be induced to do anything.

Nowadays the rational members of our society consider possession to be superstition – along with the notion of sin. But in the days of the New Testament, Christ and his apostles were always casting unclean spirits out from people who were paralysed, dumb, mad and otherwise unsound. Mental illness, according to Sahaja Yoga, is nothing but possession. If you go to extremes the negative entities will get you. When you do not move far from the centre, the chakras are not distorted and your life manifests in harmony and balance, but when your attention swings violently from right to left, and vice versa, the resulting tension causes disintegration, physical disease, or nervous breakdown, neuroses and psychosis. Spirits can enter easily into a distintegrated system through the ajnya (forehead) and nabhi chakras.

According to Sahaja Yoga negativity is as contagious as flu: as viruses are to the physical system, negative entities – 'boots' – are to the psyche. They are parasites the nervous system, sucking the vital energy and upsetting the mechanism. Symp-

_____

audiences would be swept up in a stream of hypnotic intoxication and torrents of spirits would flow through him into the hysterical crowd. The Nazi emblem, the reversed swastika, is well-known for its association with black magic.

toms of possession are immaturity, shakiness, irrationality, uncertainty, lack of confidence and nervousness. You become arrested, separated from the Self. Once a devil gets into you it starts to suck your energy, lowering your resistance so that more and more devils can enter, then you become an action station from which all the devils can jump into other people. What seems to be a run of bad luck may simply be an invasion of devils, and since the negative entities may spread from the person who is suffering the attack to yourself it is therefore contagious. Sometimes quite an intelligent spirit may penetrate you. He may not have completed his work and wants to operate through you. Mataji had known someone who had hidden in a cemetery during the war, he had been entered by the spirit of some Hatha Yogi and for years had been involuntarily turning somersaults, standing on his head and performing all kinds of complicated asanas, although he had never in his life done any exercises. Writing about someone who dies under doubtful circumstances can be a very bad thing. One friend of mine was writing about a woman who had had the misfortune to die from thirst in the water butt in which she was escaping from aborigines. Pages in reference books were always falling open at the right place and all sorts of other strange coincidences occurred. The disciples nodded. They were not at all surprised. Yes, this lady probably wanted to be reborn and saved and was trying to take over her biographer.

The notion of possession seemed to me, although bizarre, to be eminently feasible. Had I not myself experienced being taken over by a devil? I had even seen it. And I had come across plenty of people whose actions suggested some sort of psychic interference. Roy had definitely seemed possessed, while the styles of Mrs Harvey and Vijay, to name two, implied a certain delusion.

The question of God was more difficult to swallow. Mataji, her disciples said, was God. 'To grant you salvation my children, I have come with all my powers,' she had assured them. That an Indian housewife somewhat on the plump side and on her own admission middle-class was the all-pervading power, the Shakti, the Virgin Mary Herself, the Holy Ghost, did not hold water for some: 'the vicar', for example, who had insisted on coming along and had accordingly been baptised by Mataji.

'That lady, according to that Swiss boy, in an incarnation of the Holy Ghost,' he had spluttered after the meeting. He was more inclined to be impressed by the Swiss boy than by Mataji: his feet, he said, were so spiritual – even if his toe-nails were a bit yellow – and his hands were beautifully cared for. He had what 'the vicar' called 'fluid' and 'the vicar' embarked on some complicated negotiation involving a bed-sitting room in the apartment of some Egyptian princess. The Swiss boy, however, was not interested. His only concern was Sahaja Yoga. He, like the other disciples, was always seeing Mataji in visions. One told me that Mataji had been working on his chakras and had asked him to hold his breath. Then something seemed to grow in her, to come out of her physical body and stand over him. It was difficult to describe the apparition, because although it looked familiar it was outside the human dimension, but it seemed like a sort of universal personality or archetype. Another boy had had the following dream before meeting her. He was fighting with a strong and evil man when suddenly there came the sound of a hunting horn and a lot of animals rushed out of the forest. After them stepped men dressed in scarlet and gold clothes leading white hounds surrounded by birds and doves and more men and women dressed in scarlet and gold riding white horses. And finally there came a very beautiful woman also dressed in scarlet and gold riding a white horse, wearing a diamond-shaped ruby on the left ring finger. Behind her a magnificent stag with golden antlers shining in the sun broke out of the forest. Then came the king. He was invisible and surrounded by four men who formed a square. Behind him came a riderless horse which was his. He had still to manifest and mount it. Now the dreaming boy knew that evil had no chance.

Did I believe that Mataji was the Goddess? In a word: God? I can honestly say that I neither believed nor disbelieved it. I simply ignored it. To this end I may or may not have had a bonus, able as I was to blot out of my mind anything that I did not like. Any aspects of Sahaja Yoga, anything that Mataji said that seemed questionable, I simply dismissed, and this happened almost unconsciously.

It seemed to me that all these things were unimportant, like some television programme going on at the other end of the room, or the continuous buzz of flies on the ceiling. The real thing seemed to be this stream of energy. Besides, the technique made one feel good. Mataji herself, however, certainly believed it. 'I have always known who I am,' she said. 'I have come to save the world. The sun, the moon, the stars the sea, all this has come from me. This has to be realised.' People have never recognised their saviours – look how Christ was treated. Now, this time, everyone had better recognise her and be saved. The Swiss boy believed it and so did the small dark one, the one who had been so aggressive to Roy, who was Greek. Indeed the Greek could not understand how there could be any difficulty. 'I mean, what is it?' he asked, shaking his head, bewildered. 'I mean Mataji *is*, she just *is*.'

Soon after the seminar at Easthampstead a Sahaja Yogi circular arrived. This was about an Indian festival called Navratri, celebrated to commemorate the goddess Bhagavati, the Mother of the Universe. 'This auspicious celebration recalls the victory won by the Great Goddess, thousands of years ago, over the hosts of demons who had gained the overlordship of the Earth.' Today, it continued, most of these demons have reincarnated as fake spiritual leaders to mislead 'the naive, all too naive, seekers. It is more than ever appropriate to duly commemorate Navratri asking the Goddess to protect all the children. We in London are immensely privileged and blessed to be in a position to hold a puja* in the holy physical presence of the Mother of the Universe who has incarnated in the gracious form of H.H. Mataji Nirmala Devi'.

The puja was celebrated in Finchley. Three of us novices were honoured by being delegated to wash the Mother of the Universe's feet from which, we were told, flow powerful and purifying vibrations. First we made a pudding with flour, honey, sugar, ghee, water, milk and yoghurt, and with this we massaged the feet; next we anointed them with red dye and painted them with swastikas – the sacred symbol of the triumph of spirit over matter. After lunch came another purifying ceremony – a havan, which consisted of throwing flowers, ghee, rice and scented powders into the fire to cast out 'boots.' Afterwards there was no doubt that I felt marvellous,

* Many words derived from Sanskrit may be spelt alternatively: thus pooja or puja.

energy rushing through me and not a hint of unease lurking anywhere.

Mataji's teaching certainly gave me a new dimension. 'You cannot imagine the beauty of human beings,' she would say (and indeed I could not), 'but how often you conceal your beauty in moods. Thank God for the beautiful flowers: the flowers don't have moods. You must laugh at yourselves and your silly moods – don't play all that melancholy music, all that romantic nonsense, don't treat yourselves so seriously, use humour. Look, at yourselves. Ah! here's vanity, ego: come along, recognise yourselves, how you're working. See the humour and the joy of life. Move into another sphere: act through radiation rather than action: by radiation this is how it is going to be done.'

There is no doubt that I received results, or should I say sensations? The first came about a month after the seminar. I had been sitting for a while, quite peaceful and relaxed, and I experienced a definite movement of energy, a strange sort of cool, radiating, glowing energy, which ran up both the outer channels within me and lifted up into a balloon in the head. The mind was still there churning out thoughts but pushed to one side so that, instead of being involved and identified with them, you could see they were like flies buzzing around. After a little a radiant shaft of energy shot up my centre so that I felt taut, erect. You felt there was a supporting rod travelling up the backbone, and with it came great elation. The whole of my body rejoiced; it felt as though every pore, every vein, every nerve was joining in the Alleluiah chorus of *Messiah*. All the body united in this expression, there was a definite widening of area, a feeling of space, of losing the outlines of the body and a very definite feeling at the top of the head, a gentle disturbance. It felt so comfortable, so safe, as though I was protected by waves of gossamer. And later the centre of energy remained, a cool clean core to which you could refer back. Then two nights later, my body went absolutely hollow. I felt empty, a clean clear instrument. And outside there was suddenly a wild winter whirring, and a flock of geese passed over the house to their feeding grounds – and this was in Putney. These moments of stillness and beauty were unfortunately only flashes in the pan. More often, emotions, anxieties and habits would reclaim my attention and I would identify with them rather than with that clear-flowing spirit, which all too easily disappeared from the mind. Even so it was strangely luxurious to set out for Caxton Hall or Finchley and know that no one would dissipate you, no one would demand anything from you, that you were going to restore and refresh yourself, return exhilarated, charged with energy. It was rather like setting off for a holiday. And there was a magic: the cold winter night outside and inside a warm delicious cosiness, so soothing, so relaxing.

Sometimes Mataji would massage our spines. Sometimes at certain points a throbbing, a pulsation, would be clearly invisible under the skin: look, she would say, the kundalini is pulsating, it is blocked at this point, you can see it. Three large bumps rose up on the neck of one disciple: this, said Mataji, is all his guilt, he has taken on the guilt of the world. She rubbed the bumps and gradually they became less. I myself apparently suffered from a bad liver (no wonder, from all that drink). I must sit cross-legged while Mataji sat with her feet applied to my side. My whole body heated up. Next she gave me a scalp massage and a lovely clean force travelled up, competing with the discomfort of the heat and the aches induced by prolonged sitting in such an uncomfortable posture.

December brought several letters from Vijay on the romantic writing paper, this time depicting two people perched on a rocky cliff. 'Now or any time you're just a thought away from me.' Since leaving him on Allahabad railway station in February there had been silence, but now it seemed the winter rains were lubricating old channels in his mind. He had been posted from Allahabad to somewhere in the Himalayas near a tiger reservation and I must go and stay with him for at least a month. 'I shall forever remain yours and you must be mine as well,' he reiterated in his old vein, 'therefore it's God's wish to have come in each other's lives so please remain mine and you will see that it's not just a thought, but a reality which shall end only with our lives.' My last visit had been very quick, not interesting as he had expected it to be, yet his wife was still asking about me, she was sure we were in love, indeed she had wanted us to be alone in Allahabad to make love. Poor thing, it seemed to me to have been the last thing she would have wanted!

I wrote back a prim little letter; I was indeed returning to India but with a group (Mataji was going to India in January and I was travelling with her); I had completely changed and was interested only in God. I had given up all notions of adulterous affairs. Vijay was undaunted. He replied that he knew the 'old lady' with whom I was to go around. Indeed he had taken her out with her disciples during the Kumbh Mela in the jeep one night to meet Deoraha Baba (words fail me at the idea of Mataji at the Kumbh Mela surrounded by all those 'horrible people'. Vijay meanwhile was still determined to come to Delhi to meet me at the airport and retained his possessive, proprietary air. 'Your love and relations is very pure and not hidden,' he assured me, 'certainly not adulterous.' Indulging in shallow, hard-drinking society companions made a person cheap and degraded, he was glad I was going to stop this. Why wouldn't I think of marrying him? 'I am seriously thinking in this line, only if you permit.' Meanwhile would I do him a favour? And he listed some articles he would like me to bring him: lighters, air pistols, sleeping bag, 'steel or gold case', 'spray/ordinary scents for me of your choice'... Here seemed to me to be the prime example of self-delusion. Whatever I said, whatever I did, whatever I wrote, made absolutely no difference to what he thought. Reality, to him, was whatever went on in his head. Here again the essence of madness was encapsulated: you thought and acted quite regardless of the climate of opinion, of how others thought and acted.

Before we departed for India there was a New Year's Day celebration. New Year's Day 1979 was one of those rare glittering white days that come to London with a fresh fall of snow. Never had I seen Putney more beautiful. The roads lay untrodden, overhead the trees were like white lace against the azure sky. The air seemed to crack with energy. I was filled with exhilaration even before I reached the celebrations. I felt absolutely free, liberated. Anything seemed possible. And the feeling stayed with me all day, growing stronger, clearer. When I returned in the evening it was as though I were floating, levitating, zinging; there is no other word for it. Even Roy could feel the effect. 'I love your vibrations,' he said. 'I *love* them.'

Shortly after this, Mataji left for India. Three weeks later I set out to join her in the company of a Jungian psychiatrist, a Parsee, the product of an Oxbridge education who was now absolutely committed to Sahaja Yoga. Certainly there would have been no room in our luggage for a single item on Vijay's list. We were loaded to the hilt, carrying with us cheese, chocolates, sausages, plastic tea-sets, safari and dressing up suits, piles of saris, cassettes and films. We had been delegated to take Mataji's extra luggage together with presents for all the other Sahaja Yogis in India. Books, however, were notable for their absence. Sahaja Yogis do not read books, or at least they are not encouraged to do so – bad for the agnya (the small dark Greek had burnt all his books the moment he met Mataji). Innocent humour, though, is encouraged and the psychiatrist had brought with him a volume of *Peanuts* against the journey, when he was not immersed in that he was telling me of the forces of evil ('they are everywhere'). According to him, ninety percent of the world's population is mad – due to its being possessed. Only a few nights ago he had had a dreadful dream, a boy from the Carribean had appeared with his throat slit and tried to stifle him. He had woken with the dream and the terror engrained in his memory, and had spent the morning saying mantras until at last the pressure had released – he was often going on about the pressure releasing.

That trip to India was in a sense two journeys – physical and metaphysical, We were there, Mataji told us on the first day, to go deeper into ourselves, to achieve peace, joy and divinity. We should see only beauty and joy in everything. Now only Sahaja Yogis are our family, our only responsibility.* No one outside Sahaja Yoga is important. Mataji is our mother and we are her children: her antennae, her projections; we are the wires transforming the energy from the source. What joy we should receive from our fellow yogis! We must try and feel more love towards one another. We must above all be positive, strong, not afraid of anything. We must be *exceptional* people. We must have authority. Here we will be secure, all our physical and material necessities will be cared for: we need not, must

* Actually Mataji places a high value on the ordinary family structure. In no way does she try to alienate you, but encourages ties with your parents and children.

not, worry about material things. God will take care of those. Why should we worry about money? Our job is to enter into the spirit: Mataji is the core into which we must surrender ourselves, into which we must dissolve, this is how we are going to ascend. We must cleanse and purify ourselves so that the energy can flow through. We must use every opportunity to establish ourselves. We must go out and fight negativity. We are the foundations of tomorrow's universe. We must keep diaries in which to write down everything that Mataji says, just like the Gospel – comprehension is not necessary.

We were a motley crew, we European Sahaja Yogis, we founders of tomorrow's universe, about ten of us altogether, with among us the small dark Greek, Philip from Birmingham who had a music hall sense of humour, and a Scottish lady who spent the time practising her shorthand and talking about her Arabian friend, Mr Daz. There was very little about Mr Daz that we did not know: how he slept in a cupboard on a shelf and ate bread and water with a little black dahl in the evenings. Certainly Mr Daz must have enjoyed more privacy than we did. With Sahaja Yoga, being a collective movement, privacy was a thing of the past. But this lack of privacy was by no means the same as Rajneesh's. The idea of joining someone in the bathroom for whatever function would have been horrifying to a Sahaja Yogi. This was not so much lack of physical privacy as psychic. We should do nothing on our own, everyone must do it (the result seemed to me was that no one ever did anything). In Bombay we lived in a modern tower block. The men slept in one room which during the day was used for meditation and Mataji's darshan, while we women slept, as many sometimes as ten squashed together, with all the luggage, which consisted mainly of dirty washing.

You should look like an English lady, Mataji had told one girl. Accordingly she had travelled to India with tweed coats and skirts and little dresses and now these were all dumped round the room since there was nowhere to hang or to put anything. A young Indian Sahaja Yogi called Ardhout was charged with caring for our physical needs, guiding us to meetings and about the country on journeys. We nearly drove him mad. Washing? we would ask each morning, pointing to the increasing pile. Yes, yes, yes, he would say, she is coming. No problem. Certainly, there *should* have been no problem. India is above all a land abundant in washermen and washerwomen. But by next day no one would have come. Washing? Yes, yes, yes, he would say again impatiently. 'All these questions: I am getting a bad agnya.' Just as Sahaja Yogis do not read, neither do they plan. Planning is a waste of energy. Everything works out automatically. We'll see how it works out, one would hear, over and over again. So we waited for the washing to work out. But the washerwoman never did materialise and in the end we had to resort to the dry cleaning firm in the road below (it turned out to be the most expensive in Bombay).

The guru is supposed to exercise you in all kinds of ways, some subtle, some obvious, Mataji, apparently, is always devising big and little tests for her disciples; anything out of the ordinary, any dilemma, was pronounced to be 'Mataji's maya'. The whole of that trip seemed to me to be a series of tests for our powers of observation and detachment. Never before had a sense of humour come in so useful. There were often, for example, twenty people queueing in the morning to use the bathroom (Rajneesh's policies might have been positively practical here). Matters were not improved by the fact that all over India, no matter where you are, the water and electricity are turned off from ten in the morning to some time in the late afternoon, so there was no question of nipping in later when everything was quiet. Ardhout would be running up and down. Hurry, please, everyone, we have to go to the programme ... the train ... the bus. You must have had a bath, you must have clean clothes. The easiest thing was to go round in a daze. No doubt I wasted a lot of energy laughing to myself about how other people would have reacted. Horace for example with his need for privacy, plans and routine, would have gone mad and there was another man who was obsessed by exercise, always in the gym or skipping, swimming or dashing about on a horse, he would have gone mad too, and in this I nearly joined him, since all the time we were in India we were expected to consume large meals, yet had hardly any exercise at all.

We now lived in a new world, governed by new values in which the unconscious played a large role. Let the unconscious come through, we were counselled. And indeed it seemed that the unconscious had come through for a few people. One who hitherto had not had a note in her head could sing beautifully, while another could draw miraculously. We were, above all, governed by vibrations. Food, for example: one would not concentrate on the cooking, on the taste, texture or bouquet, but on the vibrations of the food. All gross things, it seemed, had a subtle echo. There were some strange little bits of hair and stick lying round our room, together with jars containing what looked like the dregs of dirty water. These belonged to the Greek. The hair was Mataji's, the sticks, it seemed, she had chewed on some occasion. They all, he assured me, had quite exquisite vibrations. As for the water, it is considered most auspicious to drink the liquid in which Mataji's feet have been washed, while the puddings, the unguents, which are stirred upon her feet during the pujas are carefully conserved as panaceas against all ills. Nothing is considered more beneficial than the leftovers from Mataji's plate: the residue is reverently passed round after meals and shared out. Vibrations, vibrations, vibrations, everything was a question of vibrations. The greatest threat of all was that we would lose our vibrations. I never quite knew what that meant. Every so often we would have our vibrations tested – this meant that you knelt with your head on Mataji's feet and everyone stood round to see what was the matter, rather like putting out your tongue for the doctor. Left swadistan, (lower stomach) people would chorus, nabhi, very bad mooladhara (genitals).

Much of our time was spent in public, as it were. There would be large meetings in Bombay. First of all there would be a lecture and then we would proceed to heal people or to 'work on' them as it was called. The Indian Sahaja Yogis had a much easier system for testing a patient's defects, they would place their hands on the person's head where all the chakras of the body are represented, recognising imbalances by heat in various parts of the cranium. We would travel in trains and buses out to the villages, or up to hill stations, through woods of red blossom and fields with haystacks on stilts. Philip chattered all the way. Are there any shops? he would wonder. The Scottish lady, who had taken against him announcing that he had tried to touch her up and would not leave her alone – would look up from her shorthand with a cackle. 'Go on, lay another egg,' Philip would urge. 'Have you ever been on one of those speak-your-weight machines? Out comes a little card: there's two of you on there, it says, will one of you get off?' 'My agnya is catching with so much talking,' Ardhout would say.

We spent a lot of time in the villages. The women would come to be blessed by Mataji, the barren ones being pushed forward. Women in Europe don't like their children, Mataji told them. They drink, they become like men. The village women in their bright saris, coloured flowers in their hair, looked amazed. There was no doubt that these people in the villages really celebrated the appearance of Mataji. It reflected their attitude towards authority. The worship of gods, goddesses and gurus is accepted as part of Indian life and, it seemed to me, lies mirrored in the behaviour of the Indian family. It is a normal thing to find children venerating their parents, who are in a sense guru figures, just as the guru is a mother or a father figure, the two are interchangeable. In the West the majority neither esteems nor believes apparently either in parents or God – and, if the attitude towards God is ambivalent, towards a goddess it is more so, she has definitely been relegated to paper, where she lies safely between two covers, shrouded in mystery, smacking of Celts, deographers, mist and mountains. But in those villages Mataji was welcomed as the living Goddess, the Devi, of that there seemed no doubt. Those celebrations were some of the most stirring I have ever seen. Everything – eating, singing, music – was performed in praise of the Goddess, in praise of God. First there would be a great reception committee. A bullock cart would carry Mataji; the bullocks streaked green, adorned with embroidered cloths, their horns painted; the cart decorated with palm fronds and potted plants, escorted on either side by ladies balancing on their heads water pots containing coconuts and smoking incense. Then the band: drums, pipes, fiddles and an unmelodious instrument like a long drainpipe which every five minutes or so was banged on the ground, affording a loud explosion. Finally, would come all the village, dancing, whirling like dervishes, throwing up in the air clouds of red powder, crushing the herbs at the side of the road so that the fragrance of bruised mint rose with the incense as the dancers gyrated to the central square of the village where the meeting would be held.

They were packed, those meetings, people would squeeze into unbelievably small spaces, some perching in trees like parrots. Mataji would be introduced in whatever tongue was local to the area. The gist would be that living without God was like eating food without salt – insipid. Without God we are incomplete and unbalanced. Now, through Mataji, we may be connected to God. It is like a bank, if we don't have a bank account we may not draw cheques. If we don't have a connection with God we may not draw divine energy. After Mataji's lecture there would be the usual group meditation. In those villages nearly everyone would feel the cool breeze. The simpler people are, Mataji would explain, the easier it is, the stronger the experience. Certainly, it was elating: being in the presence of hundreds of exhilarated people is a powerful experience.

We ourselves spent much time in the sea with Mataji – nothing, she said, was more cleansing than the sea. Indeed all the elements – earth, air, water, fire and ether – could be used since they are all components of our bodies. So we bathed, but not in the Western sense, since Mataji and Sahaja Yogis believe that exposing the body to the sun is harmful – bad for the liver. Thus we bathed in our clothes, or rather, with the January sun sinking behind the palm trees, we stood up to our waists in the luke-warm water, since Indians are on the whole frightened of the sea and unable to swim. Philip, it seemed to me, had started to grow breasts. He was apparently planning a sex change operation. This caused consternation within the segregated circles of Sahaja Yoga, since it seemed that he preferred to sleep in the ladies' quarters and had done so once or twice before being removed. Mataji pronounced that he had been penetrated by the spirit of some lady who was taking him over – clearly the village gossip, which would explain all his chattering. Later that morning a dark haze rose out of the sea: that, said Mataji, was all our bad vibrations, and everywhere in the sparkling air little lights flickered. On one occasion we stood on the sea shore, when it was supposed to be low tide. Look! everyone exclaimed. The sea is coming to meet us, look, it is coming up right to Mataji's feet! It is a real miracle; high tide when it is supposed to be low! Much as I would have liked to see large waves enveloping us, in all honesty I could see no difference. The Indian Sahaja Yogis were furnished with copious tales of miracles performed by Mataji, countless tales of healing, cases where it had been thought there was no hope, of husbands being rescued from the grip of heart attacks, cancer and so forth.

We covered a great deal of ground that trip. Mataji had a programme at the Kovalam Beach Hotel in Kerala. How beautiful it was in Kerala, with purple bougainvillea frothing, cascading, against the blue seas and skies, striped chipmunks everywhere and crows cawing in the orange evenings. How astonishing those sunsets were, the sun sinking into the sea, turning the sky to vermilion, pink, then grey, like satin. And how comfortable the coconut forests in whose cool shade the villages sheltered, intersected by sandy paths, lagoons and canals. As for the Kovalam Beach Hotel, it was farcical! There we were in this luxurious honeymoon resort, complete with swimming pool, bars, musak and the most appalling food and service (all the cooks, it seemed, had gone to Dubai, indeed a plane came weekly to recruit workers). There we were, this spiritual group, the Devi and her disciples, in this most sybaritic and materialistic of places, consuming prawn cocktails (prawns swimming in unspeakable thousand island sauce). One of the Indian Sahaja yoginis had very sensibly developed anorexia; she sat through each meal immobile in front of the disgusting platefuls. We had been joined now by the psychiatrist's mother, an invalid, a diabetic with a bad heart and bad eyesight, who for five years had been unable to lie down at nights, and by two decidedly portly middle-aged ladies lumbering around a bit like elephants; one, whose name I heard to be Miss Moriarty, went nowhere without wheeling behind her a small canvas bag loaded with goodies in case she required a snack – biscuits, sweets, roasted vermicelli and other savoury Indian titbits.

There had been some confusion in promoting Mataji's tour and only a small circular had been placed in the rooms, discreetly concealed beneath the laundry list and bar tariff. Honeymoon couples, it seemed, were not interested in self-realisation. No one turned up for the morning session and we had to go out and canvas, something I found acutely embarrassing. Nearby there was, I discovered, a hippy beach, much

214

like any other hippy beach in India, the freaks lying out naked in the sun, dosing themselves with acid and hash and reading *War and Peace*. Some staggered along to the evening sessions, half-naked. 'Wow!' gasped one called Cloud, who was wearing a dress covered with black skulls. 'I met a giant chessboard on the way here.' Most of the Indian Sahaja Yogis were very shocked by the hippies. 'Why do you ask us to treat those horrible people?' they asked Mataji. 'What have we done to annoy you?' 'Our nabhis are catching from all those drugs, all that sun, our mooladharas...' And indeed most of the hippies were suffering from hepatitis, stomach troubles and unsatisfactory love affairs. The Indian Sahaja yoginis sat round with lemons clutched to their heads, or sometimes they sank to the floor in a fit of Victorian vapours. Actually the Indian Sahaja yoginis were altogether rather like Victorian ladies, very inert, interested mostly in shopping, new saris and marriage. This last topic seemed to be one which the Devi herself found totally absorbing and she spent much time arranging matches for her male followers.

Back at Kovalam, the final straw to our vibrations was a visit to a village nearby. We drove out through the beautiful forests to the shores of a lake. There in the middle of the trees a table had been dumped down, decorated with a vase of flowers. One of the first of the villagers to arrive was a boy with a chain round his ankle and a very sinister-looking head, all shaved and raw, plastered down with cow-dung. The whole place was riddled with black magic, someone hissed. The oldest inhabitants, so frail they could hardly sit in the chairs provided for them, were placed in front of Mataji, where they trembled with heaven knew what affliction. The village, it appeared, was possessed. Those not afflicted with asthma were down with leprosy. That village, together with the hippies, nearly finished off the poor Indian Sahaja yogis. As for myself, I felt queasier and queasier as the day progressed until I was suddenly and inelegantly sick outside Mataji's room. Next day I still felt awful. Thoughts raced through my head. What on earth was I doing here with all these inert people? Caught something, they all said. Go and sit in the sea and clear yourself out. I did.

One evening I came across an extraordinary sight in the swimming pool. The psychiatrist was standing knee deep, his

215

hands held out towards the moon. His eyes were starting from his head, his hair was moving backwards and forwards (releasing the pressure from the agnya, and he was discoursing to a couple from Dakota on death: on which occasion the soul breaks into two, the being and the energy, the being then goes off to wait somewhere until it is ready for its rebirth. It has taken millions of years for us to evolve from an amoeba to a human being, the psychiatrist told them, at least our centres are ready to be awakened now that we have reached the human stage. At this, the couple from Dakota looked doubtful, as though they suspected that neither the psychiatrist nor I could possibly be human at all.

At the end of our stay in Kovalam we drove to Cape Comarin to watch the famous sunrise and to perform a puja on the beach. The Tamil Nadu country was beautiful – bright green rice fields fringed by high brown hills whose ridges, silhouetted against the sky, made the faces of gods and giants. It was a day of elephants and drums; garlands of sweet flowers; monkeys with erect tails and huge banyan trees all gnarled, their branches writhed and knotted, hanging down like tendrils, on which small girls swung, their cotton skirts billowing. We visited temples at sunset, where orange light filtered through carved, traced windows, throwing exquisite patterns over the ground. Less romantically, I shared a room with Miss Moriarty and the psychiatrist's mother. We lodged at the Tamil Nadu Tourist Bungalow where neither of my companions was pleased with the facilities. Only one glass, they grumbled. No water, what nonsense! Neither the psychiatrist's mother nor I slept a wink. The former spent the night propped bolt upright on my luggage; I meanwhile crammed everything available into my ears against Miss Moriarty, who, when not rootling about in her canvas bag for snacks, was snoring as lustily as a litter of pigs. Nor was the sunrise next morning in the least spectacular, since the line of sea was obscured by a bank of cloud. Nevertheless the puja, which was to ensure abundant harvests in India, or something of that sort, took place according to plan. Soon we were back in Bombay where Miss Moriarty's canvas bag burst open and all her snacks were distributed over the airport floor.

We were off again, almost at once, to Wardha in the north of

216

Maharashtra, where we spent a few days with Mataji's sister and husband, both of whom have devoted their lives to the cause of Gandhi, whose famous ashram is nearby. We had come especially for the anniversary of Mataji's father's death, in honour of which a competition between the surrounding village schools was being celebrated: devotional freedom songs, whose theme was liberation from British rule. The children had an incredible sense of rhythm, accompanying the singers with tablas, sitars, cymbals and harmoniums. Most of the audience, however, paid very little attention. Some talked, some tried to start the overhead fans with long poles, some tried to open the ventilators with what looked like huge grass-hooks and one sat heavily against a cupboard exhibiting Gandhi's cottage industry and broke it. The competition went on, what with the prize-giving by Mataji and the presentation of garlands, until 7.30 and then it was time to listen to more songs, this time rendered by Mataji's sister.

Next day we were to visit Gandhi's disciple Vinobabhave. We drove through flat country made lush and green by recent rain, and were ushered in to the presence. Vinobabhave reclined on a bed seeming very frail, wrapped in a yellowish blanket with a green hooded cap over his head. Did we know a language common to all people? he asked. 'Yes,' answered one of my bolder Sahaja Yogic brothers. 'Divine vibrations.' The sage paused a moment. Divine vibrations were rather difficult. He knew a language much simper than that. We should all clap our hands. now, who was the oldest among us? Philip (who later dropped his handbag down Gandhi's well) was fifty-seven years old? In our language we were always so many years *old*, said Vinobabhave, Annie Besant always said that she was so many years *young*. Anyway, he would teach us his language. He gestured that we should get up, get down, get up again and then go out: and that was sign language and the end of the performance. We all trooped out. 'A crackpot' was what Mataji called him.

In the middle of Gandhi's ashram there was a most beautiful tree radiating such cool vibrations that they could be felt refreshing the air for really quite a distance. The whole place was marvellously peaceful, the huts made of a cool, calm, brown mud. In the corner was a long pair of tweezers for catch-

217

ing snakes and a special box with which to convey them to the fields, where they would be liberated.

Much of our time on that trip was spent as the guests of various Indian Sahaja yogis. For our hosts nothing was too much trouble. Sometimes we would arrive in a place at four o'clock in the morning, but for them there was nothing unearthly about the hour. We would be received with guns firing salutes, bhajans, music, cups of tea, garlands and meals galore. The huge quantities of food we were expected to consume became something of an embarrassment. Even in the middle of a sight-seeing tour we might suddenly be conducted into a shop, an office, a tourist agency, and there cups of coffee and plates of idlis would materialise. They are so pleased to be able to feed you, Mataji would say. Damn pleased, one of them endorsed. Living like this was absolutely the other extreme to England; from being perpetually exhausted by doing too much one had moved to doing nothing physical at all. It was a case of too much food and too little exercise. Our days often consisted of meal after meal with perhaps the occasional waddle up some dusty hill to see a temple dedicated to a goddess – who was of course only Mataji in one of her previous lives. More often than not there would be a substantial breakfast with one of the disciples, then, if we were on progress, there would be a meeting in some village, in a marquee perhaps, set up in the village square, with the schoolmaster keeping his children in control with the aid of a long stick. Next there would be a massive lunch, eaten cross-legged on the floor, after which everyone would rest during the heat of the afternoon; the goats, the bullocks, the horses, would all be tethered under the shade of the banyan trees, mattresses would be brought and everyone, even the chickens, would sleep. Then out we would set again. In the setting sun the dusty thorny land of Maharashtra develops a soft radiant beauty: there is a feel of continuity as the long lines of bullock carts loaded high with bundles of sugar-cane bump home along the dusty roads. As we progressed, the lack of exercise made me more bourgeoise than ever, more and more exercised by my lack of activity. I would get up early and pace round the roof. I even performed some forbidden asanas (Sahaja Yogis do no exercises – bad for the swadistan). Then I would sneak down to the kitchen for some warm milk with which to mix my bran, collect a bucket of hot water and wait furtively by the bathroom door to slip in – along with everyone else who was doing the same. All of us were indeed developing a certain awareness, albeit about mundane things.

Once Mataji held a programme in a sugar-cane factory. Her throne was decorated with bougainvillaea and green branches were stuck into paint tins. The hall, which was huge, was packed; children were squeezed in, sitting crammed in every available space. Afterwards we were presented with silk embroidered shawls, garlands and coconuts. There we were, about twelve Europeans queueing up in that huge hall, whose air was thick with incense, to receive our presentation, and down came the word: 'We'll be able to get some washing done at the next stop!' After the ceremony we were led to a guest house where stainless steel tables groaned under mounds of assorted fruit. At last it seemed that there was a host who understood our problem. What a relief not to be facing another huge meal! So we ate the fruit gratefully: bananas, grapes, chickoos, apples. Half an hour later our hosts reappeared: now, please, it was time to move into the next room for dinner.... And there we were again, all those piled-up plates, all those succulent yellow curd dishes, sweet cakes, dahl, vegetables, salad, poppadums, chapatis and so on.

We stayed a while in Rahuri, a strange modern university built in the middle of that undulating thorny land. Out there in the distance the birds honked, the air rang and echoed with space. The university buildings rose up out of the dusty plain but already the walls were green with creepers and the gardens filled with luxuriant trees and bushes. Some of the professors were conducting interesting experiments with vibrations. For a year one had been treating his plants with small amounts of potash, nitrogen and vibrated water. There was no doubt that his banana and coconut trees were large and lush, while those of his neighbours, which had received only fertiliser, without the vibrations, were no match. Nor was this good banana country, yet the bananas in his garden were huge and juicy.

Down the path was Professor Chavan. He had a bottle-brush tree which during one year had doubled in size. His garden overflowed with roses, pomegranates and that perfumed climber, Queen of the Night. Either yogis should become scientists, the professor declared, or scientists yogis. As it is, yoga is a synthesis, seeking to make whole, while science is an analysis aiming to break into parts. So how can science hope to investigate yoga? How can a part examine a whole? Professor Chavan saw vibrations as a whole new science and was devising the means to experiment and measure the effect of vibrations on humans, animals and plants. But how can you explain vibrations in quantities? How can you measure them? There are at present simply not the facilities. It is, as someone has described scientists trying to measure gravity waves, the indefatigible in pursuit of the indistinguishable. Professor Chavan had been making considerable investigations into the functioning of his own energy and had, he said, devised a means of controlling and monitoring it at any point that he desired. He was so sensitive that he could locate on his fingers the exact spot where he had contracted a constriction on any chakra and could clear it accordingly. Often he would introduce Mataji at the lectures; no longer, he said, did he need to plan, to think at all, the necessary words flowed down from the unconscious.

Dhumal was another who often introduced Mataji; he too spoke fluently and powerfully. He was a farmer aged thirty-eight who, he said, had received his realisation in 1973, six years before. He had established a healing centre here in Rahuri where he achieved spectacular results, curing five or six polio victims, one gall-bladder patient and another suffering from cancer of the stomach. He ran his farm by a mixture of orthodox agricultural methods and vibrations. He vibrated his seed and his irrigation water: he dressed his crops with a balance of potash, nitrogen, potassium and vibrations; he never used insecticides or pesticides and had never been troubled by pests or diseases. Since vibrations, he said, his yield had increased by twenty-eight percent. He employed old-fashioned bullock power which, he claimed, was more suitable for cultivating those light soils than tractors, which pack down the ground, spoiling the drainage by suppressing the root action of the plants, so that eventually the land becomes exhausted and eroded. Vibrations plus these organic methods afforded him a yield of ninety-five metric tonnes of sugar-cane per acre, while his neighbours, he said, working with tractors and without vibrations produce eighty tonnes.

By now most of us, in spite of vibrations, had developed heavy colds. Sniffing and coughing, our party arrived in Poona where, for reasons of her own, Mataji decided it would be a good idea for me, escorted by the Greek, to pay a visit to the ashram of Rajneesh. 'You must be back for lunch,' shouted Dhumal, who was inclined to be bossy. 'That is compulsory.' But it was almost lunchtime before we had even arrived at the ashram. Sporting cardboard labels saying PRESS and ushered by a receptionist called Darshan to a great pavilion, we watched all the orange sannyasins dancing round to music, singing: 'Wake up, wake up, how long can you ignore, Bhagwan is knocking at your door?' All ages were engaged in this pursuit, from quite young children to geriatrics: one lady cavorted round with her baby strapped to her back and one venerable gentleman leaping about was plainly well over seventy. 'Celebration,' said one of the disciples, 'this is a great celebration, it's really wild.' After lunch everyone listens to a discourse delivered by 'Bhagwan'. For this people lay on the floor or stood on their heads. Rajneesh's voice had a hypnotic timbre with a strange hiss to it, he hissed out the esses. In this particular discourse it seemed that he was suggesting that Christ was something of a gourmet (and misunderstood by his mother): 'He isss the only messssenger from God who eatss, drinksss and enjoyssss: all that God hasss given man hasss to be usssed: renounciation hasss been a cursse: the world hasss not to be renounced: nothing issss to be denied.' At about three o'clock, in the middle of all this, there was suddenly a great gust of wind that rushed through the pavilion, knocking down one of the notice-boards, swirling round and dying down; and an image of Mataji came very clearly into my mind. As we left the pavilion we bumped into one of the boys who had been in Devon on Sat Prem's course. He was here, he said, with his wife. They had sold their house in Holland and given the proceeds – something like seventy thousand pounds – to Sat Prem, who had vanished.

Everything in that ashram was a whirl of activity. Rajneesh believed in keeping people occupied; there were approximately fifty different courses that you could take, to support *your* Quest', as Bernard Levin had noted, covering every sort of meditation, dance and martial art – to say nothing of pottery, dressmaking, jewellery, leatherwork and so on. It was like a meditation department store. When not meditating, potting, dressmaking, etcetera, disciples relaxed in the 'temple of smoking' or in Poona's luxury hotel, the Blue Diamond, which was situated coveniently close-by, with its swimming pool, iced gateaux and coffee shop, in which one of the sannyasins seemed to be changing his orange knickers. Couples could everywhere be seen 'denying nothing', standing in clinches in the middle of the road, staring into each other's eyes, stroking each other's backs and moving rhythmically together. All the sannyasins sported Indian names to show that they had rejected their old personalities. One of the exercises consisted apparently of not using the first person singular: everything must be geared to breaking down the old personality, the enemy, the ego, which stands between the sannyasin and his enlightenment, thus he must not refer to himself as 'I'. Conversations were inevitably inclined to be somewhat confused. Also the sannyasins would often break out into hysterical laughter in the middle of a conversation. I knew from my own experience with Sat Prem that this sort of treatment is uncomfortable, the whole of one's identity undergoes a crisis, and it seemed to me that many of these people were in a state of panic. My Greek companion, who had spent much of his time sprinkling the floor with vibrated powders, was absolutely clear in his view of Rajneesh's ashram at Poona. It was a giant holiday camp, he said, wherein people's irresponsibility was being sanctioned, and energy dissipated in the name of spirituality; people were hearing exactly what they wanted to hear. What Rajneesh was doing was sympathising with everyone in their difficulties and problems – and charging for it.

We must return early tomorrow morning for Rajneesh's darshan, urged Darshan. 'It is most important for you to hear Bhagwan speak.' This was unfortunately out of the question since we were to catch the train that night. We had created a furore by failing to turn up for lunch – which had that day been a special feast. 'We were just going to inform the police,' shouted Dhumal, hustling us off to the station. 'Yes, yes, yes, there have been many cases of people vanishing from that

222

place.' Mataji remained unruffled, however. 'I tested your vibrations,' she said. 'I could see that you were quite all right. At three o'clock we all gave you a bandan.'*

I had returned with brochures and leaflets. Now several Sahaja Yogis joined in a chorus: 'You must get rid of those at once, burn them – very bad vibrations.' So apparently had we. 'You are catching on your heart from that place. Did you argue?' asked one who was a poet and supposed that we had been spreading round Sahaji Yogic propaganda along with the coloured powder. 'Did you tell them about Sahaja Yoga?' The subject of Rājneesh and his ashram inspired a reaction from those Sahaja Yogis that was almost unbelievable. Everyone had a 'Rajneesh Story' to tell. 'I saw a group of those people in red,' said one Indian girl, 'and they were openly smoking cigarettes, ugh!' she shuddered. She was lucky, it seemed to me, that she had not seen them 'openly' doing several other things. 'You have caught boots from that place,' moaned the Indian girls, 'our vishuddis are catching,' and they sank back against the wooden seats of the train, clutching their lemons. Next day the heavy cold that had been passing through us caught up with me and I lost my voice. 'Your vishuddi is catching from that place,' they said to me, 'completely blocked up: just see.' It was conveniently forgotten that everyone else had had heavy colds and had been blocked up before getting anywhere near 'that place'.

Mataji now had to go north to spend a few days with her granddaughter who was ill, and we had some time off for sightseeing in the foothills of the Himalayas. Again I crossed the Ganges plain, brilliant as before with young wheat, golden with mustard and now far away on the horizon that great range of mountains. I loved those foothills. Mussoorie with its carved green painted houses, its Tibetan population, had the heady atmosphere of the Swiss Alps; from its heights, away in the distance, you could see the wild snowy peaks of the Himalayas themselves where holy places like Gangotri and Badrinath were still cut off from the world by walls of snow. But down here it would soon be spring, the rhododendrons were in bud and the bergenia in bloom. From Rishikesh the peaks of the Himalayas seemed more tempting than ever, for this is one

* Circular protective gesture made with right hand.

223

of the main centres whence to begin the pilgrimage into the mountains. These days, buses and cars can drive most of the way and no doubt the Himalayan pilgrimage – like most things to do with God – is now a major industry, yet a strange wild yearning swept down from those peaks, as stirring as the hunting call of geese passing on a winter's night. The air here felt cool and clear, the earth aromatic; bird calls echoed, rising away into the forests, wave upon wave into the distance. And here the Ganges flowed down fresh from the snows, opaque, greenish, icy to the touch, yet after a few minutes strangely warm. And as I stood with my feet in those swirling milky waters, that smelt so faintly sulphurous, I felt all my blocks flowing away. I felt clear and absolutely clean. My spirit rushed through me, it was like the Ganges, it was the Ganges. I was one with the Ganges, with the river, the mountain, the air. I was clear, cool, dissolved, as free as the emerald parrots that flew into the sunrise. I could understand now the faith in the cleansing powers of this holy river. For a moment I had been one with the universe. I had been purely a flowing, swirling current of energy.

We walked, the Greek and myself, some of the way to Hardwar – not without difficulty. Indians are a nervous race, they are frightened of the sea and now it seemed they were frightened of the land as well. Hardwar? It is very dangerous to walk. Dacoits, said one, elephants, said another. Apparently the dacoits and the elephants dash out of the forest and attack the passing traveller. The country was cool and verdant, remarkably like England at the end of February when everything is beginning to stir, soon green would shoot through and overcome the black stalks of last year's growth. But here peacocks graze in the dead undergrowth, along with the cows, and there is the redolence of azaleas and white trumpeted flowers. The trees are filled with green parrots and brown birds, which seem quite nondescript until they spread out their wings and you see the flash of blue. Hardwar was beautiful, reminding me of Venice. Here the Ganges rushes and hundreds of chains dangle from the banks and bridges from which to suspend oneself for the holy dip. Everywhere trees of brilliant red blossom flamed against the sky and those green parrots flew in and out of sunsets and sunrises. And how beautiful is the night in Hardwar, ringing with bells and bhajans and all the river filled with hundreds of small flickering lights, swirling away with the current down towards Benares, Allahabad and the sea.

I felt I could never tire of the Himalayas, just as I would never tire of the sunsets or the birds in India. Even Delhi was filled with birds, though not always attractive ones. Our garden seemed to be a vulture park, about forty vultures perching ominously, hunched up, in the branches of one of those exotic red blossomed trees. There were flocks of laughing birds and there was even an eagle at the Imperial Hotel. One American lady had teased it, she had thrown it the bones from her chicken salad sandwich, and the eagle had swept down with its hooked beak and its enormous wing span and removed her knife, fork, plate and sandwich in its talons and flown away. As for the sparrows their trust was extraordinary. They had built a nest in the fan that hung above our main room, there they would drop bits of feather and straw all over the floor and hop down chirruping, no matter who was there or what was going on. There was one particularly beautiful young man from Patna, very gentle, very clear, totally without mannerisms, with a fine profile and fairly longish hair. He had about him the air of a saint. He would sit cross-legged, meditating underneath the sparrows' nest and the sparrows would hop down to retrieve their straw and feathers which would land in his lap.

It was so easy to be diverted by the trivial, to go on about the dirty washing, the bathrooms and physical discomfort. But there is no doubt that during that trip to India I did become more aware of subtle dimensions. It was possible now to feel the vibrations flowing from the sun, the moon, from certain places: temples, hills, trees and from people – and in spite of the physical conditions I felt good. I slept beautifully and worries and 'catches' were abnormal. By that I mean that my normal state had begun to be a clear flow and any tension or unease was registed as unusual. Once in Bombay a few people had been sitting with Mataji who was reading the paper. One man was reciting in Sanskrit a mantra for the stomach chakra. I was conscious of this curious energy sweeping up me, very soothing, very exilarating, very strong. I looked round, everyone was sitting as before, while this glow was filling me, creeping up and filling me with ecstasy and clarity. One moment I was sitting there normally, the next I was taken over by this force. It was so physical that I could not believe that other people were not feeling it as well, but they were sitting quietly as before and Mataji was continuing to read the paper. Gradually everything subsided. On another occasion we were at a meeting, in a cool hall lined with portraits of eminent men of India, and that radiant energy suddenly shot through me again, entering through the palms, filling the heart, rising up to the throat, shining like a light inside me. Somewhere a fly settled on me, my eyes ran, someone coughed but all this seemed very far away, irrelevant, unreal; the only thing that mattered was this vibrant stream of energy rushing through.

I was aware now of the difference in feeling when I was clear and when I was not. When I was clear I felt relaxed, peaceful, buoyant and elated; I literally enjoyed myself, not necessarily through contrived means; I enjoyed the birds, the flowers, the squirrels, the sun, I celebrated with them all; my mind was more or less silent and I was filled with a sense of well-being. When I was blocked, my attention was diverted either by physical manifestations – a headache, perhaps, sickness, a sore throat, a cold – so that I was physically debilitated, or I was subtly, psychically attacked; my mind whirled, I was assaulted by doubts and worries; I was tense and restless, wanting to go somewhere, do something, anything, to get away from myself, and in the extreme I was exhausted. Unlike Professor Chavan who, no doubt, could clear himself in the space of minutes, I had to work hard. First locate the trouble, then treat it. Once, for example, my left eye started to twitch violently. It would only happen spasmodically, so that after a time I would forget it, then it would start again. Gradually, and so subtly that I would hardly be aware of it, my mind would be filled with unease, there would be nothing concrete which I could isolate, just this general feeling of unease and tension. So the twitching stayed for about three weeks. Eventually I decided to attack it with the standard Sahaja Yogic weapons of fire and water. After about two hours there was a violent pain in my left eye, a great fluttering and heat, and then a stream of water issued forth and the twitching had gone.

And at the end of our two months, on 21 March, at the vernal equinox, came Mataji's official birthday celebrations. The music played as the rituals of the puja were carried out, the washing, the anointing of the feet, the decorating, the presentation of garlands. Now, instead of the energy coursing upwards and out, it was flowing in, my body was sucking in the vibrations, down to all the chakras, round and into pains, aches and restrictions, soothing, stroking, pressing, until they flowed away into the river that rushed through me. Again I became that energy, with no outlines. Everything apart from that energy flowing through me felt absolutely unreal.

Entering the world again from that sheltered environment came as a shock. For a start all was not well back in Putney. Instead of applying himself to his A-levels my youngest son had sunk into inertia, due to an orgy of joint-smoking, and meanwhile the lavatories had blocked up (a symbol, the psychiatrist said later, of bad mooladharas). For three days in the wind and snow we were obliged to use the garden while the plumber, selected from the yellow pages, arrived each day without the correct tools and at last presented triumphantly a bill for four days' work. Yet apart from the cold the inconvenience seemed nothing as compared to that of India; it could do nothing to shake my equanimity. In retrospect there seemed however something strange and rather woolly about that equanimity: it was more like a state of daze.

On his return from India the psychiatrist came round to do what he called clearing the place out. The house, he said, felt very heavy in the head, a very bad agnya, a very bad mooladhara also ('put a bandan on the toilets before you use them'). We went round the house blowing a conch horn and ringing a bell – the conch and the bell are apparently weapons of the divine which attack, on a subtle sonic level, bad entities. One of the cats puffed up his tail the way cats do when they see something they dislike and peered at the ceiling, hissing. Either the cat was possessed, said the psychiatrist, or it had seen something; in his view it was likely to be the former (Sahaja Yogis do not care for cats, left-sided creatures, they say, in touch with the subconscious and the world of the dead).

Roy meanwhile was ill again. I had written to him from

227

India about Mataji's reception in the villages and my own experiences. He had written back about my obsession with 'crass superstition' and 'that woman'. Now he was going round as white as a sheet and absolutely tortured. 'The unconscious will deal with him,' said the psychiatrist airily. It did: Roy stumped off to his parents saying he could not bear the regime.

For the next seven months I tried to absorb myself in Sahaja Yoga. I rose at six in the morning to meditate and again in the evening I 'took vibrations'. For the most part I felt marvellous. More than ever I responded to nature. One day, while I was meditating, a thunderstorm broke. It was one of the most exhilarating experiences I have ever had: the crack of thunder, the shock of lightning, the hissing of the rain seemed directly to charge up my system so that I vibrated with vitality. Afterwards a thick warm mist rose up, the atmosphere was tropical. The steamy heat was body temperature and as I walked in the evening light to the river, glimmering, grey like a Whistler painting, the air enveloped me like a cashmere blanket, so that I melted, dissolved into the mist, became one again with the universe.

On the whole I still found it easier to become one with the universe than with people, although now, using this technique, it was possible to by-pass the usual means of communication and enter into another's stream of consciousness. Once I was working on a man:* He sat with his feet in salted water which on the principle of the Victorian mustard bath draws out all the impurities, while I worked up his spine on the chakras. After a little I felt a flow of energy surging up me; as for my patient, his neck kept creaking like a floor board, even though he was sitting motionless. It seemed to me that the whole of the void, that area round the stomach, filled up completely and I felt whole, marvellously secure, comfortable, and more: I felt as though I were having a beautiful love affair with this man, that we had just made love, because this was an experience that incorporated many aspects, eroticism, love, ecstasy. I felt absolutely in harmony with him, that we were one. And this was without any sort of conventional contact. Most important

* Women working on men and vice versa was in fact not encouraged, Sajaha Yogis are nothing if not sexist. Men are supposed to work on men and women on women, although why this was so was never very clear.

of all it had nothing whatsoever to do with personality.

It should perhaps be mentioned here that sex, unless you are married, is absolutely discouraged in Sahaja Yoga. The primordial energy, Mataji is always saying, the kundalini, has nothing whatever to do with sex, and anyone who says it has is satanic – part of the tantric campaign to pollute the world. The whole topic is considered very inauspicious. After all, Mataji was often asking, what is so great about sex? Even the mystic trances of St Teresa she dismisses on account of their erotic element: St Teresa, she says, just wanted to go to bed with Christ! Yes, sex, the erotic, is definitely out. So are cigarettes and alcohol. Pubs are the worst: pubs the very heart of England, the very image of well-being in the British subconscious, are crammed with 'boots'. Sahaja Yogis have various stories of their reactions to these taboos. The psychiatrist, for example, used to be something of a connoisseur of wine; just after meeting Mataji he went to Germany and bought a bottle of some fine vintage, but he found he simply could not drink it and would tell with pride how he poured the stuff away. Another told how he had tried to make love to his girl friend, but fell back with a searing pain in his prostate. Mataji had told them not to drink, not to make love; she had told them they would not be able to; and they could not.

As for myself I did sometimes drink still; not often but occasionally I would play truant to remind myself what it had all been like. The point was that I *wanted* to cut out alcohol; I was researching after all, I was using my body as a laboratory and I had to see what would happen. The last thing I wanted at this stage was to revert to my old habits. Besides discovering that cutting out drink and the friends that went with it meant a yearly saving of about a thousand pounds, I found now that I could actually monitor the effect of alcohol within my system. There is nothing new in knowing that we drink as a panacea against the day's nuisances and we do not require Sahaja Yoga to tell us that alcohol is an unreliable agent – it can certainly bring harmony and a sense of well-being but it can just as easily act as a poison causing disintegration. Now, badly-made wine disrupted my centre of gravity and whipped up my thoughts so that they whirled about like fragments of paper in a gale. I could feel the energy rushing up and down my body well into the night, so that next day I was exhausted. Yet fine wine consumed in the company of exhilarated people could definitely have a clearing, exhilarating effect. In other words the spirit in which the liquor is consumed is contagious; you imbibe this along with the liquor itself. The alcohol seems to open up subtle conduits through which the subconscious minds of drinkers may communicate. Thus drinking in the company of debilitated, disintegrated people can result in your ending up disintegrated and debilitated yourself. It is a psychic tranference of mood (or 'boots'), and herein lies the Sahaja Yogic horror of pubs.

I had occasion to witness both these effects. The first was when some friends, who for tax reasons had emigrated, returned briefly and threw a party. It was by all standards a most generous affair, oysters, champagne, sole and bottle after bottle of wine, and excellent wine it was too. Among the guests there was a man of about fifty-five; even before we had started dinner he was drunk, by the end of the evening he was a wreck. Here were these friends full of good-will, wanting to dispense hospitality and good cheer, and all that happened was that this man became more miserable than ever, or so it seemed to me. He had all the material comforts in the world, yet he was desperate, divorced, threatened by his approaching death and as a panacea to his loneliness begging to sleep with me. What should have been a bracing celebration ended by enclosing him more than ever in his own sense of isolation.

The other time was exactly opposite. Four of us had sailed in a boat to France. Our host was Ian, my companion of the Kumbh Mela, who was, he explained, passing through a materialistic phase; he was going to make a great deal of money and lead an extremely glamorous life for the next three years, after which he was going to pursue his spirit. The conversation on the voyage out was worldly: the state of the country and Sir James Goldsmith's table manners. I had little in common, I felt, with my fellow travellers. Then that night we went to dine in one of those restaurants that are starred in the Michelin. I had forgotten the excitement of a meal in a serious French restaurant and the real enjoyment that can come from a dinner that is carefully selected and well cooked. As we sat down to the table we were each of us separate entities, well disposed towards one another but with no real sense of communication. But under the agency of that marvellous food and golden wine I felt that we were united. It was in the real sense of the word a religious experience, that meal bound us together, if only for that evening; it was a celebration, a communion of our spirits, we enjoyed ourselves and left elevated by the shared experience. For the first time I could understand what the communion service, the Eucharist, is meant to bestow.

That summer mail from India brought diversions. One of my correspondents was Miss Moriarty: would I kindly buy some liqueur chocolates ('I love them') and a couple of bottles of rum essence? Then a book on Dadaji arrived, a collection of pieces from 'top-most' people who had been dazzled by him during his world tour. Kushwant Singh, it seemed, had been persuaded to take up his pen again and, according to him, Horace, the 'celebrated novelist critic', was one of many to have fallen under Dadaji's spell. In a piece entitled 'The Eastern Messiah shines over the Western Horizon', another 'top-most' person, the President of the World Spiritual Society, reported that Dadaji had taken Londoners by storm. 'His divine presence amidst the mystical Krishna's fragrance with charming and captivating smile uplifted the morale and confused minds of thousands of people in this troubled island.' The President of the World Spiritual Society said that, like thousands of Indians settled abroad, he had sometimes been cheated financially by so-called sannyasis coming from the motherland, misguided by saints and scholars holidaying regularly in Western countries, but now 'we in the Western world truly believe that a Divinel Light has emerged from the India subcontinent that shall shine over the world for thousands of years to come'.

Abhi Battacharya had also written: 'My dear Philippa Pullar of Truth ... Dadaji has shown all manifestations of him or God or truth, destiny of Creation, man, all beings, planets, stars, moon, sun, trees, rivers, what not.' He is the breathing existence of the life of the universe – a reality, a science beyond the science of man. He had come: this Dadaji: this family man with a toy shop in Calcutta: this sort of Advent had never happened in any civilisation since the Creation was willed by Him.

231

Dadaji is that truth. He moves to his created beings all over the world to teach us the significance of creation: life: the reality of truth. He was, said Abhi Battacharya, just about to approach his created beings in Neasden: his arrival was imminent.

Mataji was not impressed by the approach of this particular personification of Truth, this rival Advent, this Light, albeit 'Divinel,' who by a trick of fate was promising to arrive in the adjacent road to her own ashram. I should inform the police, she said. I should write to them telling them that a criminal, a forger, was about to enter the country.

Matters were by no means uneventful either within Sahaja Yogic circles. A certain number of disciples belonging to Maharishi Mahesh Yogi had been drawn to Caxton Hall. It seemed that within their flock there was conflict. One couple who had run a centre for the Maharishi's courses in levitation, invisibility and so on had strange stories to tell. Over the years the couple claimed that they had paid over thirty thousand pounds in course fees, they had been swept up by an over-whelming enthusiasm for enlightenment, which they were assured would come, if not during the next course, during the one after next. Now they were still unenlightened while the Maharishi, they said, was probably one of the world's richest men. To take the siddhi course alone you paid three thousand pounds. When you started this intensive training, they explained, you got these 'blissed out' phases, sometimes with visions – god, goddesses, lights; but these were matched with very bad times which in the trade are known as 'unstressing' (built into the system are all the strains of one's karma, not only from this life, but all the past ones, you must cleanse these, exorcise them, before you can be liberated). If you complained how frightful you felt, you were assured that this was quite natural – indeed the more frightful you felt the deeper you were supposed to have gone and the better it was. However, some people felt so frightful that they ended up in hospital – with all the symptoms of possession.

More and more of these people came to the meetings and indeed they did seem to be possessed. In front of Mataji they would shake and burst into tears and hysterics, their bodies would contort and go rigid. One boy jumped like a frog, hopping about and shaking with muscular spasms, another growled like a lion. Their treatment was standard. They would sit with their feet in salted water, with lemons in their hands. Gradually they seemed to heat up, the heat would start in their hands, spreading to the centres in which they were said to be possessed: agnya, vissuddhi, heart. The psychiatrist (whose speciality was mantras) would stand reciting and others would work on the chakras. After a while the spasms would start. The patients would fling their lemons across the room and try to leap out of their chairs. Some were worse than others, and some mantras seemed to be more dynamic; at the mention of Kalki for example they would scream and try to escape from the room. Upon the application of bells, conches, Mataji's bangles, shoes and other vibrated articles, they would tremble and groan. At all times it appeared as though they were in great pain but this apparently was not so. It was possible to address the spirits themselves, who spoke through their hosts in strained voices. For example when one spirit was asked why it was there, the reply came: 'Because it is my function to do what I'm doing.' 'Who commanded it?' 'The Maharishi.' On being asked to leave, the spirit said:' No, I'm to stay here until otherwise ordered by the Maharishi.'

I, too, was facing difficulties. The time had come for me to start writing this book. I wanted to slip away and begin. But no, this apparently was not permissible. What about the collective? Momentum: Solitude: Quite unnecessary. One didn't think about it, one simply sat down and the stuff would flow down from the unconscious. But it seemed to me that there was a snag to this argument. The stuff that had flowed down from the unconscious in the past to the pens of my brother Sahaja Yogis was not good enough -- or anyway it was not acceptable to my literary advisers. They did not like the tone, they said. I myself had tried to write a short introduction to Sahaja Yoga, and Mataji, for a newspaper, bringing in, as I imagined, a nicely-balanced, scientifically-based explanation of kundalini. I had shown it to Horace and to a philosopher, both of whom were appalled. Don't talk down; don't berate us; where is your sense of humour? I suppose you think that is as unimportant as clearly you find your mind? (Horace's contribution.) 'I had hoped for something elegant,' the philosopher added. Be more subtle. This kundalini (and by the way I shouldn't use foreign

233

words), this kundalini should just sneak up on you. As for the yoga part of it, not even *Yoga Today* would print that, it was the worst sort of hagiography. The whole thing sounded crankish. And Mataji? She should be popped in just in the last paragraph, subtly, she too should sneak up on you. It was most ironic: here I was trying to write about this subtle thing and being urged to be more subtle – and by people who on Sahaja Yogic terms were operating very grossly indeed. As for Mataji, she had no intention of being 'popped' anywhere. She saw herself as the focus of my book. We had discussed the shape the book should take. There should first of all be an autobiographical piece, this should be like the Old Testament, here I should establish the fact that I was a serious seeker, then go on to prophesy the Coming. The second part should be the journey, the search during which naturally I had seen through all the false prophets. The third should be Sahaja Yoga and Mataji herself.

In the event it seemed that the collective had no intention of allowing me to write anything at all. I must dash off to Neasden, Leeds, Birmingham. And when I was not doing that, could I have so and so to stay for a night? a weekend? indefinitely? In spite of everything I did manage to establish a very small trickle of momentum, but then I must hurry off to Scotland. Mataji, the collective said, wanted particularly that I should go. I did not want to, I said. We all know, said the collective, that if Mataji wants you to go, you will. I went.

The woods were beautiful there, the sun shone on the leaves, making them glitter and fall in dappled light on the soft grass and bracken of the glades. Everywhere was the sound of rushing water and brown peaty streams flowed through the glens, pouring over the rocks in cascades, at that time of the year the night hardly darkened, the sky remained a brilliant blue over the loch. The house was less beautiful – crammed with 'boots'. One little girl kept on seeing small red figures with horns, tails and carbuncles sitting on her cupboard. Another girl felt as though she were being smothered. When she closed her eyes there were all these bristly hairy things with yellow pustular eyes coming very close to her face, smothering her. They looked at her with such yearning, such tortured expressions, as though they needed her attention. Then again a woman would come, more golden, but also smothering. I saw none of these phenomena and, apart from feeling permanently exhausted while I was there, I was unaffected. My youngest son, however, who had roused himself to enjoy a Sahaja Yogic summer, never recovered. Shortly after his arrival he was smitten with, in Sahaja Yogic jargon, bad 'catches' – terrible neck-ache, terrible headache. I was only in Scotland for three days but he remained there for a week and then travelled north to Caithness, where a month later I met him since I was preparing another article for the American magazine. Neither he nor I enjoyed ourselves. I returned with the most frightful cold while he had sunk again into inertia, so much so that he spent almost the entire two weeks travelling down the west coast of Scotland asleep.

Meanwhile a boy from New Zealand and his Indian bride (the result of Mataji's Bombay matchmaking) were staying in my house and had enjoyed a Sahaji Yogic dinner party in my absence. The dinner party had rampaged through the house complaining of the vibrations. It was all those books, they said. The psychiatrist telephoned. I must do something about the vibrations in the house, he said, everyone had caught bad agnyas, while he himself had contracted a bad nabhi and had been violently sick. I must get rid of all the books for a start, to say nothing of the pictures, (they all had bad vibrations as well), the cats, the garden and the house. The trouble was, Mataji had said, that I was retaining too much of my past life. I should buy a nice flat and move into that. I felt far from collective.

I knew that if I were to write anything at all I must go away. I decided then to spend the winter in Ireland. About a week before I was due to leave, Mataji, who had been for a few weeks in India, returned. There was absolutely no doubt that seeing her was both a soothing and an exhilarating experience. Power seemed to radiate from her, and at the same time, like a psychic hoover, it sucked all the cobwebs and dust that had accumulated within my system. She put her hand once on my knee and a soothing balm seeped through me, making me relaxed and quiescent: All this inspite of the fact that, together with several other highly privileged Sahaja Yogis, I was there to do Mataji's housework. During her absence her maid had left and we had been invited round to mop and mend – to be invited to hem Mataji's pillowcases or to sluice out her kitchens was considered in Sahaja Yogic circles as the highest tribute. I was going to Ireland? Why? To write my book? Why did I have to go to Ireland? To write a book one should not be disturbed. It would be better if I stayed in London. However, if I had to go would I come to the ashram tomorrow since she had something important she wished to dictate.

Neasden was the last place I wanted to go, especially since I had so much to do before leaving. Yet I went. There were a number of others there, some of them hot and shaking as a result of their 'horrible gurus" practices. What have the other gurus given you? Mataji would ask. They have not given you your realisation: they have not given you the actuality of experience. She looked closely at me and for a moment I was overwhelmed by a most unpleasant sensation, everything swam before me and her eyes were very large, seeming to hone in. 'You are catching on your left heart,' she said. 'God is angry with you because you have not written anything about Sahaja Yoga.' And then she proceeded to dictate the following impeachment of one whom I shall call X, which was so extraordinary that I give it here in full.

'We the undersigned who have visited X, for many years, at various times, have found certain things which are disastrous to your being. We feel duty bound to inform you all because we know that he has tremendous hypnotic powers by which one remains illusionless believing that one has found truth. To begin with X used to talk about thoughtless awareness: about God Almighty: His love: Kundalini – but this was the first trap by which we, the seekers of the West, were enamoured. He attracted us Westerners with his sex theory since we were blindly believing Freud and had accepted so-called liberation as the aim of life. We could not not resist such a temptation: having a guru to teach us how to be sinful and unrighteous. Gradually we found out that we were much better masters in perverted sexual behaviour than this Indian pseudo-intellectual but still we stuck on to him because of our consciences which all the time pricked whenever we tried to overcome our so called inhibitions. According to Freud this

236

was conditioning of the mind but we felt it was some innate resistance of our being that we were trying to overcome by having a guru who sanctioned all kinds of sinful activities. As a result of the practices of X we developed impotency and his hypnotic methods exploded our sex desire. We became mad with the disintegration of our bodies and our desire. So many of us became schizophrenic and dropped out. We became very superficial, ambitious and dishonest to ourselves. Though we were very hypnotised we could see that none of us – nor anyone of you – have achieved anything by surrendering to the dirty desires of X. He would take us in privacy, make the women nude and use them. He always wanted to touch the private parts of men and women alike, he always liked to smell the private parts on his fingers which he would then lick: all this filth we accepted because we thought it was our test of endurance. He exhausted our money: we had to pay for this trickery which leads you nowhere. Some of us had to work for hours together to find the money. Many things surprised us like this. Some women believed that he was their husband in previous lives. They have donated all their property to him. X acted also as a pimp for many wealthy old Indian men and women and he employed younger boys and girls to be used by these old men and women. X himself cannot bear the fragrance of flowers or any scent and calls himself God, yet we know that one name of God, one aspect of God, Lord Vishnu, Suganda Priya, means fond of good flowers, good scents. Here is a God who does not like the smell of flowers yet enjoys the smell of private parts! He is a patient of diabetes, yet eats like a glutton. He has a huge silver plate at least 24″ in diameter with 20 bowls in it and he cannot sit in ordinary chairs – it is said that a sannyasis is always very light in his weight and movement, even though he may be tall and hefty. Besides this he appears 20 years older than his age, which is just the opposite to divine personalities. Whenever you talk to him about money or material possessions his eyes widen with interest and he can go on talking about wealth for hours together. If he knows someone has money he becomes unusually attentive. He has left us bankrupt, physically disabled, hysterical, mentally degraded. We cannot do anything in life. We are some of the first who used to come to him for all those years and this is the result. We feel that real

Indians are much wiser and saner people than we and they understand spirituality while the Westernised Indians may be trying to copy us. We admit that we have been real fools and stupid people and that we also told a lie to others and made them believe in this wretched fellow. And our life is a curse now. We are writing this letter to warn you against this X and his dirty designs. He pampers your ego, supports your wrong style of life by creating divorces in the family. All Indians look upon disciples of X as great aggressors of their own culture. They say we destroyed so many old cultures: America, China, Japan, and now you are trying to destroy Indian culture through this satanic fellow. Now we realise that we have aggressed on our own innocence and are also aggressing Indian people by our foolish egotistical ideas of liberating them of their sanity and wisdom. There are many people who are missing, who tried to go against or tried to express the truth behind this iron curtain. We do not know if they are dead or living. We know for certain that this man has guns and other weapons with him. Why should a holy man have guns to protect himself? Why should an ascetic live on people's money like a parasite and amass such wealth? We request you to face yourself truthfully and find out if you have become less materialistic, less aggressive, thoughtlessly aware?'

The ways of the Devi, I was assured by the psychiatrist, are mysterious. They certainly are. My job was to type out this singular document. If this was one of the Devi's tests then I failed it completely. Doubts and catches came flowing in. I did not like it at all. I was not sure that the Devi and all the Sahaja Yogis, myself included, were not mad. What on earth *were* we doing? And yet I returned again to that central force of gravity, that purifying energy which seemed every day to grow stronger. If this were the reality then nothing else mattered.

A few days later I left for Ireland. It was exactly what I needed. Quiet; ravishing, purple mountains; fuchsia still scarlet in the hedges and the sea birds blown by the autumn winds like drifts of snow across the grey skies. Each day seemed to me more fragrant, more delicious than the last. I could draw great draughts of restoring silence. How wonderful it was to hear only the roaring of the surf, rather than that of aeroplanes! On most days I felt quite clear and the energy rushed through. Sometimes it was as if I were astride a marvellously sensitive horse which responded to the lightest touch; it was as if I had harnessed this sleek and rippling beast, the sunlit country lay open before me, and anything and everything was possible. I seemed to have the strength of surf roaring up the beach, green waves pounding against the cliffs, sublime, endless. This really did seem to be the power of God. The energy streamed higher and higher, erotic, exhilarating, spiralling like fragrance from incense sticks, like the blue acrid turf smoke that rose up in the evenings from the chimneys. How idyllic it was, that internal energy streaming and the landscape changing, yet motionless, into which I dissolved! There were rare still days when the purple mountains reflected in a sea whose surface had the sheen of satin, when there was no sound in that clear space, just the distant surf and the birds, singing birds like robins and calling birds from the reedy beaches. There were blue days when the sky was azure and the sea deep blue green, when light streaked like paint across the mountains. There were wild windy days when the crows were blown up in clouds like the burnt fragments of paper from a bonfire, and icy days when the heavy clouds parted to show the mountain peaks covered in snow; and there were days when drops of water lay in the hedges and on the grass, catching the sunlight like prisms, glittering more richly than emeralds and rubies.

Slowly but surely I started to write. The days passed in a flowing rhythm. I had been there about six weeks when I received a telegram. That day had been more beautiful than ever. The sea was duck egg blue, blown by the wind into little swirls and eddies. Everything that was white glittered that day, the painted houses, the lighthouse. The tops of the mountains were covered in snow, the surf very white on the blue sea. The lower slopes of the hills were all blues and greens and yellows, and in the foreground spiky flax plants and rhododendrons, a dark and glossy green. And then through the mouth of the harbour came this very white boat, as white and glittering as the lighthouse, and on its deck men's life-jackets flamed scarlet and above in a great white cloud flew a host of sea-gulls. There was just the sound of the sea, the throb of the boat and the cry of all those gulls. And all over the bay single birds were flying above that eddying sea to join that great white cloud pursuing the boat. And when I returned there was the telegram: 'Mother going to India return at once.' I was absolutely astonished. What on earth could my mother, aged eighty-three, be doing going to India? But the misidentification was only momentary; it was Mataji, whom we must all call mother, who was going to India. Now I was in a quandary. Here I was writing the book, yet I did return.

Just before I left I dreamt of a dark evil woman with great power. She drew me to her, sucking me towards her as though I were a piece of iron and she a magnet, and then she tried to press her finger to my forehead. I twisted and shrank away, reciting Mataji's name. She put her finger into my mouth, I bit off the tip. 'There!' she screamed triumphant. Then she started to make love and there was a violent and jerking orgasm and I woke up.

It was an appalling journey back to England almost as if the unconscious did not want me to return. I was driven by a friend – the one who is obsessed by exercise – who had arrived with his skipping rope and his book about his great-aunt. The great-aunt's family had been great travellers. They were always setting out with a retinue of cooks, footmen, maids, fourgons and feather mattresses across Europe. Their journeys were nothing to ours, which took so long that we had ample time to work on his book – mine having temporarily come to a full stop. As Lord and Lady Orford struggled through the nineteenth century, their fourgons capsizing, their carriages threatened by brigands, our windscreen shattered and, unshielded, we jerked our way across the south-west of Ireland, our engine having been irredeemably flooded by my skipping friend who kept leaving the choke out. Certainly Lord and Lady Orford in their snug upholstered carriages were far better protected than we, rain drove freely through the shattered windscreen and, when we travelled through a puddle, of which there was an abundance, mud and ordure shot into our mouths. As Lord and Lady Orford trotted at last triumphantly into Rome we were towed on to the ferry at Rosslare by a tractor. Our journey which should in the twentieth century take twenty hours, had lasted four days.

Thus I arrived only a few hours before Mataji's departure. She and her minions were busy packing. The psychiatrist who was travelling with her, and who was to be married a month later to a specially selected bride from Delhi, was running round with his allocation of luggage which included babies' bottle warmers, nappies and chocolate. Mother Theresa meanwhile, who had just won the Nobel Prize for Peace, was coming in for a wigging. Mataji who had once travelled with her on the same aeroplane did not think much of her at all – very materialistic she had found her. Now they were even bringing out some Mother Theresa record – just imagine that!

She had called me, she explained, to see how the book was progressing. She was anxious that I should make very clear the fact that I was a serious seeker. I had always known what I was looking for. I had seen at once that all those other gurus were not pure. When I had met Mataji I had seen at once that she was pure. Here was purity. She was that. And now she had something else to dictate: a list of gurus and how they befuddled the seekers – all this should go in. Unfortunately the document has since disappeared. All I can remember is that Krishnamurthi muddled people with words and ideas while someone else made them eat his faeces. Shortly after this I terminated my experiment in Sahaja Yoga.

PART V

I had terminated my experiment in Sahaja Yoga; but so what? I had changed certainly. I had enjoyed experiences, glimpsed new dimensions, but still wanted knowledge that as far as I could see no living person was going to give me. I felt the need to return to the safety of paper. I was drawn back once again to books. I resumed my old haunts: the India Office, the British Museum.

The first fact I managed to unearth was that Sahaja Yoga is a Tantric cult! Actually Mataji did not conceal this. 'We are the real Tantra,' she would say (while adding of course that any sexual practices within Tantra were schemes of satanic forces); but since no one had ever really heard of Tantra it did not mean much.

So here, first of all, are some brief words on Tantra itself, which is said to be India's most ancient cult, dating from the Harappan culture of 600 B.C. Until 1930 little was known of Tantric philosophy in the West. It was Sir John Woodruffe, under the pseudonym of Arthur Avalon, who translated many of the scriptures, known as Sastras, and published his pioneer works *The Serpent Power* and *Siva and Sakti*. During the past forty years there has been considerable academic interest in the subject – in a world of rapidly dwindling resources from which to draw theses, scholars are moving into this neglected branch of study. Much of my information is drawn from Lalan Prasad Singh's thesis: *Tantra: its mystic and scientific base*.

To discuss Tantric philosophy fully would require volumes. The most important point to make here is that the aim of all

242

Tantric procedure is to rouse the dormant force (known as kundalini) lying within the initiate. In other words Tantric discipline incorporates techniques for harnessing human energy. The body is used as an instrument to channel the vital energy (known as prana) through the parasympathetic (the sushumna). The spinal cord acts as a conductor and the vertebrae as insulator so that the glandular system may be employed to transform and store energy.

There are many different schools to be found sheltering beneath the umbrella of Tantric philosophy, some of which teach different ways to reach the same goal. Sahaja Yoga, for example, is a 'right-handed path' which strictly forbids physical contact to achieve its end. But some of those known as 'left-handed paths' do involve rituals employing skulls, cremation grounds, corpses at midnight and, worst of all, *sex*. But these exercises are not performed for sensory gratification, as always they are to generate power. The point of employing skulls and corpses as aids to meditation is, ironically enough, purification. The gravest impediment, it is believed, to 'Realisation' is attachment to objects which are perceived by the senses, hence the use of such unsavoury items is to help detach the senses and to draw the mind away.

Briefly the theory runs as follows. Everything in creation, including one's own body, is divided into opposites, positive and negative, passive and kinetic, male and female. The feminine side is passive, magnetic and absorbing and if it comes into proper contact with the masculine side a circuit is established, a reaction occurs and power is generated. The effect is the same when a predominantly masculine personality is brought into the magnetic field of a predominantly feminine one. This is seen as the mystic transmutation of the male and female principle of Siva and Sakti and sometimes is acted out literally with a male and female physically coupling.

Before the kundalini can be successfully raised the body and the mind must be purified. For this the mantra and yantra are employed. The yantra is a physical form, a devised symbol upon which to focus the attention thereby making the mind 'one-pointed'. The mantra is an incantation; an ideal sound visualised as letters and vocalised as syllables which creates sound vibrations that have the power to raise the kundalini. Vibration*, an essential component of Tantra–instruction, aims to expand human consciousness so that it may comprehend vibrant realms unapparent to the ordinary person. By fixing the mind in the yantra, by chanting the mantra, the nervous system may be soothed by vibrations and the sense organs and secretions of the body kept in order; mental activity may be sublimated and the kundalini aroused.

Significantly, one of the schools within Tantra is the Sakta cult, the worship of God in the form of mother. Here is the idea that Sakti is the power, the feminine principle personified as the Goddess, the Devi. Several cults contain an inner circle which encourages a group mind, while 'Sahaja' is a key word cropping up in both Hindu and Buddhist Tantra. One teacher even uses it as a mantra. Its meaning is given as a state of mind which is desireless and motionless. 'Sahaja Samadhi' is the goal of all yogis, the final and most blessed state when the individual has become completely merged in the Self.

My conclusion is that Sahaja Yoga is a 'right-handed' Sakta cult wherein a collective mind is encouraged. Mataji is the feminine principle personified. Her image provides the yantra, while incantations in praise of herself, together with a company of gods and goddesses, make up the mantras. The name itself Sahaja is auspicious, symbolising the final heavenly state to be achieved.

Secondly I came across the work of a contemporary who describes himself not as a mystic, nor as a saint, but an ordinary householder who has felt the full force of kundalini. Gopi

---

* Both orthodox science and Tantric philosophy combine in saying that matter is nothing but a seething mass of energy, waves and vibrations. The difference between a colour and a sound, between a cosmic ray and a television picture is frequency – vibration. Where there is action there is vibration and the nature of the action is judged by the waves it creates. No two vibrations are the same. The visible world is nothing but a pattern of waves which vibrate collectively upon the sensory plates. Sound. Touch. Smell. Thought. Everything is vibration. Moreover all the sense organs are simply instruments of the mind. In other words colours, sounds, smells, tastes, shapes, forms, figures, time and distance, together with all the emotions are products of the mind. All are received through the senses and are impressed upon the intellect which forms its own concepts.

Krishna* supplied for me some of the missing fragments which now made the jig-saw puzzle fall into place.

Like all men of spiritual maturity he emphasises the importance of evolution – and here I hailed Gopi Krishna with delight for he attacks my old enemies, the scientists, the men of progress, for their narrow-mindedness in denying any reality that does not fit into physically demonstrable concepts. He blames science for the present explosive situation in the world which has been caused by nothing but wrongly-directed energy.

Here is his argument. At the first glimpse of evolutionary theory, God had been shown the door and from then on the evolutionists concentrated their attention and energy on organisms. The orthodox biologist is not prepared to allow consciousness the least position in the scheme of evolution.† He is concerned only with the play of atoms and molecules as modified by actions of nature and environment. The only way that a full-scale disaster can be averted, is for science and religion to work together and for the leaders of the world to receive the vision of reality through the rise of kundalini. At present the strongest, most competent, members of society exercise themselves in ambition, power and financial ends, while it is the inadequate members of society who turn to spiritual guests.

Yet in the past it was the man of talent and the mystic who have been responsible for the progress of mankind – Einstein, Socrates, Buddha, Christ and Mohammed, to name five. But among the mystics there has been endless conflict over the state to be attained, the god to be worshipped and the mode of conduct to be observed. Far from being a harmonious force, religion has been the cause of war and havoc. Even so, in essence, all religions teach that same thing: the human body is an instrument for harnessing the vital airs in order that the individual may evolve, transcend from the gross human stage

* He has written twelve books, published by Kundalini Research Foundation, most important of which are *Kundalini: The Evolutionary Energy, Kundalini: The Biological Basis of Religion and Genius, Kundalini: The Secret of Yoga,* and *The Dawn of a New Science.*

† What was so destructive to faith was the fear encouraged by many scientists that evolution could only be a materialistic process, that rational beings had occurred by accidental mutation over the ages.

245

and rise to a higher, more refined level of understanding, merging with the cosmic consciousness.

Through his experiences Gopi Krishna has realised that the cosmic consciousness is formless, but becomes for the individual whatever shape or image that individual imagines it to be. Different images of God are devised to help him purify his mind and direct his devotional ardour. Thus he sets up a tangible symbol with which he can identify, on which he can concentrate and into which he hopes to dissolve.* In other words different symbols are devised to suit different tastes and cultures, the Buddha, the icon, the cross, the mandala and so on. Fixity of attention, whether upon a god or a goddess, a symbol or a diagram, is the cornerstone of every religion, occult practice and mind control technique. Success lies in focusing the imagination and directing the vital energy to that point.

The arousal of the primordial energy (Christianity's Holy Spirit, Ramana Maharishi's 'I' consciousness and kundalini are all the same force under different names) is the key to all religions. It has been a secret closely guarded through the ages, travelling round the world, transmitted from one generation to another, adapted according to culture, moral values and the intellectual level of the population. It is contained veiled in riddles, symbols and allegories, in the Vedas, the Bible, classical mythology, alchemical doctrines and other scriptures. All the mysteries have the same lever, the same goal. All aim to discover the precious essence under different names, the gold, the wine, the elixir of life, the great unknown quantity, the mysterious x of algebra. Now Gopi Krishna calls for scientific research into the subject and to this end has set up the Kundalini Research Foundation.

All religions would seem to me in essence, to be an adumbration of the central Tantric experience. Even the ceremonial bathing at the Kumbh Mela, at the Sangam, the confluence of the three rivers, is a symbolic representation of the inner purification that occurs when the kundalini awakens and the three channels of the nervous system converge at the agnya chakra.

* Most religions have developed from nature worship, from worshipping the primordial energy in the form of nature; gradually the various aspects of nature developed into atmospheric, terrestrial and celestial beings endowed with man's image.

Here the Ganges represents ida, Yumuna, pingala and Saraswati the sushumna. Sir John Woodruffe has pointed out that pre-Reformation catholicism contains all the ingredients to Tantra. Christ is Siva, the male principle; the Virgin Mary is Sakti, the female principle. They and their symbols are the yantras upon which to focus the mind; the psalms and the prayers chanted in rhythmic plain-chant are the mantras, while churches and cathedrals are symbols of the body, running from the font, representing the mooladhara, up through the nave, the choir and the corona to the rose window, the sahasrara, the thousand-petalled lotus. The circumnavigation of holy shrines and wells is still retained in Ireland. There are endless parallels, it is enough to quote Clement of Alexandria: according to him Christ said that the kingdom shall come when the two shall be one, and that is without as that which is within and the male with the female – neither male nor female.

Every religion teaches the necessity of cleansing the mind and the body. This is because if the mind, and therefore the nervous system, is not pure, in other words not properly balanced and working harmoniously, when the primordial energy is aroused, mental and other frightful disorders may ensue – anything from neuroses to insanity – because of the poisonous hormones released into the system.* (And this is of special interest in the light of what is to follow with Roy.) Gopi Krishna himself had an appalling experience which he relates in *Kundalini*.

The range of manifestations of an active kundalini, it seems, can be as vast and as varied as the range of intellect. If nerves

* Hormones are secreted from every endocrine gland and influence the output and use of energy, while in turn their efficiency is directly affected by the state of mind. If a system becomes upset the balance of hormones is disturbed. Of all the glands the two most important are the pineal and the pituitary. The pineal gland (the sahasrara chakra) is the mystery gland of modern psychology, controlled some believe by the moon, the action station for all the subsidiary glands of the human structure. The normal secretion of this gland has a mystic influence on both the mind and body and can bring about spiritual ecstasy. Normally the pineal gland secretes about three drops of hormone in 24 hours which goes into the pituitary gland (the agnya chakra) the controlling station for the unconscious mind. If the conscious mind is filled with impure thoughts and ideas, with lust, greed, anger and malice, the hormones are burnt up and wasted. If the mind is pure then the system is drenched in bliss.

are not pure, even the slightest degree of awakening can lead to nightmares and tormenting sensations of burning. Furthermore, obsessive delusions may attend the rising of this energy because of an incompatible way of life. In mentally unhygienic conditions, congested cities, for example, or polluted air and water, the mechanism continues to work but instead of spiritual genius the environment produces such a phenomenon as drug addiction. According to Gopi Krishna there are not a few products of yoga who hover on the border of madness; the same subtle forces act to create the brilliance of saints and the aspirations of maniacs, and the division between these two states is thin. Everywhere, mental hospitals are crowded with people filled with grand ideas of their own spiritual, intellectual and artistic excellence. Side by side with demented poets, philosophers and inventors are lunatic visionaries, clairvoyants, prophets and godmen – to my knowledge the Virgin Mary (another one) is alive and ill in a Cork hospital. Some claim to be God, or to be in direct communication with Himself; others tormented by guilt live cheek by jowl with the devil.

And one day the living example of this walked in. Just after Christmas Roy returned from France, whence he had been precipitated by the unconscious, displaying all the signs of a severely disturbed nervous system. He had lost so much weight he was almost emaciated and you could see the poisonous chemicals working. He would be suddenly thrown into fits of panic. His heart would thunder. Sweat would pour from him and his body burned. He could concentrate on nothing. His impressions of colours, voices and smells were distorted. The world had gone grey, he said. The stench of Hell was in his nostrils. He had returned to die in my arms. It seemed that he would swell up and a strange alien force glower down through his eyes. His face would darken – by this I mean that he gave out the impression of darkness together with a strange essence akin to fragrance, the sweet smell of jasmine, yet jasmine that was dying and slightly disgusting, smacking faintly of rotting meat. His eyes were wild and staring and, whatever you said, whatever you did, wherever you went, his mind ran along the same tracks: his life was ticking away; he had done nothing with his life. At night he dreamed of long

248

lines of people being received into Hell; going through the gates, writhing, being sent to Hell, all of them, because of him, because he had not lived in the Truth. He saw their terrible expressions, heard their cries of pain as they entered the flames. He was standing judgement, he said. He had himself been received into Hell. Again his heart would thunder. Again 'the March of Angels' would ring out through the house. He was overwhelmed by panic. He was persecuted by Satan, the communists, the I.R.A., you name it, it was persecuting him. He could not bear the ticking clock, that reminded him of his life ticking away. And he would lie on his stomach, wriggling, making love to imaginary bodies far more real in his mind than myself lying there beside him.

Soon he was back in hospital. There the doctor was Satan's agent looking him up and down with hard piercing eyes, taking an inventory of his life. He himself was a man of vision thrown into the company of fools. 'They give me all these meals, when what I need is spiritual food,' he kept on saying. Indeed they did have a lot of food in that hospital, huge four-course meals. They would sit there, the patients, eating these huge meals, some crying, some hunched up and silent, others talking away – about the communists, the I.R.A., their drugs, no one with any form of communication between them: it struck me as being rather similar to many conventional dinner parties.

Just then I came across a book called *How to Live with Schizophrenia* by the doctors Hoffer and Osmund. Schizophrenia, they believed, was a disease, a biochemical disease, and was curable by dietary control and high doses of vitamins. Roy's doctors, however, were not impressed. Rubbish! they said: that was all rubbish! What was clear once again was that the medical profession seemed to know very little about schizophrenia and very little about the nervous and the endocrine systems. No one seemed to understand how or why the glands converted hormones into poisonous chemicals. The medical world was divided in its opinions. Much expensive research would be carried out into one theory, one eminent professor would advance a school of thought and all the others would dismiss it. It seemed to me remarkably like the world of religion and occult circles. Even the name of the condition was wrong, Hoffer and Osmund argued, since the term implied that something was divided or split when in fact the personality was not split at all. All, however, were agreed that something different was circulating in the blood of schizophrenics to that of other people, which resulted in various manifestations: skin changes, fatigue, depression, listlessness, glazed eyes and changes in the way that patients saw, thought, felt and acted. In other words there was an interference in the sensory mechanism so that the patient perceived sounds, tastes, smells, colours and so on differently. Some felt that people were plotting against them (one woman believed that the National Front was after her, spraying her with poison and prodding her with venomous umbrellas, bugging her house and her telephone and bombing her letter box). Some felt they were in a position of high authority; some supposed that they were brittle and would break like glass if they moved. All doctors were in agreement that something interfered in the way that messages were being delivered to the brain so that the sensory perceptions received a distorted picture; thus a person might act appropriately to the information he received yet inappropriately to his situation. All were in agreement over this yet the causes of schizophrenia remained unestablished, current ideas ranged from stress, poverty and inheritance to disrupted family situations. Some said it was sociological, some psychological, some biochemical.

The biochemical hypothesis (which is dismissed in orthodox circles) is interesting here in conjunction with the information that Gopi Krishna and Lalan Prasad Singh reveal about the functioning of the nervous system. One of the biochemical theories is that for unknown reasons the adrenal gland produces large quantities of adrenalin which floods the system, throwing the patient into fits of hyperactivity and panic. Again within the biochemical field there are many hypotheses, but they are all based on the common assumption that certain chemicals stop pursuing the normal procedures. For example adrenalin can turn into a toxic and changeable hormone called adrenochrome, which can in turn be changed to two compounds, the harmless and beneficial dihydroxindole and the poisonous adrenolutin. One biochemical treatment consists of trying to neutralise the poisons by administering large doses of vitamins, thereby converting the poisons into non-toxic chemicals.

The only hypothesis that Sahaja Yoga would advance is that all schizophrenics are possessed, to say nothing of their doctors. And in this context it is interesting to read the following case reported in *The Schizophrenias yours and mine*, published by the Professional Committee of the Schizophrenic Foundation of New Jersey:

'When ill I suffer from severe hallucinations and the physical presence of much felt ghosts within my body. I feel I am possessed to a very uncomfortable degree. I have spells of extreme discomfiture, usually in the evenings, which last for as long as six or seven hours in which I am forced to lie down and sweat it out in extreme fear and discomfort. I can hardly restrain myself because of the violent and teasing movements of the spirits in the locality of my buttocks and pelvis. During this frightening period I sweat a lot and have difficulty breathing. I also have tightening of the chest when the spirits encroach upon me there. I hear these ghosts, as well as see them, their acute presence is felt every minute of my unhappy existence and I am in a state of misery at all times because of them.'

No doubt there is such a thing as a psychic attack, and of particular help in this matter is the late Dion Fortune who wrote a book called *Psychic Self Defence*. What she has to say is of importance here since it explains the technique that may be used by some gurus and occult operators; it is also interesting when compared with the Sahaja Yogic theories of magic. I have drawn my own conclusions in those passages enclosed within square brackets. The general public, she says, has no conception of the sort of things that are done by people who have a knowledge of the human mind and who set out to exploit it. (Certainly from my own experiences I discovered that it is virtually impossible to find out anything about the workings of the occult world, it is so veiled, with each operator ready to put down the next: no other way is right, no other technique apart from his own is correct or safe.)

The essence of a psychic attack, or a psychic influence of any sort, is to be found in the principles of telepathic suggestion. This falls into three categories: auto-suggestion, conscious suggestion and hypnotic suggestion. None of these becomes

251

operative until the subconscious mind is reached and if they succeed they owe their success to the acquiescence of the conscious personality. The subconscious mind belongs to a much earlier phase of evolution than the conscious, to a phase prior to the development of speech; to address it with words is like speaking to a man in a language he does not understand. We must make a mental picture of the thing we want done and hold it in the consciousness till it begins to sink into the subconscious which will understand the picture and act on it in due course (and here again are the principles lying behind all religious and occult symbolism, also of modern mind control methods). Suggestion does not make its appeal to consciousness but aims at the springs of action in the subconscious and manipulates them there.

Different kinds of suggestion are distinguished not by the difference in end results but by the gate through which they enter the subconscious mind. Auto-suggestion originates in one's own consciousness, it is given by one's own conscious mind to one's own subconscious, hypnotic suggestion enters the subconscious directly without impinging upon consciousness at all. In most cases, suggestions are not recognised as coming from outside but are only discovered after they have matured in the subconscious and are beginning to take effect. But before anything at all can happen one's protective aura must be pierced, which always occurs from within by the response of some emotion – fear perhaps, desire, etcetera. So first the magician must establish some sort of rapport. [In the case of modern gurus this is easy for it is part of the contract that the disciple must open himself, surrender himself willingly to any influence that the guru brings to bear.] Next a focus must be established to direct the force by using an object impregnated with the victim's vibrations. [With the guru this works the other way, the disciple takes some object pertaining to the guru, a photograph, a medalla, a locket and focuses his attention through this on to the guru.] The more devout the disciple, the more potent the force becomes, but if he doubts the guru, or his mind is filled with thoughts, then his energy is diluted. An unfocused imagination and thereby an unfocused energy is not much use.

The stuff of telepathy, then, consists of the induction of

vibrations. Since emotion is electrical in essence it may be focused by the occultist into a beam and concentrated. First must come some sort of telepathic hypnotic suggestion. Next comes the employment of some physical substance as point of contact, or magnetic link. The attacking, or the influencing, power can now be directed either as a thought form, which is a current of force transmitted by the mental concentration of the operator, or it may be reserved in a kind of psychic storage battery, acting on the same principles as the glands of the body, which may be a talisman, or a locket, a photograph or an artificial elemental. The last is created by the mind of the magician and unlike the thought form it possesses an independent life of its own; but, as with an electric battery, its power slowly leaks out through radiation and, unless recharged, will weaken and die. Artificial objects associated with any form of ceremonial operation are invariably highly charged with magnetism and are ultimately linked with the force they are serving. Sometimes books which are brought out on a particular occult school [or guru] are magnetised so that they form a magnetic link between the reader and the order [or the guru]. The trained occultist himself has an exceedingly magnetic personality which may prove highly disturbing to people who are not used to high-tension psychic forces. And, if the mind of a trained occultist is a considerable weapon, the group mind of a religious community, the collective mind of an occult group, is potentially very powerful indeed, especially if concentrated by means of ritual.

So, by my calculation, a clear thoughtless state where the attention is directed upon the guru is ideal for psychic manipulation. And it is precisely the state which is worked for in many modern methods, where the focus of the meditation is the photograph of the guru. A guru can only work efficiently when his subject's conscious mind is quiescent, either when he is asleep, or in a meditative and/or hypnotic state, and the subconscious mind is open to suggestion which, in the case of sleep, may be manifested in dreams.*

* In the past, orthodox Christianity recognised the dangers lurking behind these passive techniques of meditation. Quietism, a non-activist faith specialising in interior life, was condemned and branded as heresy in 1687. The way of contemplation was acquired by the cessation of every operation and

Meditation, as the Shankacharya said, is a gimmick, a panacea, and like all panaceas it seems to me can be addictive. Even the dynamic Christian technique contains its own dangers and swings easily, as I have seen, into the realms of fantasy, psychosis even. You get so much in the habit of creating your own images, your own world, that instead of dissolving your ego you inflate it, you become the creator, deluded by your own caprices and self-importance. Your creations may become real to you but they bear little relation to the truth. In other words what you imagine may be perfectly appropriate to yourself, but not to anyone or anything else around you. Here surely is a dilemma similar to that of the schizophrenic? The power to distinguish between the products of your own imagination and the external world is eroded.

Certainly the mind has potentialities which are not widely understood. At the normal level of functioning it is constantly being diverted by a bombardment of various stimuli: thoughts, wishes, needs, desires, noises, lights, pressures, conflicts, smells, tastes, touches. But with special training these sensible messages may be sublimated. Then a yogi may accomplish with his mind all that can be done with his physical organs. Suppose a man in London wants to see what a friend in New York is doing? With special concentration and practice of his psychic powers, he will be able to do this. He may penetrate all form with his mind. Every man has the capacity to do this, he has only to develop it. He may train the imagination to visualise and quicken images that he will see, hear, taste and touch.

The Silva Mind Control teaches you to do exactly this: to pierce the physical barriers of matter and penetrate into objects, walls, metal tubes, vegetables, fruit, animals and other human beings. It teaches you to raise 'counsellors' to help you with diagnosing and healing illness. Its techniques are precisely those which lie behind any religion. You take the symbol and focus the imagination upon it, quickening your

---

by removing the mental images upon which orthodox Christianity feed. Here lay the heresy. It is interesting to note an article written in the *Cambridge Review* of January 1975 by J. Stern, who spoke at a conference on Transcendental Meditation, in May 1974 (at which the Maharishi also took the floor). Here parallels are drawn between the dangers of Quietism and those contained in the passive techniques of T.M.

image by connecting it to the electricity of your mind, animating it literally with positive energy. By concentrating on a thought or a symbol with a properly focused imagination the thought or the symbol becomes reality and the body transforms it into action. One lady (who had nothing to do with the Silva Mind Control) told me how she had conjured an earth elemental. First she imagined it, then she quickened it, next she put out a saucer of water on the mantelpiece for it and, before she knew where she was, there was the earth elemental and she could not get rid of it.

Let us return to the gurus and look in a detached way at some of their teaching. Surrender, they say: this is beyond understanding: you cannot understand, this is beyond the mind. You cannot know, therefore you must trust the one who understands these things. It is the ego that stands between you and enlightenment. You must surrender your ego. And the gurus set tests for you and if you fail it is because of the ego. There'll be no results until you have surrendered your ego, they say, broken down your values, cleansed yourself of your personality, been reborn – or in the case of Mataji: 'if you doubt me it is because of negativity,' or, 'you are possessed.' All too often there are indeed breakdowns. Instead of the ego dissolving harmoniously into the absorbing body, the disciple disintegrates. For it is, as Gopi Krishna says, generally the inadequate members of society who seek groups and gurus, who seek to be made whole. Yet enlightenment is a strenuous process and requires robust and mature systems. Most people are in no fit state. Those that have not become so insensitive that they have deadened their systems are emotional and/or mental and/or physical cripples. With the disintegration of the ego the person breaks up as well, there is no centre of gravity, no standard of reference and he will be prepared to do anything.

The tragedy in Jonestown, where Jim Jones ordered hundreds of his disciples to commit suicide is an example. And there have been other scandals. In Switzerland members of the Divine Light* were accused of conspiring to murder someone through black magic, and most recently there has been the case of drug smuggling under the auspices of Rajneesh. Headlines

* *Tribune de Genève*, Monday 23 April – Friday 28 April, 1979.

in the *Daily Star** screamed out that British girls were being made to smuggle drugs into Europe and if they refused, would be forced to sell their bodies on the streets of Bombay. Brainwashed, one mother claimed. Her daughter had been brainwashed, the whole purpose of the discipline at Poona was to take away the personality under the guise of discovering the inner being. Poona was in her opinion nothing but another Jonestown†. The *Daily Star* article was followed by a piece in the *Daily Telegraph* by one of the girl's psychiatrists, Dr Gomez. The girl's programme, she said, contained some of the mind-bending ingredients used by the Nazis. She progressed from swaying and chanting in the dark, to sessions of questions to which there was no answer; staring without blinking into another's eyes for periods of thirty minutes, to holding a tennis ball in her navel for seven hours; praying for three days, to dancing until she collapsed; the Tantra group in which she must have sexual intercourse with fourteen others each pretending to be a different animal, to the samadhi bath – an exercise endured in solitude, darkness and silence where she was immersed in salt water so that even the sense of gravity was absent. After this the girl agreed without question to carrying cannabis to London for money to return to the ashram.‡

What is to stop anyone from honing in on God? Making God into a business? A kind of God Board pedalling energy in the same way as the Gas and Electricity Board? A God Board for the distribution of God, or in some cases, rather than the distribution, it seems to be the appropriation of other people's

* Wednesday 6 February, 1980.

† As this book goes to press the orange sannyasins are leaving Poona. The saint has gone marching out. On 31 May, 1981, Rajneesh left India. He has entered his 'silent phase'. Rumours fly about: guns, drugs, he has been arrested. He has been expelled. He is in New Jersey looking for land. He is in America looking for life. He has sciatica/leukaemia/slipped disc/venereal disease/cancer of the larynx. He is dying. The speculations multiply. The newspaper articles pour out of India.

‡ At the time of writing, the latest tragedy to be reported came on 28 September, 1980, in the *News of the World* and concerning one of Sai Baba's disciples. After his involvement with the guru, his parents claim that his career fell apart, he walked out of exams and he was haunted by fears that people were following him. Finally he put his head on the railway line and was run over by an express train. On the same page the Silva Mind Control also came in for criticism.

energy. The answer is: nothing. God is an industry providing a livelihood for thousands, if not millions, of souls, from orthodox churchmen to begging sadhus, from spotty Andrew to the God Child sitting on the steps in Tiruvannamalai. Provided one has the necessary air of authority there is nothing to stop anyone from teaching or exploiting that mysterious power called God. A recent article in *Yoga Today* counted something like seventeen various gods, goddesses and messiahs currently operating in India and the West. God is as good a resource as any to turn into a commodity and exploit for one's own use. And the charge may not be always financial, it can be more subtle, but no less potent.

There is a point midway along the mystical path which is most difficult to pass, Paul Brunton wrote in *A Search in Secret India*. It often happens that the person whose devotions have brought him to this point believes that he has reached the highest goal. This condition is fairly common among dedicated enthusiasts who may experience sudden but temporary states of ecstasy and emerge with the awareness that something colossal has happened. It takes little more for him to imagine himself as a messiah and, displaying all the signs of psychosis (by this it is meant exaggerating everything pertaining to himself), he makes claims to spiritual greatness, founds new cults and sets himself up as a great spiritual teacher. This is a point which is well-known to hypnotists who are warned during their training about what is known in the trade as the Messiah Syndrome.

It is as easy to conceive naive ideas of purity as it is to conceive them about materialism. The root of all impurity lies in the ego, therefore the only real purity is absence of ego, absence of self-interest. One who desires to appropriate and control the energy of thousands of people is no less greedy, no less ambitious, no less anxious for power than a politican or a businessman, a factory farmer or a property developer wishing to control thousands of pounds – even if he does swallow no meat or alcohol, smoke no cigarettes and enjoy no sex.* He may be satanic, or he may be self-deluded; psychotic perhaps,

* A dream of Roy's is interesting in this context. He was preparing with some punks to go on a journey. At one point he and the punks filed past two American groups of Jesus freaks, each devoted to a different leader and obvi-

for psychosis need not necessarily be uncontrollable – it has been said that the difference between certain gurus and the patients in mental hospitals is that the gurus know how to focus their delusions and control their energies while the patients of mental hospitals lie at the mercy of their caprices and their nervous systems.

No doubt many gurus appear to operate in a different dimension to most of us, throwing out an illusion of freedom by which anything is possible. As Bernard Levin has said it is a very definite effect which is easier experienced than explained: a torrent of love-imbued energy bathing you in a refulgent glow of wisdom and love, forming a pool in which to soak yourself.

These are sensations which are so unfamiliar and so delicious that it is easy to become addicted to and obsessed by their source. Certainly there are casualties of the modern guru and cult wave. But again there are people who feel comforted by belonging to a guru or a group, who find they can live stronger, healthier lives under the umbrella of their protection. By delegating responsibilities to the guru many difficulties in life are automatically eradicated. For example, perhaps one of the most formidable problems is making decisions. These are all taken care of, the idea is that you do nothing,

ously in competition for their souls. Each offered sex as an inducement to join their group. But the proffered girls were neither particularly pretty, nor were they in any sense ugly. Then Roy and the punks became involved with the followers of another leader of this sort and came up against the man himself. He was in fact an Easterner, probably an Indian, who spoke to his disciples in a booming Texan voice, delivering biblical messages similar to revivalist Christians'. Roy supposed that he would be of no great yogic development but when he started to test him this man assumed a suit covered all over with rubber suckers and enveloped his head with a World War II air pilot's helmet and goggles, and then started to exude a great deal of power. Nor was it beneficial, although his followers were greatly aroused. Roy saw them as they were, hideously ugly and deformed through their dependence on him. This man was a drug to them and they could not do without him. Roy felt this great force prevailing on him to surrender but he managed to resist and scream out to the punks that they should get out immediately. It was a close escape. Roy was particularly interested in this dream and it was he who pointed out that Peter Brent in *Godmen of India,* had interviewed an American disciple of a famous guru. 'He's got like great teats all over him,' this disciple had told Peter Brent, 'and we just suck and suck that heavy goodness out of him.'

everying will work out. The notion that you are the 'doer' is merely an attitude of mind. If you can let go all will be well. But on the other hand the real root of our trouble lies in attachment to people and things around us. And here it should be said again: some gurus become yet another source of addiction, it seems to me, and another obsession for their disciples. Moreover the irony is that by advancing the destruction of their disciples' egos some gurus may be promoting their own.

The final part of my researches came when I paid my annual visit to the Mind and Body Exhibition and happened upon the ionizer, an instrument which seemed to me to throw light on to the subject of vibrations and go far in providing a scientific explanation as to how they worked.

Ions are natural phenomena and are formed where there is sufficient atmospheric electricity (which may be variously caused by radioactive elements in the soil, by cosmic rays, by electric-magnetic waves from the sun, lightning or the splitting of drops of water in a waterfall) to detach an electron from a gas molecule. (The air consists chiefly of oxygen, nitrogen and carbon dioxide molecules, each consisting of one or more atoms which are made of a central core, or nucleus, of positive charges, surrounded by an equal number of moving negative charges known as electrons.) The molecule from which the electron is detached becomes a positive ion while the freed electron becomes attached to an adjacent molecule to form a negative ion.

In certain meteorological conditions both the number of air ions and the ratio of positive to negative ions can increase. Such a situation commonly precedes ill winds like the Föhn, the Sirocco and the Mistral. The characteristic complaints are lassitude, depression, migraine, nausea, insomnia, irritability and respiratory disturbances. Thus the term 'under the weather' means exactly what it says. It has been found that, while an excess of positive ions has a deleterious effect, negative ions produce a sense of well-being (and here there is a paradox since negative ions are good and positive bad).

Ill winds are not the only phenomena to cause electrical imbalances within the nervous system; air pollution, overcrowded stuffy rooms, synthetic fibres and plastic, central

259

heating, air-conditioning, smoking and driving cars all do so as well – by producing negative fields which attract positive ions. The ionizer is a machine which can electrically charge the atmosphere with negative ions; its function being medical is to eliminate cigarette smoke and pollution thereby reducing fatigue and respiratory problems in buildings where crowded conditions, smoke, plastic, and modern air-conditioning bring about a high level of positive ions.

Medion Ltd who market the ionizer, believe it is the low level of negative ions in the air we breathe that may cause modern stress problems. Research has shown that positively ionized air raises the level of serotin in the blood (causing depression, tension, irritation and anxiety), while negative ions stabilise the frequency, increase the amplitude and synchronise the electrical wave forms in the brain's alpha rhythms, encouraging relaxation and relieving tension.* In short: negative ions seem not only to have a soothing effect on the nerves, balancing the endrocrine system and, being linked with the parasympathetic, reducing the rate of the heart beat and the blood pressure, but also they have a beneficial effect on plants and animals which thrive in air well-endowed with negative ions.

It seemed to me that the similarity between negative ions and the vibrations of Sahaja Yoga is striking (the ionizer even emits a cool breeze). By channelling the pranic energy through the sushumna, the parasympathetic system, one must be acting as a transformer of energy, charging oneself with negative ions and, furthermore, holding the charge so that one is radiating out beneficial ions. This would explain the healing aspect of Sahaja Yoga, also the Indian experiments at Rahuri with plants and plant yields. By the same token people who are not functioning efficiently may act as an ill wind emanating debilitating positive ions. Again while certain people may hold a charge of negative ions, so can particular trees, temples, holy

---

* The American National Aeronautics and Space Administration Molecular Biophysics Laboratory has shown that each normal cell of the human body possesses a surprising degree of negative electrical charge. It has also shown that cancer cells have a very much reduced charge, while Dr Kuster at the University of Frankfurt has demonstrated the inhibiting effect of ionised air on the growth of cancerous tumours in mice.

shrines, wells and mountains; and if you are tuned correctly you can pick up these electrical vibrations, these negative ions, in the form of a cool breeze. In other words negatively-charged atmosphere is similar to prana – André van Lysebeth in his book *Pranayama the Yoga of Breath* identifies ions with prana itself.

All yoga, then, and all religion, I believe to be electrical in essence. All techniques aim to channel the vitality through the body so that, instead of dissipating his energy, a man may use his body as a transformer, putting himself on charge, tuning up his nervous system so that an accumulation of power may be generated.

Is it not ironical that human beings have devised techniques to harness currents of water, to catch waves of radar, radio and television, even to split the atom, achieving not only the means of capturing nuclear power but of destroying the world, while their own bodies, the most extraordinary of all potential magazines of power, lie untapped?

In spite of my haphazard schooling, my education – or what passes as the formal training of my mind – stays with me. I am conscious of seeking ways to shape this book into a nice conclusion. I have posed the problem, I have set out my proof. But where is the answer? I have no logical reckoning, nothing below which I can draw a line and sign off: Q.E.D. After all I have not yet fallen into an ecstatic coma, nor have I been flooded with illumination. But I have been awarded glimpses and from these I have learnt a great deal.

I can say with authority that I *know* the difference between a nervous system which is working harmoniously and one that is not. With the latter I could feel my vitality curdling, knotting in my arteries, so that the overall sensation was one of disintegration. I was aware only of evil, and the personification of this, the devil, actually appeared himself. Everything combined to trap me; even the sky seemed to be a blue prison pressing in and crushing me. But when that internal energy is properly controlled everything external, however muddled it may seem, falls automatically into place. When that vitality flows there is no such thing as fatigue, or impossibility. Everything operates as though by clockwork. Buses come. People smile. Whatever you do works. It is the difference between heaven and hell. It is perfectly possible, it seems to me, to live in a heavenly condition: it is a question of technique and application.

I had to make three journeys out to India before I discovered that what I had been looking for was the way in. Only then, and at rare moments, could I begin to lose my subjective preoccupation with myself and dissolve into the sun, the sea, the heat and the dust and experience that union which is the root of all things.

Each time that energy rose it incorporated everything marvellous I have ever felt. Those rare moments of stillness; the relief you feel when you have completed something that you feel may be good; the joy that springs from the fragrance of flowers; the vigour of a spring day ringing with birds, blowing with apple blossom, vibrating with vital earth; the feeling of liberation that rises with a beautiful dawn, or open spaces, or certain music. It was as though Elgar's Allegro for Strings were sounding through every nerve and sinew. I was refreshed, relaxed, poised, fulfilled – all these words meant exactly what they said. I billowed with the clouds, celebrated with the birds, resounded into space with the cries of the curlew. The hiss of the rain and the hiss of the fire became one, blending with the hiss of blood in my veins. Now there were no limits: I was free.

I have put this in the past tense because, since finishing with Sahaja Yoga, I have not devoted the time and the attention necessary to raising this force. Yet when I am alone and still, especially in the country, I am conscious of that vitality resounding within me.

There is after all no need to go anywhere.